A-level Study Guide

Drama

Revised and updated for 2008 by

Melissa Jones

Revision Express

Acknowledgements

Melissa Jones would like to thank past and present staff and students from the Drama Department at **Saffron Walden County High School** who have contributed to this publication in so many ways. Thanks also to Graham and to Michael for their support during the writing of this guide and to Naomi Jones for her professional insight.

The Publisher is grateful to the following for their permission to reproduce copyright material: Faber and Faber, for permission to use an extract from *Our Country's Good* by Timberlake Wertenbaker.

Series Consultant: Geoff Black and Stuart Wall

Project Manager: Hywel Evans

Pearson Education Limited

Edinburgh Gate, Harlow

Essex CM20 2JE, England

And Associated Companies throughout the world

www.pearsoned.co.uk

© Pearson Education Limited 2007, 2008

British Library Cataloguing-in-Publication Data

A catalogue entry for this title is available from the British Library.

ISBN 978-1-4082-0668-3

Second impression 2008

First published 2007

New Edition 2008

Set by Juice Creative Ltd

Printed by Ashford Colour Press Ltd., Gosport.

Contents

How to use this book

Specification map
Provides a quick and easy overview of the topics that you need to study for the specification you are studying

Exam themes
At the beginning of each chapter, these give a quick overview of the key themes that will be covered in the exam

Exam themes

- The language of drama and theatre
- The playwright and social context

Theatrical revolution

This section covers one of the most important eras in the development of the theatre. It looks at the European pursuit of truth and reality through which important practitioners and playwrights emerged. You may be studying Stanislavski, Brecht or Artaud as well as the playwrights Ibsen, Chekhov or Strindberg. This section examines the social context and development of their approach. This period shaped modern acting and playwriting.

Action point
A suggested activity linked to the content

Action point

To learn more about the Royal Court, see *The Royal Court Theatre and the Modern Stage* by Philip Roberts, *Taking Stock* by Max Stafford-Clark and Philip Roberts or the chapter '1956' in *Changing Stages* by Richard Eyre and Nicholas Wright.

Realism and naturalism

The theatrical revolution in Europe was led by the playwrights **Ibsen**, **Chekhov** and **Strindberg** and by the practitioners **Stanislavski, Brecht, Artaud** and **Craig**. Emile Zola, a French novelist, was the first, as early as 1873, to criticise the frivolity of theatre and advocate an approach he called 'naturalism'.

'Drama is dying of its extravagances, its lies and its platitudes . . .'

Checkpoint
Quick question to check your understanding with full answers given at the end of the chapter

Checkpoint 1

Define, in your own words, the difference between **realism** and **naturalism**.

The Norwegian realist playwright **Henrik Ibsen** shocked the audiences of his day with plays about venereal disease (*Ghosts*) and the role of women in society (*A Doll's House*). He sought to highlight the ills of society; the romantic need for the happy ending was swept away, Hedda shoots herself and Nora leaves her husband and, more shockingly, her children.

In *Miss Julie*, **Strindberg** advocates the use of *real* objects in scenic design and comments that *'theatrical characters . . . ought to be challenged by naturalists, who know how richly complex a human soul is . . .'*. Realism could be defined as selecting and distilling observations from real life, while naturalism is a more philosophical engagement with the essence of humanity. Stanislavski was criticised as overwhelming the text with naturalistic detail, which inhibited communication with an audience. Chekhov, the Russian dramatist who worked closely with Stanislavski at the Moscow Art Theatre, famously complained that the director had ruined his play *The Seagull* with an overly detailed and cluttered set design, which allowed little room for actors to move.

Links
Cross-reference links to other relevant sections in the book

Links

For a detailed discussion of practitioners, see pages 24–39.

Mise-en-scène and design

The design of stage settings during this period was detailed and natural. Sets for plays in the 18th and 19th century relied on two-dimensional painted 'backcloths'. Realism demanded accurate detail. Strindberg's *Miss Julie* is set in a kitchen and in his Preface he admonishes the theatrical convention of painted pictures of pots and pans on the backcloth.

Realism, naturalism, expressionism and symbolism refer to specific genres and styles in late 19th- and early 20th-century European theatre.

Examiner's secrets
Hints and tips for exam success

Examiner's secrets

In your notes it is important to write about the chronology of Stanislavski's life only as it relates to his theories. You will not gain credit for simply repeating historical facts.

→ **Realism:** making the set, characters and plot *appear* to be real life.
→ **Naturalism:** influenced by Zola, aiming to make the theatrical event a detailed and *precise* 'slice of life'.
→ **Symbolism:** reacted against realism and focused on the use of *images*.
→ **Expressionism:** an extreme emotion dramatised through *symbol* and *metaphor*.

Watch out!
Flags up common mistakes and gives hints on how to avoid them

Watch out!

The practitioners associated with this theatrical revolution do not necessarily fit neatly into boxes. The changes in style evolved and it would be wrong to place anyone emphatically in one category.

Topic checklist
A topic overview of the content covered and how it matches to the specification you are studying

Topic checklist

	Edexcel		AQA		WJEC	
	AS	A2	AS	A2	AS	A2
The language of drama and theatre	○	●	○	●	○	●
Greek and medieval theatre and Commedia dell'arte		●	○		○	●

Revision checklist
Allows you to monitor your progress and revise the areas that you are not confident about

By the end of this chapter you should be able to:

1	Understand approaches to playwriting.	Confident	Not confident **Revise** page 10
2	Analyse the nature of audience and explain 'suspension of disbelief'.	Confident	Not confident **Revise** page 11

Acting and directing

Stanislavski, whose work is discussed more fully in another section, is credited with the revolution in the craft of acting during this era. He sought to develop a science of acting which he named *The System*. In his many books, notably *An Actor Prepares*, he gives a minutely detailed account of how the actor should approach a role. Stanislavski strove to find 'truthful' acting and his work at the **Moscow Art Theatre** shaped the style of acting that we see today.

British theatre in the early 20th century

In Britain, it was regional repertory theatres that tried to establish a non-commercial permanent home for the classics and innovative contemporary drama: The Abbey in Dublin and The Gaiety in Manchester. In London, however, theatre remained in the domain of managers who wanted to retain a traditional approach, the antithesis of the new European practice.

Actors like **Henry Irving** and **Beerbohm Tree** had continued the 'star' system tradition. Playwrights such as **Oscar Wilde** (*The Importance of Being Earnest*) illustrated social snobbery and **Noel Coward** (*The Vortex*) dealt with scandalous themes, but their plays remained in a conventional and comic style.

Only **Granville Barker**, who had an analytical approach to text, and **Shaw** paralleled the social realism of the European writers. Granville Barker's *The Voysey Inheritance* dealt with the moral problem of a man who realises that his father's fortune was acquired through deceit and trickery. Shaw, influenced significantly by the work of Ibsen, wrote about prostitution in *Mrs Warren's Profession* and had his work rejected by the censor. Other plays focused on the emerging role of women in society.

Theatre-going was essentially a middle-class activity. Theatres retained the ornate auditoriums and proscenium arch stages of the past and plays depicted a section of society rather than encompassing its entirety. Even Shaw's *Pygmalion* portrays a common flower seller's attempt to rise in social class by learning to speak like a lady; it does not expose the hollow superficiality of polite society or the truth about the underclass.

The seeds of change were sown after the Second World War (1939–1945) when the Arts Council was formed in 1946. This gave regional theatres increased funding to rehearse and to experiment with new plays and removed the pressure of 'weekly rep'.

The real revolution in British theatre was to come from the Royal Court Theatre, founded by **George Devine** in 1956.

Grade booster
When you are recording and evaluating **research** it is important to link this research to the text or devised piece, showing how the information was **embedded** into your work. Research for the sake of it has little theatrical value.

Take note
The **protagonist** is the principal character in a play.

Example
'Today we worked on a difficult scene. Our aim was to affect the audience emotionally and to leave them feeling moved and helpless. David had found the scene challenging and slightly embarrassing. We dimmed the lights in the studio and recounted sad moments from our lives. One or two were close to tears. David then improvised his monologue and we all closed our eyes. He seemed to lose his embarrassment and the speech was very moving. After this we all wrote down the line or phrase that we had found the most emotional and gave them to David. He created his final speech from our list.'

Terminology
Weekly rep, short for repertory, meant that a theatre company would stage a different production every week. They would rehearse one play during the day while performing the previously rehearsed play at night.

Exam practice   15 minutes   answers: page 21
Select a modern play that you are studying or preparing for performance. List the features of **theme**, **style** and **character** that have been influenced by the practitioners or theatrical movements discussed in this section.

23

Grade booster
Examiner suggestions on how to get the top grade

Take note
Extension notes on the core content

Example
text to come

Terminology
text to come

Exam practice
Exam-style questions to check your understanding of the topic content with full answers given at the end of the chapter

Specification map

Edexcel		AQA		WJEC	
AS	A2	AS	A2	AS	A2
○	●	○	●	○	●
	●	○		○	●
	●	○	●	○	●
	●	○	●	○	●
	●	○	●	○	●
○	●	○	●	○	●
○		○		○	
○		○		○	
○		○		○	
○		○		○	
○		○		○	
○		○		○	
○		○		○	
○		○		○	
○		○		○	
○		○		○	
○		○		○	
○	●	○	●	○	●
○	●	○	●	○	●
○	●	○	●	○	●
○	●	○	●	○	●
○	●	○	●	○	●
○	●	○	●	○	●
○	●		●	○	●
○	●		●	○	●
○	●	○	●	○	●
	●	○	●	○	●
○	●	○	●	○	●
○	●	○	●	○	●
	●		●		●
			●	○	
	●		●	○	●
	●		●	○	●
	●		●	○	●
	●		●	○	●
	●		●	○	●
	●		●	○	●
	●		●	○	●
○		○		○	
○		○		○	
○		○		○	
○		○		○	
○		○		○	
○		○		○	
○		○		○	
○		○		○	
○	●	○		○	
○	●	○		○	
○	●	○		○	
○	●	○		○	
○	●	○		○	
○	●	○		○	

Drama and theatre in context

This chapter begins by examining the language of theatre before giving an overview of the history of theatre and play writing. Theatre history encompasses the physical development of theatre buildings and stages as well as the advances in technical effects. Importantly, this chapter explores the changing nature of audiences, the concerns of playwrights and the significant practitioners who have influenced performance and directing.

Your A-level course will involve the study of plays and practitioners from different historical periods as well as analysis of plays in performance. This chapter will be especially valuable where your specification asks you to compare a contemporary production with productions of the play in other historical contexts. Most specifications ask you to respond to the social, cultural, historical and political context of plays and this chapter will assist you in contextualising the plays you perform, watch or study.

Exam themes

- The language of drama and theatre
- The playwright and social context
- Design of theatres and stages
- The nature of audience
- Development of acting and directing

Topic checklist

	Edexcel		AQA		WJEC	
	AS	A2	AS	A2	AS	A2
The language of drama and theatre	○	●	○	●	○	●
Greek and medieval theatre and Commedia dell'arte			●	○		○	●
Elizabethan and Jacobean theatre			●	○	●	○	●
Restoration to the 19th century			●	○	●	○	●
Theatrical revolution				○	○	○	●
Modern theatre	○	●	○	●	○	●

The language of drama and theatre

This section explains the key features of plays, the art of play writing and theatrical genres. It is important to use the correct terminology in examinations and this section explains how and why certain terms are applied to stages, plays and technical elements. The section also gives an overview of acting, directing and design and explains the nature and composition of audience. Examination questions often ask you to consider the impact on an audience.

Plays and playwrights

The evidence

Historically, plays were written for particular audiences or theatres. The **play text** refers to the original play while the **performance text** is the version that includes the variations that actors and directors have brought to the play during rehearsal. Modern plays are often organic, with the **playwright** working with the director and the actors and rewriting sections as rehearsals progress. Plays should be considered in their social and historical context; drama echoes the concerns and culture of the era.

The **Greek** playwrights Aeschylus, Sophocles and Euripides created tragedy for a competitive festival and the first writer of comedy, **Aristophanes**, parodied leading figures of his day. In **medieval** England, drama evolved from the Church and concerned religion and morality. The most celebrated playwright of Elizabethan and Jacobean theatre, **Shakespeare**, wrote **tragedies**, **comedies** and **histories**.

Following the closure of the theatres during the Puritan era, new playwrights emerged. The **Restoration** playwrights focused on comedy that was, in fact, a serious criticism of contemporary life. **Racine** and **Corneille**, from France, influenced early 18th-century writing, but actor managers, like **David Garrick**, who staged versions of the classics, dominated the late 18th and the 19th centuries.

There was little new play writing, but **Gay's** *The Beggar's Opera*, written in 1728, was a great success and the plays of Sheridan, **Farquhar** and **Goldsmith** are examples of incisive comedy from this era. **Melodramas**, such as *Maria Marten* (or *The Murder in the Red Barn*), were hugely popular in the 19th century. They were romantic and sentimental, with music and song accompanying the dialogue. **Music-hall** was part of the non-literary development of the 19th century; this genre included a variety of 'acts' rather than a scripted play.

During the same period European dramatists **Ibsen**, **Strindberg** and **Chekhov** wrote 'problem plays', discussing controversial social questions. Their plays were in the **realistic** style. Ibsen influenced the work of the Irish dramatist, **Shaw**. The English playwright **J.B. Priestley** raised moral issues, but the theatrical revolution of post-war Britain changed British theatre.

Writers at the **Royal Court Theatre** questioned social values and attacked the ruling classes and there was an explosion of writing from young playwrights, both male and female.

Experimental theatre flourished during the 1960s and 1970s and the plays of **Pinter**, **Stoppard** and **Hare** are classic examples of this period. The number of female playwrights increased and feministic issues were raised by writers like **Caryl Churchill** and **Sarah Daniels** in the final decades of the 20th century. Many plays written during the 1980s attacked government policy and social deprivation. Modern theatre is an eclectic mix of styles and forms, which continues to reflect the social and political concerns of the day.

The nature of audience

The **audience** is the collective term for the group of individuals who attend a theatrical performance. Members of the audience traditionally **suspend their disbelief** when they watch a play. This means that for the duration of the performance they ignore the fact that they know they are in a theatre and that the characters and situations are false, allowing themselves to engage in the world of the play.

Brecht sought to remind audiences that they were watching a play using a technique usually translated as 'alienation' but literally meaning 'make strange'.

As you revise your texts and use this book you will discover that audiences have a collective, as well as an individual, identity. Audiences in **Restoration** theatre went to the play to be seen, Shakespeare's **groundlings** went to be entertained, while a modern audience at the **Royal Court** might be seeking intellectual challenge.

Stages and theatres

It is very important that you write about theatre spaces and stages using the correct terminology. Many people connect the word **stage** with a **proscenium arch** theatre: the picture frame surrounding an end-on platform on which the play is performed. As many theatres were built at the time when this was the popular form of staging, it has survived as a general term for all theatres. There are, however, many different forms of theatre space, each one producing a different experience for the audience.

The **amphitheatre** or **arena**, which originated in Ancient Greece, is a fan-shaped auditorium that looks down on the performance space. A **thrust stage** juts out into the audience, who surround it on three sides. **The Globe** was the original thrust stage but it is also used in many modern theatres.

In **theatre in the round** the audience surround the action and a **promenade** performance moves the audience from one location to another, following the play's action. **Traverse** productions have the audience seated on either side of the action, which takes place in a channel between the spectators. Theatres can be described as **intimate** if they seat a small audience close to the action or **fringe** when they present plays outside mainstream theatres.

Site-specific productions are performed in non-theatrical locations such as barns, warehouses or factories and **street theatre** takes plays to the people.

When you are considering a style or location for your own work you should explore different staging opportunities. Try to see a wide variety of theatre during your course or revision period. The **Edinburgh Festival** held annually in August is an excellent way to see an impressive range of new and experimental work performed in diverse venues.

Checkpoint 1

What is the difference between **thrust staging** and **promenade theatre**?

Take note

Fringe theatre has often been performed in pubs, for example The Brockley Jack in East London, The King's Head in Islington and The Finborough Theatre in Earl's Court.

Directing and acting

It is a common misconception among examination students that directors simply tell actors where to stand and that actors merely follow these instructions and learn their lines! The craft of actors and of directors has evolved over time; the creation of a piece of theatre is a complex and multi-layered event.

Checkpoint 2

What is a **rehearsal**? Write your own definition.

Rehearsal today is a process through which the play is explored, shaped and revealed; the **final production**, the production that the audience see, is the result of this process. It is important that when you are writing about the **rehearsal process** in an examination or portfolio, you analyse the techniques and experiments that lead to the final shape.

Links

For Stanislavski, see page 30.

Similarly, actors develop character through a variety of methods. A practitioner whose work has influenced the craft of acting is **Stanislavski**. His system for acting became the foundation for **Lee Strasberg's** 'Actors' Studio' in America, which in turn gave rise to **the method**.

Design

Theatre design has a specific language. You should ensure that you use this accurately when writing about texts, in your own performances or in evaluating live theatre. Examples of performance space have been discussed above and you should use these terms precisely to describe the actor/audience relationship.

The term **proxemics** refers to the positioning of people in relation to each other. This can be used to discuss the actor/audience relationship or the relationship between characters on stage. Other parts of the stage have specific names: the off-stage areas to the side are the **wings**; the area where the audience sit is the **auditorium**, which in traditional theatres is divided into the **stalls** (seats on the lower level in front of the stage), **the circle** or **dress circle** on the level above and in large theatres the **upper circle** (sometimes affectionately known as '**the gods**' because of the great height). Your seat in the theatre will obviously affect your experience of the production.

Some stages slope towards the audience; this is known as a **rake**. The wall at the back of the stage is known as the **cyclorama**; this is often made of cloth and used by lighting designers to create mood or location.

Backcloths, on which scenery is painted, are an outmoded form of scenic design, confined mostly to pantomime. A **trap** is a small door in the floor of the stage, first used in Elizabethan theatre; traps can be used as graves or for entrances from below the stage. **Tabs** are the curtains at the front of the proscenium arch, separating the audience from the actors. The end of the play or act is sometimes referred to as **the curtain** and the time when actors take a bow to the audience is the **curtain call**.

Lights are referred to as **lanterns** and the bulbs that go into them are **lamps**. When referring to costume and set you should use words such as **shape**, **texture**, **period**.

Links

For more detail about lighting terms, see page 138.

Exam practice   15 minutes   answers: page 26

Imagine that you are deciding how to stage one of your texts. You are considering **traverse** and **promenade**. Compare the advantages, disadvantages and practicalities of these types of staging.

Greek and medieval theatre and Commedia dell'arte

This section gives an overview of the origins of theatre in Ancient Greece, looks at the beginnings of British drama in the Middle Ages and introduces Commedia dell'arte. These areas are important, even if you are not studying a text from this period, because they are the foundations of theatre. You will find that many elements of theatre practice have their roots in these historical periods.

Theatre in Ancient Greece

Theatre originated in Athens. The first tragedy sprang from a choral lyric sung in honour of the god Bacchus. In the 6th century BC **Thespis** introduced an actor and created conflict between the chorus and the actor. Many of the terms associated with theatre have developed from this era – Thespis gave us the term **thespian**.

The plays were performed in **amphitheatres** built into the hillside. The **theatron** (literally, 'viewing-place') is where the spectators sat. Mathematics played a large role in the construction of these theatres as their designers had to be able to create **acoustics** in them such that the actors' voices could be heard throughout the theatre, including in the very top row of seats.

Playwrights wrote a trilogy of plays for the festival of the god of wine and song, Dionysus, and there was a prize for the winning playwright. Three main playwrights emerged at this time: **Aeschylus** (*The Oresteia*), **Sophocles** (*Antigone*) and **Euripides** (*Women of Troy*). **Aristophanes** wrote comedies such as *Lysistrata,* and **Menander** was the chief representative of 'New Comedy'. Writers addressed current debates and concerns in their plays – Sophocles in *Antigone* and Euripides in *Women of Troy* address the issue of war.

In Greek tragedy the **protagonist** was usually at the mercy of the gods. Greek drama used the technique of the **chorus**, who acted as a **narrator**, recounting events and commenting on the action. Aeschylus had only one actor, with a second and third performer being introduced by Sophocles and Euripides respectively.

The acting area was circular and known as the **orchestra**, while the terms **scene** (the 'skene' was the building directly behind the stage) and **proscenium** originate from Greek theatres.

The comedy and tragedy **masks** have their origin in the theatre of Ancient Greece. The masks were used to show the emotions of the characters in a play and to allow actors to switch between roles and play characters of a different gender. The Greeks also had the first technical effects, the **deus ex machina**, a crane which enabled the gods to 'fly'.

Many conventions of Greek drama can be seen in theatre throughout history and in the theatre of today.

→ The **Olivier** auditorium at the National Theatre is based on the theatre at Epidaurus in Ancient Greece.
→ Dramatists use a **chorus** to comment on the action. See **Brecht** and **T.S. Eliot**.

> **Take note**
>
> The **protagonist** is the principal character in a play.

> **Checkpoint 1**
>
> What was the **orchestra** in Greek theatre? What does this word refer to today?

→ **Masks** are a feature of plays from many cultures. See **Kathakali** and **Commedia dell'arte**.

→ Plays debate the issues of the age.

Medieval theatre

This period is often referred to as 'the dark ages' in which very little literature was written. The beginnings of drama in Britain took place in the churches (**liturgical drama**), where priests 'enacted' sections of the service in Latin. In the 10th century the **Quem Quaeritis**, the story from the New Testament in which Mary Magdalene and her companions discover Christ's empty tomb, was performed in churches and cathedrals at Easter time.

Eventually liturgical drama encompassed many stories from the Bible performed at diverse times of the year, according to local custom. Plays in the church, performed by ordinary people, were very popular on holy days and at fairs. They became filled with humour as a way of capturing the audience's attention. The Church reacted by throwing out all those 'ordinary' actors and instead produced full and complete performances themselves.

Church buildings themselves were too small to contain many people, so plays moved from the altar, to the porch, to the churchyard and eventually to public streets and open spaces. The further the plays moved from the church, the weaker the clergy's control. By 1210 a papal edict forbade the clergy to act in churches.

Take note

The term **mystery** came from the French *mystère* meaning craft or trade.

Processional drama developed in the 14th century, celebrating the feast of *Corpus Christie*, a day-long festival. **Mystery plays** (reenactments of Bible stories) were presented in the local vernacular, instead of in Latin. It was customary for each of the **guilds**, representing a certain group of craftsmen, to present a short play. The play related to the occupation of the craftsmen who performed it, e.g. Noah's Ark was entrusted to the boat-builders, the adoration of the Magi to the goldsmiths.

The actors stood on a **pageant wagon** which moved on wheels. In the course of the procession a certain number of **stations** were appointed, the pageants stopped and the plays were performed. The function of calling the people to order was entrusted to a tyrant, e.g. Herod, the murderer of the Innocents; or to Pilate, who dressed in grotesque clothing and, armed with a sword, raged about among the audience, imposing silence.

The guilds became very competitive in trying to create impressive wagons, with constructions such as a '**hell's mouth**' with fire and smoke. There are several **mystery cycles** in existence today, notably in York, Chester and Wakefield. Later in this era, **morality** plays told stories, such as *Everyman*, which taught Christian living and exposed human vices.

Take note

Allegorical means symbolic representation. *Everyman* represents mankind and he is confronted with his vices, such as gluttony and sloth.

These plays used **allegorical** stories. The influence of this form of theatre can be seen in **street theatre** and **carnival**. The gathering of spectators around the pageant wagon in an inn yard influenced the construction of the early Elizabethan theatres such as **The Globe**. A modern allegorical drama is David Campton's *The Cagebirds*, which uses characters called

'The Guzzler' and 'The Wild One' to comment on the human condition. York and Chester continue to stage their **mystery cycle** using amateur actors in large-scale community events.

Commedia dell'arte

Beginning during the Renaissance and lasting into the 18th century, travelling troupes performed the **Commedia dell'arte** – the Italian comedy. The company's ten or more actors each developed a specific type of character, e.g. the Captain, two old men (Pantaloon and the Doctor), the **Zanni** (valet-buffoons). Since all wore **masks**, their roles were eventually called *masks*. Along with these comic characters were the lovers. Female parts were originally played by men, but later played by women.

The actors had specific comic business (**lazzi**) that they developed. Before going on stage, actors would agree on a basic plot and a general idea of how it should be performed. The improvised performances were never subtle: the humour was often bawdy and coarse.

An important part of every play, given always to the most expert and popular actors, was the lazzi, which often had nothing to do with the play itself. It might include clever pantomimic acting, acrobatic feats, juggling, or wrestling. The **stock characters**, e.g. rascally servant, the old man, the lady's maid, which appeared in every play, always wore a conventional dress, with masks. In general these masks can be classed under four or five headings: Pantalone and the Doctor, both old men; the Captain, a young man of adventure; the valet or jester, usually called Zanni; the hunchback Punchinello; and another old man, somewhat different from the first two.

Checkpoint 2

What is **liturgical** drama? What are **mystery** plays and **morality** plays?

Checkpoint 3

Explain the terms **lazzi** and **stock character**.

Exam practice   15 minutes   answers: page 26

Look at the play you are studying or preparing for your practical exam. Are there any features in this play that might have been influenced by any of these periods of theatre history? If the play was written in one of these periods, list the conventions of theatre at the time. How will this affect your ideas for performance?

Elizabethan and Jacobean theatre

This was a significant period in theatre history and it is very likely that you will be studying a play from this era. It is important to understand the political background to Shakespeare's theatre and to know how the physical characteristics of the theatre had an impact on play writing. Examination questions require you to have a sound knowledge of cultural and social factors.

Elizabethan or Jacobean theatre?

English Renaissance theatre is often called Elizabethan theatre. However, in a strictly accurate sense, the term Elizabethan theatre covers only the plays written and performed publicly in England during the reign of Queen **Elizabeth I** (1558–1603).

Elizabethan theatre can be distinguished from Jacobean theatre (King James I, 1603–1625) and Caroline theatre (King Charles I, 1625 until the closure of the theatres in 1642). In practice, however, Elizabethan theatre is often used as a general term for all English drama from the **Reformation** to the closure of the theatres in 1642, thus including both Jacobean and Caroline drama. As such it can be synonymous with English Renaissance drama.

Shakespeare's theatre

Theatre developed in its shape and structure from the medieval pageant wagons. The concept of a platform surrounded by the audience became the **thrust** stage and the tiers mirrored the spectators who stood on the balconies looking down into the inn yard. The first theatre was built in 1576 in London by the actor James Burbage; it was called The Theatre. Acting was not regarded as an honest activity, so the theatre was constructed outside the city boundaries. It was later moved to the South Bank and became **The Globe**. In 1996 a historically accurate reconstruction of The Globe Theatre, built by Sam Wannamaker, was opened on the same site.

The Globe opened in 1599 with a production of *As You Like It* and continued with works by Shakespeare, Beaumont, Fletcher and others. In 1613, during a performance of *Henry VIII*, a cannon went off to mark the entrance of the king and a stray spark set the thatch roof aflame. In one hour, the theatre was destroyed. Reconstruction of The Globe began immediately and it was finished by June 1614. Performances continued until 1642, when the Puritans, who found theatre vulgar and intolerable, shut down all theatres.

One of the most valuable sources of our knowledge about the architecture of the theatres at this time is a drawing by Dutchman Arend van Buchell. Van Buchell used a sketch made by his friend **Johannes de Witt**, who attended a play at **The Swan**, to make his own drawing.

The stage jutted out into the pit and was raised about 4–6 feet. Its **dimensions** were 20 feet wide and 15 feet deep. The groundlings would gather tightly around the stage. In the floor of the stage was a **trap door**, used for the appearance of ghosts and spirits from graves. Elizabethans believed that 'hell' was below the ground and that 'heaven' was above.

Action point

See www.Shakespeares-Globe.org

Take note

The Swan is the name of the thrust stage theatre at the Royal Shakespeare Company (RSC) in Stratford-upon-Avon. It is also a reconstruction of an Elizabethan theatre.

The theatre was an octagonal rounded shape; Shakespeare famously described The Globe as '*this wooden O*' in *Henry V*. The rear of the stage contained two doors through which entrances and exits were made and behind them was a small back-stage structure, called the **tiring house**. The stage wall was covered by a curtain and the actors used this area to change their attire.

At times, the curtained **inner stage** was used to reveal scenes. The stage was covered by a roofed house-like structure supported by two pillars. The Herculean pillars were made of huge, single tree trunks. The pillars supported a roof called the **heavens**, which served to create an area hidden from the audience. A selection of ropes and rigging would allow for special effects: smoke effects, the firing of a real cannon, fireworks (for dramatic battle scenes) and spectacular 'flying' entrances.

Behind the pillars was the stage wall, called the **frons scenae** (taken from the name given by Imperial Rome to the stage walls of their amphitheatres). Immediately above the stage wall was the **stage gallery**, used by actors (e.g. Juliet's balcony), by the rich and by the nobility; it was known as the **Lord's rooms**.

Checkpoint 1

Can you explain how the **tiring house**, **trap door** and **stage gallery** might have been used in a production of one of Shakespeare's plays?

The actor and the audience

Theatre performances were held in the **afternoon**, in full daylight, and flags were flown on the day. Colour coding was also used: a black flag denoted a tragedy, white a comedy and red a history.

Elizabethan theatres could often present ten different plays in two weeks. There were two levels for audiences: expensive galleries for the wealthy – the very grand could watch the play from a chair set on the side of the stage itself – and an open space in front of the stage for the **groundlings**, who paid a penny to stand in the **pit**. At the height of the summer, the groundlings were also referred to as **stinkards**, for obvious reasons.

The Shakespearean **actors** generally got their lines only as the play was in progress. Parts were often allocated on the day of the performance. Often the actors used a technique called **cue acting** – a person whispered the lines to the actor just before he was going to say them. Each actor was given only his own lines and the cues, rather than a whole text.

The complete scene of the play was not explained to the actors until it was actually being performed. This technique allowed for little rehearsal time, thus enabling a rapid turnover of new productions at The Globe and a great portfolio of different roles. There were no actresses – the acting profession was not a credible one and it was unthinkable that any woman would appear in a play – so female characters had to be played by young boys.

Take note

In *A Midsummer Night's Dream* Shakespeare parodies cue acting in the mechanicals' rehearsal when Quince reprimands Flute for speaking '*all your lines at once, cues and all*'.

Plays and playwrights

Shakespeare's plays were divided into three categories: tragedy, comedy and history. Some of his later plays, such as *The Winter's Tale* (1610) and *Cymbeline* (1609), are known as **late romances**. Shakespeare's plays followed the traditions of style and form, such as **revenge tragedy** (e.g. *Hamlet*), yet his plays had originality and challenged accepted forms. His plays reflected the political turbulence of the era.

The **Renaissance**, meaning 'rebirth', refers to the period of transition between the medieval and modern worlds. In addition to Shakespeare, notable playwrights in Elizabethan and Jacobean theatre were Marlowe, Webster, Jonson and Middleton.

In **Marlowe's** *Dr Faustus* (1588), Renaissance man's thirst for knowledge is grafted on to medieval man's search for salvation. The themes have a clear link to morality plays, e.g. *Everyman*, in which Faustus is corrupted by the deadliest of sins, pride.

Webster's plays are a sombre picture of Jacobean society; their themes are corruption and human cruelty. The imagery is laden with death and decay. *The Duchess of Malfi* (1614) is a classic **revenge tragedy**, a popular sub-genre of tragedy, familiar to audiences. Ghosts, murder, the supernatural, torture and madness were recognised elements of this genre.

Ben Jonson's satirical comedies, such as *Bartholomew Fair* (1614), observed society ridiculing corrupt deceit and pretence.

Middleton's early plays, e.g. *A Mad World My Masters* (1608), were vicious comedies exposing society's parasites and painting love and sex as commodities. *The Changeling* (1622), written in collaboration with **Rowley**, was one of the last plays of the Jacobean age, with many features of revenge tragedy, including the villain, De Flores.

Checkpoint 2

Name another play by each of these playwrights.

Exam practice 30 minutes   answers: page 26

Imagine that you were directing a play from this period at The Globe in London. Suggest how you would stage three key scenes using the features of the theatre. Consider entrances and exits as well as the use of areas such as the gallery, the columns and the trap door.

Restoration to the 19th century

This period saw the first indoor theatre buildings and the style and architecture of these structures are still evident in many of today's theatres. The era saw the rise of the actor and the decline of the playwright. It was against this background that the important revolution in theatre, examined in the next section, took place. This is an important phase of theatre development, which you should understand, as it was from this period that the traditional **proscenium arch theatre** developed.

Links

See Theatrical revolution, page 22.

Restoration theatre

From 1642, for 18 years, the theatres of England remained nominally closed. There was, of course, evasion of the law and plays had to be performed in secret, by small companies in private houses, or in taverns located three or four miles out of town. No actor or spectator was safe, especially during the early days of Puritan rule. Least of all was there any inspiration for dramatists. In 1660, Charles II was restored to the throne of England after his exile in France. His 'restoration' gave rise to the term that describes this period of history.

As a reaction to the Puritan rule of **Oliver Cromwell**, the new king brought the flamboyance of the French court to England. Theatres were built indoors and the thrust stage disappeared behind proscenium arches that are still evident today. Public performances were initially presented in converted tennis courts. However, their freedom was short lived and Charles II soon reorganised the theatre by creating a monopoly through royal patent. This licensed only two companies to produce theatre in London. These theatres, **Lincoln's Inn Fields** and **Drury Lane**, became known as the **patent theatres** and were managed and directed by **Thomas Killigrew** and **William Davenant**.

Theatres were rectangular, with the stage at one end and the auditorium extending from just below the **apron** (the part of the stage that runs further out towards the audience) to the back of the theatre. The seats were classified into three sections:

1 The **pit:** the area right below the stage. It was very difficult to see all aspects of the play from here. The pit was for the audience members who couldn't pay for, or weren't allowed, better seats.
2 The **gallery:** the area behind the pit extending to the back of the theatre. The middle-class citizens generally occupied this area.
3 **Boxes:** ornately designed boxes on the sides of the auditorium were known as the best seats and were reserved for dignitaries or others who could afford them.

In the Restoration theatre, scenery became more a part of the stage. Instead of using a uniform stage, each scene was created to fit. Set and costume became elaborate and the first actresses appeared on the stage. Actresses were not regarded with much respect and famously **Nell Gwyn** became the King's mistress.

Aphra Behn was the first woman playwright. Her play *The Rover*, a comedy set in a 17th-century Spanish colony during carnival time, recreates a male-dominated society but responds with a clear-sighted

Action point

See www.bbc.co.uk/history/british/ civil_war_revolution/cromwell_01.shtml for information about Cromwell's England.

Take note

Read April de Angelis' play *Playhouse Creatures*, a modern play about actresses at this time.

and sympathetic portrayal of the female predicament. The plays performed were often adaptations of Shakespeare with rewritten 'happy endings'. Manners and etiquette were of central importance in society and the plays mirrored and satirised this preoccupation.

These plays were known as **Restoration Comedy** and were focused around intrigues and love affairs of the gentlemen and ladies of the day. Much of the comedy was about deceit and deception; plays were written with **stock** characters that represented types. The comedies were about people, not ideas or ethical hypothesis; they exposed the complexities of human experience, not a moral indictment of man's frailty. They were known as **comedies of manners. William Wycherley**, **William Congreve** and **John Dryden** were the key playwrights of the era.

Theatre in the 18th and 19th centuries

During this era, theatre took on a middle-class atmosphere. This time saw the beginnings of pantomime, which owed much to **Commedia dell'arte**.

This was the age of the **actor manager** when audiences came to see famous performers, such as the legendary actor **David Garrick**, who had a financial stake in the theatre and therefore benefitted from each ticket sold. This era also gave rise to the **star** system, where the actor rather than the play was paramount.

Theatres became enormous and some remain today. Garrick managed the theatre at Drury Lane from 1747 to 1776, during which time he produced many plays, including most of Shakespeare's work. His management produced hardly any *new* plays. He did, however, gain a reputation at the time for **innovatory naturalism**. When he played Hamlet in 1775 he had a wig maker create a 'trick' hair piece which would literally stand on end when he saw his father's ghost!

The cockpit on the site of Drury Lane was converted into a theatre during the reign of James I. After the Restoration of the monarchy in 1660, a splendid new theatre was built to designs by Christopher Wren. Having been razed by fire on 25 January 1762, it was succeeded by a larger and still more elaborate building, also designed by Wren, which housed 2,000 spectators, with the opening attended by Charles II on 26 March 1764. By the end of the 18th century, the building was in need of updating and in 1791 it was demolished.

A third theatre was designed by Henry Holland and opened on 12 March 1794, lasting for only 15 years before burning down on 24 February 1809. The present Theatre Royal in Drury Lane opened in 1812. It was a cavernous auditorium seating 3,016 people; the actors' performances became **declamatory** and lacked subtlety in such vast spaces. Another **patented** theatre – Lincoln's Inn Field – saw the first production of John Gay's political satire, *The Beggar's Opera*, in 1728. Plays were increasingly being used to pillory government figures so, under the pretext of curbing licentiousness in the theatre, Walpole rushed through the **Licensing Act** in 1737. This gave the **Lord Chamberlain** the right to censor plays. It was not revoked until 1968.

In the 19th century, the pit in front of the stage where the audience once stood or sat on rough benches, changed. Seating was installed in this area, which became known as the **stalls**. In 1865, there is a record of

---

Take note

Edward Bond's 1981 play *Restoration* is set in 18th-century England, a world of brutality and inequality, focusing on the betrayal of the working class. Bond's play is a metaphor for Thatcherite Britain.

Checkpoint 1

Name one play by each of these writers.

Links

Take note

Other notable actors of the age included **Charles Kemble**, **Sarah Siddons**, **Edmund Kean** and **Charles Macready**.

Take note

The Theatre Royal, Drury Lane, is a fine example of a theatre built at this time and still continues to stage large-scale productions today.

Checkpoint 2

What is **censorship** and why did the Licensing Act of 1737 have such a significant effect on modern theatre?

Links

See the Royal Court Theatre, page 24.

20

carpets being laid in the stalls. Matinees were introduced at this time and the scenic design became more detailed. Theatres often stayed open until midnight showing farces, tragedies, melodrama, pantomimes and other entertainment. Towards the end of the century the theatres reverted to performing a single play. The advent of the railways enabled the London plays to tour the country.

Melodrama

Melodrama was sentimental drama marked by extravagant theatricality, subordination of character development to plot, and a focus on sensational incidents. Improbable plots featured stock characters such as the noble hero, the long-suffering heroine and the hard-hearted villain. The plays ended with virtue triumphing over vice. The large theatres with their technical resources were the perfect place for melodrama. Famous melodramas included *Maria Marten (or The Murder in the Red Barn)* and *East Lynn*.

Developments in staging and design

The acoustics and lighting in the theatres in the 18th century were poor. The greater size of the theatres necessitated more elaborate scenery and increased spectacle. Garrick employed Loutherbourg, a French artist, to paint **cut-cloths** – backdrops which were cut out to reveal further scenes behind them.

Many rudimentary effects were introduced during this era, e.g. thunder sheets and ways of suggesting rain falling and wind blowing by moving silks and pieces of glass in front of lamps. One design at the Sadlers Wells theatre included real water and boats. The lavish scenic design during this period diminished the importance of the performances; audiences began to expect sumptuous design and spectacular effects.

Developments in lighting

Theatres in the 18th century were initially lit by candles but towards the end of the century oil lamps were introduced. Garrick abandoned the chandeliers hanging over the fore-stage in favour of lights behind the proscenium arch. In 1817 **gaslight** was brought in and by 1840 nearly all other theatres had followed this lead.

The risk of fire led to legislation about safety in the theatres. The blacking out of the audience lighting left the stage brightly illuminated and formed the final break between the actor and the audience.

Limelight, a term associated with being the centre of attention, was the burning of a stick of lime in a gas jet and coloured by means of painted glass slides. It was used to create special effects: sunrises, moonlight on water. Limelight was used extensively in **melodrama**.

The first electric lighting was in use by 1881.

Take note

A melodrama entitled *Gaslight* was written by Patrick Hamilton in 1938.

Exam practice   30 minutes   answers: page 26

Compare the theatre of today with the historical periods in this chapter. What are the most significant differences? Are there any similarities?

Theatrical revolution

This section covers one of the most important eras in the development of the theatre. It looks at the European pursuit of truth and reality through which important practitioners and playwrights emerged. You may be studying Stanislavski, Brecht or Artaud as well as the playwrights Ibsen, Chekhov or Strindberg. This section examines the social context and development of their approach. This period shaped modern acting and playwriting.

Links

For a detailed discussion of practitioners, see pages 29–45.

Take note

The Irish playwright **George Bernard Shaw** was influenced by the work of Ibsen.

Checkpoint 1

Define, in your own words, the difference between **realism** and **naturalism**.

Take note

There are key playwrights and practitioners who are associated with the 'isms'! **Ibsen, Chekhov, Shaw** and **Stanislavski** are allied to **realism**; **Zola, Gorky, Strindberg** and **Stanislavski** (again) are linked with **naturalism. Symbolism** is attributed to the work of **Strindberg** (again), **Maeterlink** and **Alfred Jarry**, while expressionism originated in Germany and includes the work of **Wedekind, Max Reinhardt** and the early offerings of **Bertolt Brecht**. Playwrights in America, such as **Tennessee Williams** and **Arthur Miller**, employed expressionist techniques in *The Glass Menagerie* and *Death of a Salesman* respectively.

Terminology

Mise-en-scène literally means 'put in the scene'. It refers to the creation of a stage picture, the detail of the positioning and nature of objects.

Watch out!

The practitioners associated with this theatrical revolution do not necessarily fit neatly into boxes. The changes in style evolved and it would be wrong to place anyone emphatically in one category.

Realism and naturalism

The theatrical revolution in Europe was led by the playwrights **Ibsen**, **Chekhov** and **Strindberg** and by the practitioners **Stanislavski**, **Brecht**, **Artaud** and **Craig. Emile Zola**, a French novelist, was the first, as early as 1873, to criticise the frivolity of theatre and advocate an approach he called '**naturalism**'.

'Drama is dying of its extravagances, its lies and its platitudes . . .'

The Norwegian realist playwright **Henrik Ibsen** shocked the audiences of his day with plays about venereal disease (*Ghosts*) and the role of women in society (*A Doll's House*). He sought to highlight the ills of society; the romantic need for the happy ending was swept away, Hedda shoots herself and Nora leaves her husband and, more shockingly, her children.

In *Miss Julie*, **Strindberg** advocates the use of *real* objects in scenic design and comments that '*theatrical characters . . . ought to be challenged by naturalists, who know how richly complex a human soul is . . .*'. Realism could be defined as selecting and distilling observations from real life, while naturalism is a more philosophical engagement with the essence of humanity. Stanislavski was criticised as overwhelming the text with naturalistic detail, which inhibited communication with an audience. **Chekhov**, the Russian dramatist who worked closely with Stanislavski at the Moscow Art Theatre, famously complained that the director had ruined his play *The Seagull* with an overly detailed and cluttered set design, which allowed little room for actors to move.

Mise-en-scène and design

The design of stage settings during this period was detailed and natural. Sets for plays in the 18th and 19th century relied on two-dimensional painted 'backcloths'. Realism demanded accurate detail. Strindberg's *Miss Julie* is set in a kitchen and in his Preface he admonishes the theatrical convention of painted pictures of pots and pans on the backcloth.

Realism, naturalism, expressionism and symbolism refer to specific genres and styles in late 19th- and early 20th-century European theatre.

→ **Realism:** making the set, characters and plot *appear* to be real life.
→ **Naturalism:** influenced by Zola, aiming to make the theatrical event a detailed and *precise* 'slice of life'.
→ **Symbolism:** reacted against realism and focused on the use of *images*.
→ **Expressionism:** an extreme emotion dramatised through *symbol* and *metaphor*.

Acting and directing

Stanislavski, whose work is discussed more fully in another section, is credited with the revolution in the craft of acting during this era. He sought to develop a science of acting which he named **The System**. In his many books, notably *An Actor Prepares*, he gives a minutely detailed account of how the actor should approach a role. Stanislavski strove to find 'truthful' acting and his work at the **Moscow Art Theatre** shaped the style of acting that we see today.

British theatre in the early 20th century

In Britain, it was regional repertory theatres that tried to establish a non-commercial permanent home for the classics and innovative contemporary drama: The Abbey in Dublin and The Gaiety in Manchester. In London, however, theatre remained in the domain of managers who wanted to retain a traditional approach, the antithesis of the new European practice.

Actors like **Henry Irving** and **Beerbohm Tree** had continued the 'star' system tradition. Playwrights such as **Oscar Wilde** (*The Importance of Being Earnest*) illustrated social snobbery and **Noel Coward** (*The Vortex*) dealt with scandalous themes, but their plays remained in a conventional and comic style.

Only **Granville Barker**, who had an analytical approach to text, and **Shaw** paralleled the social realism of the European writers. Granville Barker's *The Voysey Inheritance* dealt with the moral problem of a man who realises that his father's fortune was acquired through deceit and trickery. Shaw, influenced significantly by the work of Ibsen, wrote about prostitution in *Mrs Warren's Profession* and had his work rejected by the censor. Other plays focused on the emerging role of women in society.

Theatre-going was essentially a middle-class activity. Theatres retained the ornate auditoriums and proscenium arch stages of the past and plays depicted a section of society rather than encompassing its entirety. Even Shaw's *Pygmalion* portrays a common flower seller's attempt to rise in social class by learning to speak like a lady; it does not expose the hollow superficiality of polite society or the truth about the underclass.

The seeds of change were sown after the Second World War (1939–1945) when the Arts Council was formed in 1946. This gave regional theatres increased funding to rehearse and to experiment with new plays and removed the pressure of 'weekly rep'.

The real revolution in British theatre was to come from the Royal Court Theatre, founded by **George Devine** in 1956.

Watch out!

Stanislavski's work was called **The System**, *not* **the method**. Beware of referring to 'method' acting as Stanislavski's creation. 'Method' acting was, in fact, developed in America by **Lee Strasberg**, who had studied Stanislavski, but it focuses on one or two key elements of his work.

Checkpoint 2

Who was the playwright most closely associated with Stanislavski and where were his plays performed?

Terminology

Weekly rep, short for repertory, meant that a theatre company would stage a different production every week. They would rehearse one play during the day while performing the previously rehearsed play at night.

Exam practice   15 minutes

answers: page 27

Select a modern play that you are studying or preparing for performance. List the features of **theme**, **style** and **character** that have been influenced by the practitioners or theatrical movements discussed in this section.

Modern theatre

The modern theatre continues to evolve. This section explores the significant changes in the second half of the 20th century, which have shaped the theatre as we know it today. There is an analysis of absurdist theatre, an explanation of the critical pioneering role of the Royal Court Theatre and a discussion of contemporary experiment. This section is particularly important as a background to the study of unseen modern texts.

Theatre of the absurd

Theatre of the absurd has its roots in German **expressionism** and surfaced in the 1950s with a group of playwrights who included **Samuel Beckett**, **Eugene Ionesco**, **Jean Genet** and **Harold Pinter**. Their work expressed the belief that, in a godless universe, human existence has no meaning or purpose and all communication breaks down.

One of the most important aspects of absurd drama was its distrust of language as a means of communication. Language, absurdists argued, had become a vehicle of conventionalised, stereotyped, meaningless exchanges. Logical construction and argument gave way to irrational and illogical speech and to its ultimate conclusion, silence, as in Beckett's play *Breath* (1970).

Although absurdist theatre appears completely opposed to the realistic ideas of **naturalism**, the work is often founded on very precise observation of human nature and behaviour.

Angry Young Men

On 8 May 1956 a revolution took place in British theatre. At the Royal Court Theatre, presented by the newly formed English Stage Company, a play by **John Osborne** shook the middle-class audience. The play was set in a squalid London flat, with the ironing board on stage becoming emblematic of the new social realism that was to sweep the British stage. The play's protagonist, Jimmy Porter, railed against the post-war socialism that had failed to reform. The fiery invective of his attacks on the establishment gave voice to a frustrated generation.

Although the play used conventional forms, three acts, somewhat melodramatic climaxes and a box set, the critic, Kenneth Tynan, championed the play in his review: '*Osborne has presented post-war youth as it really is in the best young play of the decade.*'

The term '**angry young man**' was coined when the Royal Court press officer was asked to describe John Osborne. It quickly became a 'movement' associated with a generation of playwrights that included **Shelagh Delaney** (*A Taste of Honey*), **Arnold Wesker** (*Roots, The Kitchen*), **John Arden** (*Sergeant Musgrave's Dance*) and **Harold Pinter** (*The Caretaker*).

The explosion in British theatre continued to be centred at '**The Court**'. The Licensing Act of 1737 gave the Lord Chamberlain the right to censor plays and all new texts had to be submitted for approval prior to performance. The management at the Royal Court fought a long, crucial and ultimately successful battle against theatrical censorship by the Lord

Take note

Beckett's *Waiting for Godot* is possibly the most well-known **absurdist** play. Two tramps wait for Godot to arrive and save them from their wretched lives. He never comes; they continue to wait, day after day.

Checkpoint 1

Name one play each by **Pinter, Ionesco** and **Genet**.

Action point

To learn more about the Royal Court, see *The Royal Court Theatre and the Modern Stage* by Philip Roberts, *Taking Stock* by Max Stafford-Clark and Philip Roberts or the chapter '1956' in *Changing Stages* by Richard Eyre and Nicholas Wright.

Checkpoint 2

Why was **8 May 1956** such a significant date for British theatre?

Chamberlain's office in the 1960s. The Royal Court undermined the law by presenting controversial plays at 'club nights' where membership was obtained easily at the door.

In February 1966, the theatre was prosecuted for staging Edward Bond's *Saved*; it had been refused a public performance licence in 1965 and was one of the last plays to be censored. There was a lengthy correspondence between Peter Shaffer and the Lord Chamberlain's office in 1965 over what was considered to be religious dissent in *The Royal Hunt of the Sun*. The act was finally repealed in 1968.

In 1953 **Joan Littlewood** took over the disused Theatre Royal, Stratford East to develop her dynamic ensemble **Theatre Workshop**. Her Brechtian production, *Oh! What a Lovely War*, exposed the horrors of the First World War using vaudeville turns at an 'end-of the-pier' show, with actors dressed as clowns, to satirise the criminal irresponsibility of the English ruling classes.

Theatre today

In the 1970s and 80s, the theatre in Britain underwent a time of financial hardship. Plays with large casts and expensive settings could not be staged and even the major companies at the National Theatre and the RSC experienced cutbacks, while the Royal Court was forced to close the Theatre Upstairs. Playwrights began to write plays with fewer characters. In London's West End, stars from film and television were cast in order to attract audiences and spectacular musicals boomed.

Practitioners, such as the **Joint Stock** collective, continued to test the boundaries of theatrical form. The director **Peter Brook**, shortly after his landmark production of *A Midsummer Night's Dream* in 1970, moved to France to set up a 'theatre laboratory', concerned with sustaining experiment into form and style in theatre.

Regional theatres sprang up whilst theatres on the 'fringe' mushroomed in unconventional venues. Lunchtime theatre and small touring companies added to the rich pattern of the 1970s' theatrical scene.

In the 1970s and 1980s playwrights such as **David Hare**, **Tom Stoppard** and **Caryl Churchill** became the dominant voices of British drama. Hare and Churchill challenged the establishment and Stoppard wrote with incisive wit about humanity and emotion, sometimes attacking left-wing ideology.

Theatre since 1980 has diversified. Théâtre de Complicité, founded in 1986, combines movement, text and design to express meaning and the Canadian **Robert Lepage** is a performer and director whose work connects text, imagery and physicality in a unique way. The diversity of form, style and material makes the theatre of today a rich and varied medium. Eyre and Wright comment at the end of the excellent *Changing Stages*: '*Nothing can live in the theatre that is not conceived out of passion, nurtured on obsession, and educated in enthusiasm.*'

Exam practice   30 minutes   answers: page 27

Look back over this section and create a timeline charting the key practitioners, playwrights, theatres and landmark moments of the modern theatre. Use the internet to research parallel historical events.

Take note

The Royal Court continued to produce the work of new and contentious writers. **Caryl Churchill**, **Timberlake Wertenbaker**, **Mark Ravenhill** and **Sarah Kane** are just a few of the playwrights whose careers were launched at the Royal Court.

Take note

The National Theatre, the Royal Shakespeare Company and the Royal Court are **subsidised**. This means that they receive funding from the government to enable them to produce work that is not solely dependent on commercial success. For example, Shakespeare's plays have large casts and are expensive to produce. Theatres in the **West End** are commercial businesses and they must present productions that are viable financially.

Take note

Examples of musicals at this time are *Cats* (1972), *Les Miserables* (1985) and *Phantom of the Opera* (1986).

Links

See pages 30, 37 and 44 for more detail on **Grotowski**, **Artaud** and **Brook**, all of whom had a major impact on modern theatre practice.

Take note

In this period **Joe Orton** wrote comedies that might seem like **farce** but in fact use the form of **burlesque**. An example is *What the Butler Saw* (1969).

Take note

Michael Billington's *State of the Nation* (Faber and Faber 2007) examines the relationship between society and the theatre in post-war Britain.

Answers
Drama and theatre in context

The language of drama and theatre

Checkpoints

1 **Thrust staging** means that the stage is surrounded by the audience on three sides. In **promenade theatre**, the audience follows the action.
2 **Rehearsal** is a focused exploration of the text where actors and director investigate character, theme and staging and move towards an agreed presentation of the play.

Exam practice

Advantages of **traverse** include the fact that the audience is close to the action, they have seats, the space can mirror a journey and locations can be created symbolically. Disadvantages might be difficulty in lighting without spillage and the lack of opportunity for scenic design. **Promenade** theatre involves the audience in the play – atmosphere is created through audience participation and locations that do not need to be moved can be created in various places. The disadvantages could be that audience members have no seats, the actors have to guide the audience during the performance and it is more difficult for a director to focus audience attention.

Greek and medieval theatre and Commedia dell'arte

Checkpoints

1 The **orchestra** was the circular area in which the action was performed. An orchestra today is a group of musicians who might play in the orchestra pit in a theatre.
2 **Liturgical** drama took place in a church. Mystery plays were stories from the Bible presented by guilds on pageant wagons. **Morality** plays used allegorical figures to examine moral behaviour.
3 A **lazzi** was an extended and exaggerated comic sequence of movement. **Stock characters** appeared in all plays.

Exam practice

You might have referred to any of the following:
- The use of masks or a chorus
- A circular stage space
- Thrust or platform staging
- A performance where the actors move around with the audience remaining static
- A play with a moral story or using allegorical figures
- An exaggerated, physical comedy
- The use of stock characters

Elizabethan and Jacobean theatre

Checkpoints

1 The **tiring house** was a backstage room where the actors changed; a dressing room. The **trap door** was a small door in the floor of the stage through which actors could appear or disappear. The **stage gallery** was a balcony above the stage used for musicians or for scenes such as Juliet's balcony.
2 Marlowe: *Edward II, The Jew of Malta*. Webster: *The White Devil*. Jonson: *Volpone, Every Man in his Humour*. Middleton: *Women Beware Women, The Revenger's Tragedy* (with Tourner).

Exam practice

A production of *Hamlet*
In the scenes in Act I where the ghost of Hamlet's father appears, you might use the **trap door** and the **stage gallery** as he moves from one part of the castle battlements to another. When Polonius is spying on Hamlet and Gertrude in the 'closet scene', he might hide behind the curtained **inner stage**; Hamlet stabs him through the curtain. The **trap door** would be used again in Act V for Ophelia's grave and at the end of the play the cannons would sound from the **heavens**.

Restoration to the 19th century

Checkpoints

1 William Wycherley: *The Country Wife*. William Congreve: *The Way of the World*. John Dryden: *All For Love*.
2 The Licensing Act of 1737 affected the theatre until 1968 because the Lord Chamberlain was empowered to censor plays and could insist that parts of scripts were changed. This prevented playwrights from making political points and effectively gave the government control over what theatres presented.

Exam practice

Many theatres today retain the proscenium arch, with the audience separated from the actors, although directors often try to bring the action forward. Some theatres have constructed apron stages to enable more intimate communication with the audience. There are more diverse theatre spaces – for example, theatre in the round at The Crucible in Sheffield, the Young Vic in London and at the Manchester Royal Exchange. Lighting has developed significantly, with more realistic effects made possible by technology.

Plays continue to address the social issues of the day, with playwrights like Alan Ayckbourn making satirical observations on society in much the same way as Wycherley. There is an element of the 'star' system, as in Garrick's day, in West End theatre, where famous personalities from film and television are cast in order to attract audiences. The enormous theatres such as the Theatre Royal in Drury Lane continue to present spectacular productions with elaborate scenic effects. Plays are no longer censored by the Lord Chamberlain.

Theatrical revolution

Checkpoints

1 **Realism** is creating a scene or a situation that appears to be authentic; **naturalism** aims to present an exact 'slice of life'.

2 Chekhov at the Moscow Art Theatre.

Exam practice

In David Hare's *Skylight* the setting is a London flat. The detail of the set includes worn carpets, clutter, long shelves of books. The central character (Kyra) is a teacher and during Act I she cooks spaghetti bolognese. There is a working sink and cooker on the stage. Everything appears to be real. The play debates social values and the characters are recognisably real people: a teenage boy, a teacher in a 'sink' comprehensive and an older, successful executive.

Like Ibsen, Hare is concerned with contemporary society and he locates the play in a very specific environment – the flat must seem to be a real place, the cooking of the meal gives the scene an authenticity. However, the set does not contain everything that might be in such a flat – its design appears real while also allowing the theatrical action of the play to flow.

Modern theatre

Checkpoints

1 Pinter: *The Birthday Party, The Caretaker, The Dumb Waiter, The Homecoming.* Ionesco: *The Chairs, The Bald Prima Donna, Rhinoceros.* Genet: *The Maids, The Balcony, The Blacks.*

2 John Osborne's play *Look Back in Anger* was performed at the Royal Court Theatre. This play shocked audiences and gave a voice to a new generation of playwrights, known as 'angry young men'.

Revision checklist
Drama and theatre in context

1	Understand approaches to play writing.	Confident	Not confident **Revise** page 10
2	Analyse the nature of audience and explain 'suspension of disbelief'.	Confident	Not confident **Revise** page 11
3	Recognise and define various performance spaces.	Confident	Not confident **Revise** page 11
4	Define the purpose of rehearsal.	Confident	Not confident **Revise** page 12
5	Use the correct terminology when writing about theatre spaces and design elements.	Confident	Not confident **Revise** page 12
6	Understand why Greek theatre is considered the origin of drama.	Confident	Not confident **Revise** page 13
7	Explain how early theatre developed in Britain in the Middle Ages.	Confident	Not confident **Revise** page 14
8	Describe the characteristics of Commedia dell'arte.	Confident	Not confident **Revise** page 15
9	Explain the terms 'Elizabethan' and 'Jacobean' and name important playwrights from this era.	Confident	Not confident **Revise** page 16
10	Identify the key features of The Globe theatre.	Confident	Not confident **Revise** pages 16–17
11	Understand why the Restoration era had a lasting effect on theatre buildings.	Confident	Not confident **Revise** pages 19–20
12	Explain the importance of the Licensing Act of 1737.	Confident	Not confident **Revise** page 20
13	Understand why actor managers increased the size and capacity of theatres in the 18th century.	Confident	Not confident **Revise** page 21
14	Identify the distinguishing features of realism, naturalism, symbolism and expressionism.	Confident	Not confident **Revise** pages 22–23
15	Understand the difference between Stanislavski's 'System' and 'method' acting.	Confident	Not confident **Revise** page 23
16	Recognise the characteristics of the 'Theatre of the absurd'.	Confident	Not confident **Revise** page 24
17	Explain the importance of the Royal Court Theatre.	Confident	Not confident **Revise** pages 24–25

Key practitioners (1)

All examination specifications require the study of theatre practitioners in relation to exploration of text or as a stimulus for your own original work.

This chapter examines significant directors and designers from the 19th and 20th centuries, whose work has shaped the theatre of today. The chapter contains one section on each practitioner, with biographical detail and checklists of the key features of their theory, supported by examples from productions. The final section discusses the work of important contemporary companies whose distinctive style of theatre has influenced theatrical style. You can use this chapter when studying a specific practitioner or when revising a set text or production where the practitioner's theories might be employed.

Exam themes

- The study of the theories of a practitioner
- The influence of practitioners on the development of acting and directing
- The practical exploration of texts in relation to practitioners' theories
- The discussion of a practitioner's methods in the analysis of live theatre
- The selection of appropriate rehearsal techniques for devised or scripted work

Topic checklist

	Edexcel		AQA		WJEC	
	AS	A2	AS	A2	AS	A2
Konstantin Stanislavski	O		O		O	
Bertolt Brecht	O		O		O	
Jerzy Grotowski	O		O		O	
Edward Gordon Craig	O		O		O	
Antonin Artaud	O		O		O	

Konstantin Stanislavski (1863–1938)

Stanislavski's influence on modern theatre practice is considerable. This section looks at Stanislavski's work and the important features of **The System** and suggests rehearsal techniques that are rooted in his theories.

Concise biography

It is useful to be able to contextualise Stanislavski's work by cross-referencing important events in his life. The following biographical detail is significant in understanding the process of the development of **The System**.

Born in 1863 into a rich family, Stanislavski first performed as an actor in 1877. He attended the Moscow Theatre School for three weeks in 1885 but left because he considered the training to be poor. He was impressed by a radical production by the Duke of Saxe-Meiningen in 1890 and first met **Chekhov** in 1897 and founded the Moscow Art Theatre with Nemirovich-Danchenko. Stanislavski directed productions of Chekhov's major works at this theatre between 1898 and 1904. In 1906 he went to Finland and decided to write a manual for his '**System**'. Work on 'The System' continued and in 1912 he established the Studio, which became a centre for experiment. In 1923, aged 60, he agreed to write his autobiography, *My Life in Art;* his definitive version of The System, *An Actor Prepares*, was published in America in 1936. Stella Adler, who took classes with him in 1929, brought his ideas to America where later the work of Lee Strasberg at The Actors' Studio developed 'method' acting. Stanislavski died in 1938.

The background to The System

Stanislavski was part of the theatrical revolution in the late 19th century. His views on **realism** are well documented and he made the concept the essential principle upon which he built his work. It is useful here to reaffirm the difference between realism and naturalism: **realism** is distilled and selected from life, **naturalism** is a meticulous copy of it.

Stanislavski developed The System over a 30-year period. It began as a result of his dissatisfaction with his own performances on stage. Acting at that time was declamatory and stilted, with stock gestures and no attempt to understand a character. Costumes and sets were taken from the stores rather than designed for the particular play and rehearsal time was very short. Actors rarely learned all their lines, relying on the prompter to feed them during performances. Stanislavski called this **mechanical acting**.

The following events trace the early experiences that laid the foundations of The System. In **1888** he worked with a director, **Fedotov**, who helped him to strip away some of the mannered acting style and encouraged him to consider characterisation. The performance style, however, remained imitative. In **1895**, Stanislavski approached the role of **Othello** by focusing on one objective, **psychological realism**. His **1898** production of *The Seagull* included a detailed **mise-en-scène**, examination of the **sub-text** and an intensely psychological approach.

A glossary of Stanislavski's System

By 1911, Stanislavski had developed an approach to acting now known as The System. In its early form, it was almost exclusively a **psycho-technique** – this was the use of voice, language, expressive movement and rhythm which he developed over the following ten years. The key elements are:

→ **Given circumstances:** story, facts, names, location, epoch, historical events.

→ **Magic 'if':** this acts as a lever to release imagination. What would I do **if** I were in this situation?

→ **Units and objectives:** dividing the text into short sections under a descriptive title. Within each section, every actor has a 'want' that he/she plays in the segment.

→ **Super-objective:** links all the units and objectives into an over-arching objective for the play. It cannot be accomplished until the end.

→ **Through-line of action:** the linking of all the small objectives, which relate to the super-objective. This is how Stanislavski drew his idea of the **through-line of action:**

The super-objective

→ **Circle of attention:** an imaginary beam of light that focuses on a specific object. The actor's attention must focus solely on this area. Stanislavski called this '*solitude in public*'.

→ **Emotion memory:** finding an analogous emotion and recalling it as a way of portraying emotional truth.

→ **Relaxation:** removing external stresses from the body in preparation for adopting the physicality of the role.

→ **Action:** meaningful, purposeful activity on stage. '*Always act with a purpose.*'

→ **Tempo-rhythm:** balancing the external rhythm of the scene with the internal rhythm of the characters. *Tempo* is the speed, *rhythm* is the intensity.

→ **The method of physical action:** truthful portrayal through '**doing**' rather than internalising the characterisation. This was the foundation of **improvisation** and Stanislavski came to it very late in his career.

Examiner's secrets

When you are writing about Stanislavski in your notes, it is important to understand three things:
1 The definition of the element that you are discussing.
2 The way Stanislavski taught and used this technique.
3 How it might be employed in a contemporary rehearsal or production.

Checkpoint 2

Define **analogous**. Can you give an example of the use of **emotion memory**, citing an analogous emotion?

Relating your understanding of The System to the exploration of text and to rehearsal techniques

You should focus on the way you would use Stanislavski's ideas as an actor or as a director in preparing a role. It is important to have considered how your role or production might develop with reference to Stanislavski's System. In **Exploration Notes** you should mention and analyse techniques and evaluate how they were effective in developing your understanding of roles.

In Exploration Notes, or when writing **supporting notes** for your practical work, you might refer to one or two of Stanislavski's techniques alongside others that you drew on. You might support your points with succinct quotations from Stanislavski's works, e.g. from *An Actor Prepares*: '... *your emotional memory can bring back feelings you have already experienced.*'

Exam practice   30 minutes   answers: page 46

Examine the play that you have studied with reference to Stanislavski's techniques. Make a chart that shows how elements of The System might be employed to create roles, with reference to specific scenes or sections.

Bertolt Brecht (1898–1956)

Brecht was a playwright and a director, but it was his dramatic theories that made him a world figure in theatre. This section will examine the theory and the practice of Brecht's work and highlight his lasting influence on theatre practice.

Concise biography

Born into a middle-class family in Augsburg, Germany, in 1898, Brecht studied drama and theatre history. Sickened by the First World War he wrote *Drums in the Night* and *Baal* in 1918. His collaborative production, with **Casper Neher**, in 1923, of *In the Jungle of the Cities* was presented like a **boxing match**. In 1927 Brecht worked with **Erwin Piscator**, who began to refer to his work as '**epic**'. *The Threepenny Opera* premiered in 1928, and in 1930 a production of *The Rise and Fall of the City of Mahagonny* was picketed by uniformed Nazis. In 1930 his production of *The Mother* was toured to working-class districts of Berlin using temporary stages lit by car headlights. In 1933 he escaped Nazi Germany and moved to Denmark. The term *Verfremdung* was used for the first time in 1935 on a visit to Moscow.

Having written *Mother Courage and her Children* in 1939 he escaped from the Nazis and moved to America where he wrote and directed until 1949. Brecht opened the Berliner Ensemble in 1949 and in 1951 he used projections for the first time in a production of *The Mother*. In 1955/6 *The Caucasian Chalk Circle*, which had opened in Berlin in 1954, toured to Paris and London where it was received with critical acclaim. Brecht died in 1956.

Action point

Read more about Brecht's collaborations with **Caspar Neher**, the designer, and **Kurt Weill**, the composer.

Influences on Brecht's formative work

Piscator Developed large-scale documentaries dealing with current social and political issues. The devices he used – charts, written slogans, maps, cartoons, placards, newsreel, film and slides – signalled a significant departure in staging techniques. These were to become the fundamentals of Brecht's theatre practice.

Brecht collaborated with Piscator on the adaptation of the novel *The Good Soldier Schweik* in 1927. The story of the mournful wartime experiences of a soldier used filmed cartoons by George Grosz. Piscator is famous for his 'Living Newspaper Performances' in the late 1920s.

Sergei Eisenstein The Russian director, who moved into film in the 1920s, showed how film could have a powerful political impact. Brecht's use of **montage** has its roots in Eisenstein's *Battleship Potemkin*, which employed a montage technique.

Action point

Look at the following link to read the original FBI reports on Brecht: http://foia.fbi.gov/foiaindex/brecht.htm

Charlie Chaplin Brecht was impressed by Chaplin's lucidity of facial expression and almost formulaic presentation of emotion. Silent film was a significant influence, laying the foundations of **geste**. Brecht said of Chaplin that he '*made gestures quotable*'.

Chinese theatre The use of gesture, coloured materials and emblematic costume as symbols demonstrated to Brecht that the actor was communicating with the audience by representing, rather than becoming, a character.

Checkpoint 1

Who was **Charlie Chaplin** and why might he have influenced the development of **geste**?

Expressionism The early 20th-century German movement explored deep meanings rather than superficial ideas of reality. **Büchner** and **Wedekind** were expressionist playwrights whose tough, plain dramas had short scenes and concise dialogue.

Karl Marx His work was a guiding principle. Marxist philosophies underpinned Brecht's political theatre.

Epic theatre

The term 'epic theatre' was initially used by Piscator and encompasses the many techniques and aspects of performance and production. Essentially Brecht's theatre places the political message before the exploration of individual character.

A glossary of Brecht's theatrical style

Announcement of scenes	Written and announced before each scene
Banners and placards	Indicate place and time, comment on events
Costume	Selected garments to represent people or types
Direct address to the audience	Narrator and actors break 'fourth wall', speaking to audience
Exposed and visible lights	All theatrical illusion stripped away
Geste	An attitude expressed as a symbolic gesture; a gesture that could be read by the deaf
Half curtain	Allows the audience to see the changing of scenes – a further reminder that they are watching a play
Masks	Caricaturisation of political figures or grotesque masks for evil characters
Montage	A film term where short scenes are juxtaposed
Multi-role	The *obvious* playing of many different roles
Narrator or singer	Announces and comments, breaking the reality
Properties	Very few used but those that there are must be exact, ideally hand-crafted
Slides and film	The use of back projection or film within the production
Songs	Reflecting on the events, sometimes add humour (see also '*Spaß*')
Spaß	The German for 'fun'; Brecht often mixed comedy and tragedy
Spectators	Not an audience: those present must judge the events

> **Watch out!**
>
> It is important to ensure that the play you have seen or the technique you are using *is* Brechtian. Be careful not to use the term loosely to describe everything that is non-naturalistic.

Important Brechtian terms

Lehrstück

The 'learning plays', mostly created for the Baden-Baden festival, were presented on a concert stage. These plays argued the supremacy of the 'collective' and the need for the individual to submit to it. *The Mother* was the last of these plays in 1932.

Action point

Read *The Exception and the Rule,* a good example of a **Lehrstück**.

Verfremdungseffekt

This term was first used in 1935 and exemplifies Brecht's ideas. Literally translated, it means to 'make strange', but it is widely and *incorrectly* quoted as meaning **alienation**. The effect Brecht sought was one **distancing** the spectators from the emotion of the play, enabling them to be objective and to judge the events presented to them. The many devices in theatrical presentation were employed in order to **distance** rather than to 'alienate'.

Checkpoint 2

Write your own definition of *Verfremdungseffekt.* Learn how to spell it accurately.

Dialectic

Strictly speaking, this implies a balanced debate, with both sides of the argument presented with equal weight. The spectators are then able to critically judge the actions. In truth, Brecht rarely put forward **balanced** arguments but did show the spectators both sides of the debate.

Didactic

These are plays that are intended to **instruct**. Brecht wanted the spectators to learn more about the world. His plays were aimed at people who would not normally go to the theatre.

Historicisation

This was Brecht's practice of using a historical event to criticise society.

Exam practice   30 minutes   answers: page 46

Choose a production that you have seen or been involved in that uses Brechtian techniques. Write a concise discussion of how and with what effect the different strategies were employed. Consider the staging, the casting and presentation of roles, and the actor/audience relationship.

Jerzy Grotowski (1933–1999)

Grotowski passionately believed that theatre could address the question, *'How should we live?'* His seminal work *Towards a Poor Theatre* advocated concentration on the actor rather than on the design or technical elements of the production. His Laboratory Theatre pushed the boundaries of actor training and was a major influence on experimental work in the late 20th century. This section will examine Grotowski's experiments, explain his key theories and relate them to important productions.

Concise biography

Grotowski was born in Rzeszow, Poland, in 1923 and lived through the Nazi occupation. In he graduated from the State Higher School of Theatre in Krakow and in 1956 he took a directing course in Moscow. He studied Stanislavski, Meyerhold and Vakhtangov. In 1961 his production of *Dziady* integrated the audience into the action and his 1962 *Kordian*, set in a psychiatric hospital, treated the audience as patients. Grotowski set up the Laboratory Theatre for research into acting in 1965. and his work influenced Peter Brook's experimental projects in England. His influential work *Towards a Poor Theatre* was published in England in 1967. In 1969 Grotowski directed *Apocalypsis cum Figuris*, an experimental piece where the words develop from the action. In the 1970s he established a group, which he referred to as 'paratheatre' or 'active culture' with a spiritual agenda. In 1975 he won the Wroclaw City Prize for 'his creative activities in the realm of theatre'. Grotowski became professor at Columbia University in New York in 1982 and in 1983 he was appointed professor at the University of California. Grotowski dissolved the Laboratory Theatre in 1984 and moved to Italy where he died in 1999.

Links

See Peter Brook, page 50.

Take note

Grotowski's removal of all artifice in theatre can be compared to the revolution in the Catholic Church in 1962 when the Vatican Council removed much of the arcane ritual from the Mass. Grotowski uses significant religious terminology in his writing about theatre.

Grotowski's theories

The essential rationale for Grotowski's ideas is contained in ***Towards a Poor Theatre***. This is a complex and intense text, which will have formed the foundation for your study of this practitioner. Grotowski believed in truth; he wanted to peel away all artificiality, leaving the actor exposed psychologically and physically. His actors were put through a relentless physical and vocal training aimed at removing the artifice of 'acting' and discovering inner spirituality.

The act of theatre had an intensely religious significance and Grotowski referred to the audience as a '**congregation**', the performance as '**sacrificial**' and the actor as the '**high priest**'. He aimed to display private emotion in public and to engage the spectator in the act of theatre, shocking them into a discovery of their own 'psychic layers'.

His staging broke the traditional actor/audience barriers, placing the audience within the action and frequently requiring them to become part of the performance. The act of theatre was a shared journey of discovery.

A glossary of the main concepts of Grotowski's work

Poor theatre The opposite of 'rich theatre', a theatre stripped of artificiality, focusing on the actor and audience. All technical effects and decorative settings were removed, the text was no longer sacred and there was a sacrificial nature to the performance. Poor theatre was essentially actors and a space

The artificial Everything that is not natural, spiritual or psychological must be removed

Chamber theatre The actors and the audience shared one space. Grotowski's central concern was the actor/audience relationship, both spiritual and physical. The audience were often arranged in the space so that they could see other audience members as they observed the performance. This induced a spiritual discovery through a sort of 'psychic conflict'

Deductive not inductive Actors were to discover the 'skills within', not learn skills from others

Paratheatre Experimental work that rejected conventional texts; concerned with a spiritual agenda

Aesthetic/ascetic Combining the beauty of art with the discipline of monastic living

Secular holiness Theatre became a substitute for religion in a non-religious world

Exercises plastiques Working the joints

Exercises corporels Working on suppleness. Based on the work of Jacques Dalcroze, Grotowski's scrupulous routine of exercises worked the body through yoga techniques, twisting and contortion

Via negativa Approaching a challenge by asking *'What are the obstacles preventing me from doing this?'* rather than *'How do I do this?'* This technique was intended to ensure that actors engaged in self-discovery

Human mask The actor's face becoming contorted in a symbolic way to display emotion

---

Action point

Read the chapter 'Poor Theatre' in Peter Brook's *The Empty Space*.

Checkpoint 1

What are the essential differences between **rich** theatre and Grotowski's **poor** theatre?

Take note

There may be few examples of 'poor theatre' in your area. Look at small fringe/studio venues, where the audience is very close to the action, and touring experimental, physical theatre companies. Such productions often use 'poor theatre' techniques because they are indeed short of money and create meaning through movement, vocal sound and a minimum of technological assistance.

Take note

Eugenio Barba documented Grotowski's work over many years and edited *Towards a Poor Theatre*.

Checkpoint 2

Why do you think that although Grotowski stopped directing plays so early in his career he is regarded as an important influence on modern theatre practice?

Links

See page 34 for Brecht's use of **montage**.

Watch out!

Although there are clear similarities between the work of Grotowski and **Artaud**, it is important to remember that Grotowski's Laboratory Theatre of 1959 pre-dates his knowledge of Artaud. Critics have retrospectively linked their work and Grotowski recognised that Artaud's ideas support his theories.

Significant productions by Grotowski

Dziady (1961) The audience were integrated into the action.

Kordian (1962) The audience were placed in a psychiatric hospital and some even sat on the beds. The action surrounded them and when an inmate was 'bled', the spectators screamed with shock. Through this, Grotowski claimed that the audience experienced self-discovery.

Akropolis (1962) The audience were divided by 'moats', with parallel rows of seats facing each other. The set was a mere pile of props with no clear shape. As the performance progressed, the scene became the gas chambers of a concentration camp. (Auschwitz was in Poland.) The play used a montage technique to juxtapose scenes randomly.

Dr Faustus, Marlowe (1963) This was staged in a monastery refectory as a 'last supper'; the audience were guests. The chanting of the actors had a spirituality that was astonishing. The original text was fragmented and reordered in a montage, creating a series of flashbacks.

The Constant Prince (1965) This savage, violent play by Calderon de la Barca was presented with the audience looking down on the action, like the spectators at a bullfight. The metaphorical costuming of the victim Prince presented him as a Christ-like figure in a loincloth.

Apocalypsis cum Figuris (1969) The pinnacle of the Laboratory Theatre's work. Improvisation facilitated a journey of self-discovery for the actors who added words only at a late stage of the creative process. The words came from existing texts and included the Bible and T.S. Eliot. The play had a quasi-religious theme, a 'second coming'. The audience were seated on cushions, with the actors performing among them.

Exam practice   30 minutes   answers: page 46–47

If you have studied Grotowski or used his theory to underpin your practical project, your notes will explore the use of Grotowski's methods. For a play you have studied practically, write an account of how Grotowski's methods have informed your approach to the text.

Edward Gordon Craig (1872–1966)

Craig had a significant impact on the process and theory of stage design. His visionary ideas revolutionised theatrical design in the early 20th century. He introduced symbolism in design, which he achieved through creative use of light and perspective. This section will examine the influences on the young Craig and trace the development of his theories in relation to key productions.

Concise biography

Craig was born in Stevenage, Hertfordshire, in 1872 to actress Ellen Terry and architect Edward Godwin. He acted for the first time on a US tour with his mother in 1884 and in 1889 became an actor in Henry Irving's company at the Lyceum Theatre. His meeting with the 'Beggarstaff Brothers' in 1893, where he learned wood engraving, had a significant influence on his design ideas. Craig directed and designed *Dido and Aeneas* at the Hampstead Conservatoire in 1900, *The Masque of Love* at the Coronet Theatre in 1901 and Ibsen's *The Vikings of Helgeland* in 1903. Craig met and lived with Isadora Duncan, a dancer. His landmark production of *Hamlet* at the Moscow Art Theatre in 1911 was significant in the development of scenic design. From 1915 Craig wrote marionette plays, published *The Mask*, and exhibited in Europe. His edition of *Hamlet* with 75 woodcuts was published in 1930. Craig died in France in 1966.

Influences on Craig

Ellen Terry His mother was Henry Irving's leading actress so Craig was brought up in the theatre. His father left them early in his life and his surname came from Terry's love for the Scottish rock Ailsa Craig.

Henry Irving Irving was a surrogate father to Craig. His lavish productions at the Lyceum epitomised the realistic 19th-century tradition, where the 'star' system and extravagant settings attracted the audience.

Hubert Von Herkomer Von Herkomer founded an independent art school in Bushey, London, where he staged experimental theatre productions. Craig admired his innovative use of lighting and scenic design. Herkomer abolished **footlights**, used projected light on **gauze** and changed the levels on the stage floor as well as altering the proportions of the **proscenium** mechanically. Herkomer also recommended that the design should reflect the mood of the text. Craig harnessed and altered Herkomer's ideas in his initial designs after 1900.

The Beggarstaff Brothers James Pryde and William Nicholson worked as poster artists. They practised the art of **woodblock**, which Craig learned. In the deep **chiaroscuro** in the woodcuts, Craig saw the potential for lighting a stage – the process was likened to turning a light on a dark stage. The block represented the unlit stage and the carved white space, the light.

Isadora Duncan The dancer lived with Craig for a mere two years but her contact with Stanislavski led to Craig's breakthrough production of *Hamlet* and his collaboration with Stanislavski in Moscow. Duncan also awakened his sensitivity to the power of movement.

Edward Godwin Craig's father was an architect. He worked on providing archaeological evidence for Shakespeare's plays. Craig's Steps (see page 41) examines the common architectural element of a staircase.

Links

See Drama and theatre in context, pages 9–28.

Martin Shaw Shaw provided the opportunity for Craig's first productions; he also worked in Europe with Duncan as her musical director. Craig's designs for Bach's *St Matthew Passion* for Shaw shaped his approach over many years.

The medieval theatre Craig admired the simple style of the pageant wagons; it was the antithesis of naturalism.

Action point

Find out about the Roman amphitheatre at **Orange** in France.

The Roman theatre at Orange The visual simplicity of the Roman architectural style impressed Craig.

Craig's concepts for design in theatre

Craig's ideas for non-realist theatrical design must be set in the context of late 19th-century tradition. The revival in theatre in Edwardian England led to more theatres being built. Henry Irving was a leading actor/manager whose sumptuous productions were vehicles for the stars of the day. Little consideration was given to the way design might reflect mood or theme.

Harley Granville-Barker is credited with being the first modern director. His work at the Court Theatre began to address the need for an overall concept for a production. Craig spoke of a 'theatre of visions' and a 'real unreality'. He wanted to see a play as a sequence of moments, each making a symbolic visual statement. Lighting produced perspective and depth.

The following key developments show the journey of Craig's ideas.

Early years

Action point

Read about **Adolph Appia** (1862–1928), who was working at the same time as Craig. His ideas about the importance of design in relation to the actor and the text are very similar.

1900 *Dido and Aeneas* This production set out the principles of Craig's career – symbolist images with striking colour contrasts, a false proscenium, a concealed lighting gantry behind the false arch and no footlights. There was extensive use of gauze and cloth to create depth when lit.

1901 *The Masque of Love* The Jacobean 'masque' tradition inspired this play. It included music and dance and was played against a light grey canvas background with carefully plotted lighting.

1902 *Acis and Galatea* This used lengths of cloth and projected shadows. In a final cascade, a punctured cloth was dropped and backed by moving discs, through which lights shone.

1903 *The Vikings at Helgeland* (Ibsen) Designs included aspects of the classicism of ancient theatre, with emphasis on the vertical: the perspective dwarfed the actors. Costumes were in tones of grey with colour on huge cloaks. Some critics disliked the fact that the lighting cast shadow on faces, while others noted the symbolism of half-seen shapes. Martin Shaw composed the music.

1906 *Romersholm* (Ibsen) Craig aimed to reveal the metaphors in the play by covering the stage with sacking painted in blues and greens. An enormous window with prison-like bars provided the focal point of the perspective.

Checkpoint 2

Why were Craig's designs for Ibsen's plays considered so revolutionary?

Development of theories

1905 *Steps: The Four Moods* Craig described his drawing of a flight of steps as 'a lovely thing'. The four drawings in the series reveal an abstract modernism that leaves aside the traditional technologies of 19th-century theatre. In *The Four Moods*, Craig used light and movement to change the mood of a flight of steps ascending between two walls to an open sky. In each image, there is a sense of frozen movement, redolent of dramatic moments in plays. He wanted the actor to cease speaking and simply to move. '*Dance is the poetry of action.*' Craig returned to these ideas frequently.

1907 *Scene* It was a place where anything could happen, not a realistically created location. Craig had studied Serlio's *Treatise in Perspective* and been amazed by a drawing of huge walls on a chessboard; Craig thought again about the theatre of architecture. He experimented with raising and lowering the heights of blocks in section as well as creating a ceiling that was a mirror image of the floor and could also be raised and lowered. Lighting cast across the faces of the blocks changed the mood. The 'actors' would be two-dimensional figures who held poses while the words were spoken off stage. Craig's experiments with *Scene* led to his revised ideas of *Screens*.

1908 *The Übermarionette* The next development was the removal of the actor and his replacement with a puppet. Craig resented the control of the director over the actor and wanted him to remain remote from the role. Masked ritual was a key element of this drama. W.B. Yeats, the Irish poet, embraced many of these ideas, writing verse drama where the actor was depersonalised, with poetry and movement dominant.

Screens were portable units that were more flexible than the *Scene*. Made of wood or canvas, like stage flats, the screens were on castors, enabling easy movement. In 1908, Isadora Duncan introduced Craig to **Stanislavski**. This led to collaboration on the Moscow Art Theatre's production of *Hamlet*. This was both a momentous and a tortuous process, taking three years. The screens represented the claustrophobic inner world in one scene, then were moved suddenly and lit to become corridors or doorways. Craig used material and colour as he had done in his early days – a gold cloth covered the stage in Act I Scene ii and Hamlet was an isolated, shadowy figure against this background. The experience was fraught and the collaborators had no common language. Craig designed few productions following his Moscow triumph, but it remains a landmark in the history of theatrical design.

Exam practice   30 minutes answers: page 47

Consider the relevance of Craig's theories to the theatre today. Make notes on how Craig's ideas about design were reflected in a contemporary production that you have seen.

Antonin Artaud (1896–1948)

Artaud's contribution to theatre is encapsulated in his manifestos and writing. During his lifetime Artaud, who suffered mental health problems, constantly revised and even destroyed his work. His vision for a radical new theatre inspired experimental work long after his death. This section will trace the development of Artaud's theories, examine some of his productions and explain *The Theatre and its Double*.

Concise biography

Artaud was born in 1896 in Marseilles, France. Following a bout of depression in 1918, he was prescribed opium, which led to lifelong drug addiction. He joined the **surrealist** movement in 1924 and in 1925 became the director of the Surrealist Research Centre, but was expelled in 1926.

Between 1926 and 1928 The Alfred Jarry Theatre was formed, collapsed and was revived; during this period Artaud lived in poverty and began the **Theatre of Cruelty** experiment. The visit of the Balinese dancers at the Colonial Exhibition in Paris in 1931 had a considerable impact on his views of theatre. He began to write his manifestos in 1932 but his production of *The Cenci*, based on Shelley's poem, in 1935 failed to attract audiences. A limited edition of *The Theatre and its Double* appeared in 1937 but thereafter Artaud spent many years in mental hospitals; the second edition was published in 1943. Artaud was incensed that a planned radio broadcast was banned in 1948, by which time he was already suffering from cancer. Later that year, Artaud died of a possible overdose.

Influences on Artaud

Balinese dancers In the 1930s Bali was an exotic and little-known country; the dancers at the Colonial Exhibition in 1931 impressed Artaud. Their powerful, wordless communication, use of gesture and facial expression, the colourful masks and gamelan music had an intoxicating effect. Artaud had been experimenting with light, sound and symbolic imagery and these performers opened doors to new opportunities.

Lot and his Daughters This was a painting by Lucas van Leyden, in the Louvre. Artaud claimed a comparison with life: people's lives are threatened with disaster, yet they continue with their day-to-day routines.

The Marx Brothers In their anarchic comedy and rapidly juxtaposed images, Artaud saw parallels with surrealism: the invasion of the rational by the irrational.

Alfred Jarry (1873–1907) Jarry's absurdist *Ubu Roi* used rapidly moving scenes to tell the story of the killing of the King of Poland by the monstrous Ma and Pa Ubu. The first word was *merde* (shit) and the play, which drew on the style of the *guignol* puppets, both shocked and affected the audience. Artaud's aim was always to shock. The public dress rehearsal caused a riot!

> **Action point**
>
> See this picture at www.hobrad.com/
> lotvanleyden.htm

Action point

Find out more about the surrealist artists and about pyschoanalyst Sigmund Freud.

Terminology

Surrealism is a cultural, social and political movement. It asserts that liberation of the human mind, and thereafter the freeing of the individual and society, can be achieved by exercising the imagination of the 'unconscious mind' to the attainment of a dream-like state which is more truthful than everyday reality.

Surrealism His membership of the official movement was curtailed after a quarrel with André Breton, but Artaud was a surrealist in every sense. Surrealists saw insanity as a key to perception. They believed that the theatre should be a place not for middle-class entertainment but for emotional discovery and dreams. Sigmund Freud saw dreams as a window to the subconscious and surrealist artists created chaotic works designed to shock. Artaud believed in the power of dreams, the need to free the unconscious mind and the release gained from drug taking.

Film and cinema Artaud felt more comfortable working as an actor in film than in theatre; its influence on his work was important. He later advocated the use of modern equipment, light and sound effects that originated in his early experiences in film.

The development of ideas

Artaud had little opportunity to see his ideas in practice. He was a visionary and many of his aims were unachievable, technologically, during his lifetime. '*I want to resuscitate the idea of total spectacle*', he said. **Total theatre** is a term often employed to describe Artaud's legacy. '*But first, this theatre must exist,*' he stressed. Although it never did exist in his lifetime, few theatrical experiments over the last half century do not in some way owe something to Artaud's vision.

Artaud questioned the very fundamentals of theatre tradition: the space, the text, the design, the acting and the finances. Over six years he wrote letters, manifestos and essays, finally published as *The Theatre and its Double* in 1937. The expression **Theatre of Cruelty** is also synonymous with Artaud and often causes confusion. Artaud explains his rationale thus: '*. . . the pain which is ineluctably necessary to the continuation of life.*'

The Theatre and its Double

Why this title?
The theatre is the double of life and life is the double of true theatre.

What are these doubles?
These are metaphysics, the plague and cruelty.

→ **Metaphysics** Anything that cannot be explained rationally. Artaud references three key examples – the Balinese dancers, a painting, *Lot and his Daughters*, and The Marx Brothers (see page 43).
  → Dance and gesture could create meaning without words.
  → A painting could suggest settings and dramatic scenes.
  → Laughter was liberating and could be created using anarchic film editing.
→ **The plague** The plague was an allegory for theatre. A play should upset the tranquillity of the audience and leave them in a changed state, just like a plague. Theatre should challenge and disturb.
  → Plague was a parallel for theatre.
  → Extreme emotions arise from a lack of controls.
  → A play should release dreams and hidden emotions.

→ **Cruelty** The director, the actor and the audience combine to make theatre. This theatre must shock, disturb and amaze through its spectacular staging. '. . . *the spectator will be shaken and set on edge by the internal dynamism of the spectacle.*'

→ **actor/audience relationship** The audience were on swivel chairs surrounded by the actors who were above them. The actors invaded the audience.

→ **Sound** should assault the senses. Musical instruments were played by actors and even formed part of the set.

→ **Lighting** was a force and could attack the senses. Blinding lights shone into the audience's faces; lighting became an almost physical part of the action.

→ **Film** The juxtaposition of imagery is used to shock.

Masks and puppets were used alongside actors. Artaud called this '**magic beauty**'.

The actor must be trained rigorously, like an athlete; breathing and the voice were important. The 'forgotten' ability to **scream** must be rediscovered. Actors from the European theatre of 'words' must learn how to uncover raw emotion.

The text was replaced with 'scenarios', e.g. *The Conquest of Mexico*, the first Theatre of Cruelty show.

The performance was to be known as **The Show**.

In **language**, gesture and poetry replaced dialogue: '*gestures, postures and air-borne cries*'. Language, borrowed from surrealists, could be pure sound patterns.

Inspired by the Balinese dancers, **ritual** became synonymous with Artaudian theatre. There was also gravity in the use of ritual that was rooted in the dark and violent traditions of Greek theatre.

Example

The Cenci included shocking content and an assault on the senses. An atheist Italian count imprisoned for sodomy and incest is brutally murdered at the command of his daughter. The production included tolling bells, echoing footsteps, thunder and lightning, an oscillating metronome underpinned by whispering voices, deafening fanfares, ringing anvils from four loudspeakers in the audience. The set, made from giant scaffolding poles, had red cloths hanging like congealed clots of blood in a broken arc.

Take note

Artaud could not achieve many of his ideas as the technology of lighting was insufficiently advanced. Modern rock concerts use ideas that Artaud suggested: oscillating lighting diffused to create moods in the audience.

Checkpoint 2

Define **juxtaposition**.

Take note

Peter Shaffer's *Equus* or *The Royal Hunt of the Sun* are good examples of a late 20th-century playwright using Artaud's concept of **total theatre**.

Links

See Peter Brook, page 50; Artaud inspired his experimental work on the Theatre of Cruelty with the RSC in the 1960s.

Exam practice   30 minutes   answers: page 47

Select a play that you are studying and make notes on the visual, aural and spatial elements based on your understanding of Artaud's theories. Write your key ideas as bullet points.

Answers
Key practitioners (1)

Konstantin Stanislavski

Checkpoints

1 **Mise-en-scène** refers to the way that actors, set, props, etc. are placed on the stage. (Literally, it means 'put in the scene'.) **Sub-text** refers to the information that is not directly made clear by the dramatist's written lines. It is the impressions received by 'reading between the lines'. **Psychological realism** means that the author portrays truthful emotions that are believably the feelings of the character.

2 **Analogous** means comparable, parallel or related. An example of the use of **emotion memory**: the actor playing Dabby Bryant in *Our Country's Good* experiences **humiliation** when Ross makes her beg like a dog on all fours. The actress will not have experienced this kind of humiliation but recalls a moment when her boss in an office where she once worked publicly rebuked her for a simple spelling error in a letter.

Bertolt Brecht

Checkpoints

1 **Charlie Chaplin** was a star of the silent movies. His expressive use of movement and gesture demonstrated character so clearly that Brecht wanted his actors to use gesture to **present** a character rather than to **inhabit** the role.

2 *Verfremdungseffekt* is the term Brecht used to express his ideal: the effect of distancing – of shifting the audience's focus on the action so that they recognise that they are watching a play, not reality.

Exam practice

The Permanent Way by David Hare is an example of verbatim theatre. This style of theatre requires the audience to judge the events and to come to its own conclusions about guilt and responsibility. Brecht and Hare both express a bias: Brecht was always on the side of the victims of injustice and Hare's play presents both government policy and Railtrack officials in a less than favourable light.

In Out of Joint's production the opening scene was a rough-theatre agitprop with bold 'we're on a train' miming where individual speakers popped out from behind newspapers to articulate everyday frustrations. Immediately the audience was 'distanced' from reality. The production used back projection to recreate the platform information boards and the dramatic train crash. The actors played many roles, changing a jacket or hat and adding a distinctive prop to demonstrate a new character. The space was essentially empty, with a variety of chairs representing locations. At one point, an armchair became the truck carrying track workers onto the line. Direct address to the audience is a key feature of the text where the characters narrate their stories.

Jerzy Grotowski

Checkpoints

1 **Rich** theatre was the theatre of artifice: elaborate settings, costume, plush seating. **Poor** theatre strips all this away and relies on the actor – his/her body, voice and spirituality.

2 Grotowski stopped directing plays because he wanted to concentrate on exploring the possibilities of his 'poor theatre' and to focus on experiment and actor training. His influence on modern theatre practice can be seen in the use of an 'empty space' and physical theatre, where the actor is at the centre of the theatrical event.

Exam practice

When exploring the text of Sarah Kane's *4.48 Psychosis* we used many of the techniques from Grotowski's *Towards a Poor Theatre*. As a small, close group, we could identify with Grotowski's idea of working with a group of dedicated actors. 'Poor theatre', according to Grotowski, communicates emotion and spiritual truth without needing a narrative. *4.48 Psychosis* deals with the spiritual journey and emotional trauma of a depressive; there is no inherent narrative line. As we worked in the drama studio after college, when only a few students and the cleaning staff were around, it felt very similar to the 'laboratory' conditions. The intensity of our work was uninterrupted by movement or bells.

Our exploration work mirrored Grotowski's theories that the actor should rely on himself, not on properties, design or sound effects. Our sessions began with physical exercises, yoga and stretching. Grotowski referred to this technique as 'exercises plastiques'. He frequently required his actors to put their bodies through intense training: '… first the body, then the voice…'. We worked physically on the play, creating meaning through twisted movements, often entwining ourselves to evoke the feeling of internal torment. We also exercised our voices before exploring the range of non-verbal sound we could use, vocally creating the emotional responses, making sounds such as screaming, crying and echoing. There was also the use of percussive sound which we created by banging on the blocks or the metal supports in the studio. Our aim was to disturb an audience and involve them in the emotional journey where they discovered their own 'psychic layers'.

We experimented with reordering the text by cutting it up into sections, then reassembling the lines to create our own meaning. This had similarities to Grotowski's *Apocalypsis cum Figuris*, where the words followed the action. The delivery of the text was explored in terms of vocal variety: some sections were whispered, while other sections were explored chorally as a semi-religious chant. Grotowski's theatre was an almost religious experience. At key points in the play we felt the ascetic/aesthetic: we became 'spiritually' engaged in our own journey of discovery about the limits and possibilities of our bodies and voices, while also exploring the aesthetic potential of the play. Our work on *4.48 Psychosis* revealed the true extent of Grotowski's techniques.

My set design is stripped to the minimum: three black boxes in a studio, with the audience standing around the acting space. Between the action and the audience, I envisage a barrier of wire fencing so that the audience feel as if they are participants in the scene. Grotowski used metal and wire in his production of *Akropolis*. The 'chamber theatre' space allowed the actors to, literally, touch the audience at key points in the action. Grotowski's production of *Dr Faustus*, set in a monastery refectory, evoked the feeling that the spectators were guests. I want my audience to feel as though they are also *in* the mental hospital ward. *4.48 Psychosis* is about private emotion, which Grotowski wanted to make public. My standing audience will observe the emotional turmoil.

Edward Gordon Craig

Checkpoints

1 **Gauze** is a lightweight, thin, transparent fabric. The **proscenium** is the arch framing the opening between the stage and the auditorium. **Footlights**, rarely used today, are a row of lights at the front of the stage that shine upwards onto the actors' faces.
2 **Ibsen's** plays were naturalistic and audiences were accustomed to seeing realistic settings. Craig's designs were more metaphorical and this was at odds with the expectations of critics and audiences.

Exam practice

**A Prayer for my Daughter   Young Vic   2008
Designer: Giles Cadle**

- **Craig:** The set is part of the whole concept, costume and performance style conveyed the same meanings.

  Cadle: A grubby police office in New York, festooned with tawdry 4th July decorations, balloons, one with an ironic smile. Detritus littered the desks, empty take-away cartons. Grey filing cabinets, desks covered with papers, files. Office chairs, phones, broken furniture.
- **Craig** restructured the stage areas.

  Cadle: Traverse staging increased the sense of entrapment. Performance space sunk between two raked ranks of seating. Flights of stairs created the basement office. Actors entered from high level, descending several flights of visible stairs. A further staircase descended to a cellar room used for interrogation. Claustrophobic atmosphere.
- **Craig:** Composition and use of light. Footlights, shadow, gantry, side lights.

  Cadle: Shadows and areas of light reflected the gloom of the artificially lit office. Pools of light at desks. Light mirrors the light and dark imagery of the text. Subtle changes of mood indicated. Eerie, cold blue haze signified menace and desolation.

Antonin Artaud

Checkpoints

1 **Total theatre** combines every theatrical element in an assault on the audience's senses.
2 **Juxtaposition** is the placing together of two things so that the audience makes a connection.

Exam practice

Peter Shaffer: *The Royal Hunt of the Sun*
Peter Shaffer, influenced by Artaud, employs the technique of total theatre in this play.

Design concept: Visual, aural and spatial elements

- Gold **masks**, highly decorated, worn by all Incas. Atahuallpa's mask is even more elaborate.
- A huge **sun** slowly descends when the Inca god first appears, lit so that the rays are cast over the entire theatre.
- Inca **costumes** are in shades of yellow, russet and gold, which mirror the colours in the sun. The Spaniards are in shades of black but with slashes of red and silver, glinting in the light of the sun.
- The **lighting** creates both the heat of the sun and the cold of the Andes. A red wash of light accompanies the rolling out of the vast red cloth that covers the entire acting space at the end of Act I: The Massacre.
- **Sounds** create mood and atmosphere. For example, Shaffer writes that *'the sun gives a deep groan'* and *'terrible groans fill the air'* in Act II sc 6: here recorded sound fills the theatre and assaults the audience's senses. Sound effects suggest the bitter cold of the Andes, with wind and the creaking of ice.
- **Percussion**, such as maracas, drums, bells and cymbals, accompany vocal choral chanting from the Incas. At the massacre when *'howling'* and *'screams . . . fill the theatre'* the actors **scream** and howl but this is amplified and recorded playing simultaneously.
- Following the death of Atahuallpa, Shaffer writes: *'They [the Incas] intone a strange* **Chant** *of Resurrection, punctuated by hollow beats on the drums and by long, long silences.'* I will create a dramatic climax here, with the drumbeats getting progressively louder and the silences longer.
- **Ritual** is a key element of the play. The robing of Atahuallpa in Act II sc 4 is an example: here the removal and replacement of the bloodstained clothing is conducted with slow, ritualistic movements, enhanced by percussive sound and **humming**. The gold processions are ritualistically enacted and the massacre is enacted in a ritualised way.

Revision checklist
Key practitioners (1)

By the end of this chapter you should be able to:

1	Explain the development of Stanislavski's System.	Confident	Not confident **Revise** pages 30–31
2	List the elements of The System, with examples.	Confident	Not confident **Revise** pages 31–32
3	Comment on the influence of Stanislavski in theatre.	Confident	Not confident **Revise** pages 30–32
4	Understand how Brecht's political beliefs were formed.	Confident	Not confident **Revise** pages 33–34
5	Detail the key features of Brechtian theatre.	Confident	Not confident **Revise** pages 34–35
6	Explain Brecht's theory of *Verfremdungseffekt*.	Confident	Not confident **Revise** page 35
7	Analyse Brecht's influence on the modern theatre.	Confident	Not confident **Revise** pages 34–35
8	Understand how Grotowski's theatrical style developed.	Confident	Not confident **Revise** pages 36–37
9	Know the glossary terms that explain Grotowski's theories.	Confident	Not confident **Revise** page 37
10	Explain Grotowski's influence on contemporary directors.	Confident	Not confident **Revise** pages 37–38
11	Explain why Craig shaped modern design practice.	Confident	Not confident **Revise** pages 39–41
12	Detail the key elements of Craig's theories.	Confident	Not confident **Revise** pages 41–42
13	Understand Artaud's theory of total theatre.	Confident	Not confident **Revise** page 44
14	Explain the 'doubles' in Artaud's *The Theatre and its Double*.	Confident	Not confident **Revise** pages 44–45

Key practitioners (2)

The work of directors, designers and theatrical icons from the past informs modern ideas and theatre practice. It is essential that students of Drama and Theatre Studies look closely at directors and companies working in modern theatre and shaping the theatre of tomorrow.

This chapter examines the working practice of contemporary directors and theatre companies, which continue to influence performance, rehearsal technique and theatrical style. Some specifications ask you to consider the work of a practitioner in relation to the texts you are studying, whilst others require you to reflect the ideas of a practitioner in your practical work. The ideas of Boal will be of particular interest when working on devised theatre.

In the rest of this section, the analysis of the directors' work will be valuable to your practical work in the exploration of text and selection of rehearsal techniques. Several of the directors and contemporary companies discussed here use research and improvisation to create theatre and text – their work will be useful when creating devised theatre.

Exam themes

- The study of the theories of a practitioner
- The influence of practitioners on the development of acting and directing
- The practical exploration of texts in relation to practitioners' theories
- The discussion of a practitioner's methods in the analysis of live theatre
- The selection of appropriate rehearsal techniques for devised or scripted work

Topic checklist

	Edexcel		AQA		WJEC	
	AS	A2	AS	A2	AS	A2
Peter Brook	O		O		O	
Augusto Boal	O		O		O	
Max Stafford-Clark	O		O		O	
Katie Mitchell	O		O		O	
Contemporary companies	O		O		O	

Peter Brook

Peter Brook has influenced the practice of modern directing significantly. His central theories encompass a commitment to the text and a determination to remove all extraneous and non-essential distractions; the importance of the psychological and the spiritual for both actors and audience; a dedication to experiment as the principal method of keeping the theatre alive and vital; an embracement of multiculturalism and of the vitality of cultural stories in theatre.

Biography

Brook was born in West London in 1925 to Latvian immigrants. At Oxford University, he directed many plays and initially wanted to be a film director. At the age of 21, he directed *Love's Labours Lost* at Stratford and by 1960 he was a successful director worldwide. This included 16 years at the Royal Shakespeare Theatre.

His dissatisfaction with the state of British theatre, expressed in a series of lectures in 1968, was published later as *The Empty Space*. This is a seminal work of the theatre. Brook was much affected by Artaud and in 1962, after an elemental production of *King Lear*, Brook embarked upon an experimental period that included the Theatre of Cruelty project with the RSC. His landmark production of *A Midsummer Night's Dream* in 1970 was to be his last in England.

His objective became a spiritual quest for meaning that encompassed reinventing theatre in the deserts of Africa and adapting the world's longest poem, a Hindu story, *The Mahabharata*, into a nine-hour performance. Having left England in 1970, he founded the Centre for Theatre Research at the Bouffes du Nord in Paris, where he continues to work today.

The Empty Space

'I take an empty space and call it a bare stage. A man walks across this empty space while someone is watching him, and that is all that is needed for an act of theatre to be engaged.'

Before studying Brook's productions, it is important to consider his values and agenda as set out in *The Empty Space*. Brook divides theatre into four categories:

→ **Deadly theatre:** trapped in conventions, artificial, clichéd.
→ **Rough theatre:** Brechtian, vernacular, populist, talks directly to the audience.
→ **Holy theatre:** ritualistic, ceremonial, spiritual, mystical.
→ **Immediate theatre:** organic, vital spark, honest (his own methods).

Links

See page 51.

Action point

Look at www.bouffesdunord.com where you can find out more about Brook's Paris theatre.

Examiner's secrets

If you are studying Brook in relation to your set text or practical performance, there is no substitute for reading *The Empty Space*. See also *The Shifting Point* and *There are No Secrets*.

From *Lear* to the *Dream* (1960–1970)

King Lear, 1962

In 1962, Brook's austere production of *King Lear* heralded a new chapter in his career. He believed in **trusting the text** and **stripping all extraneous detail from the design**. The set was lit with piercing white light. The performances were detached, allowing the text to '*supply all the necessary answers*'. The audience were deliberately shocked; when one character, Gloucester, is blinded, Brook brought up the house lights so that the audience were complicit in this act of barbarism.

1964 'Theatre of Cruelty' RSC

Artaud's *The Theatre and its Double* was a confirmation of existing themes in Brook's vocabulary. Improvisation was then something of a dirty word in the British theatre, but Brook discovered a powerful theatre as reliant on **physical expression and gesture** as the spoken word. The production of Peter Weiss' *Marat/Sade* was set in an asylum where the inmates act out a brutal murder. Brook's set was bleak; the audience were positioned very close to the violent and sexually explicit action; the lighting was harsh.

A Midsummer Night's Dream in 1970 was a masterpiece of theatrical originality. The set was a dazzling white box. The actors wore white or vivid tunics. The whole design had the feel of a 'circus'; the fairies performed acrobatics on trapezes. Throughout the play, the fairies overlooked the 'mortals' from above the white box. Puck's magic flower was a whirling silver disc balanced on a juggler's stick; the midnight wood was represented by dangling steel coils.

Centre for Theatre Research at the Bouffes du Nord

Brook set up this centre so that actors could experiment rather than rehearse for a formal production. *Orghast*, performed at the 1971 Shiraz-Persepolis Festival, was a primal epic based largely on the Prometheus story, written by Ted Hughes in an invented language.

In one exercise during the preparation for *Orghast*, each actor represented a part of a single person – including, for example, 'the voice of the subconscious'. Brook comments: '*The result that we are working towards is not a form, not an image, but a set of conditions in which a certain quality of performance can arise.*'

Brook took his company of **multicultural** actors to **West Africa** where they performed *The Conference of the Birds* to people who did not share any of their languages, on carpets laid out in the sand – this became known as '**carpet theatre**'.

Take note

In some respects Brook was a devotee of Artaud, yet in others he was not. Brook's emphasis on the importance of the text is at odds with Artaud's rejection of text-based theatre. Brook's subsequent search for spiritual truth in theatre has connections with Grotowski.

Checkpoint 1

Who was **Artaud?** Can you summarise his key theories?

Checkpoint 2

What is the story of *Marat/Sade*?

Take note

The theatrical figures **Merce Cunningham, Samuel Beckett**, and **Grotowski** influenced Brook. Brook comments: '*These three theatres … have several things in common: small means, rigorous discipline, absolute precision.*'

Take note

In an interview published in *Plays and Players* in 1970, Brook comments on the rehearsal process: '*During the second week of rehearsals … the actors improvised a "happening" around the theme of the Dream. It had extraordinary force and interest, but like all happenings it can never be repeated – it was there once and gone.*'

Action point

Charles Marowitz and Simon Trussler's *Theatre at Work,* published in 1967 by Methuen, documents Peter Brook's Theatre of Cruelty project. Although the book is out of print you may be able to get it from a library, a second-hand bookshop or a website.

Take note

Michael Billington, *The Guardian* newspaper's theatre critic, commented on Brook's *'timeless questions about the subversiveness of faith, the meaning of existence and the conflict of free will and destiny'.*

Take note

The Man Who is based on Oliver Sack's clinical accounts of dealing with various disorders of the brain. Brook's production, staged on an almost bare white platform with institutional metal chairs and tables, comprised a series of scenes that showed the function of the brain. The play asked the audience to question 'How do we think?' and 'What is man?'

Brook's celebrated *The Mahabharata* was a violent epic, incorporating all cultures into the historical costume. Brook avoided using technology, creating the **elemental quality** with earth, fire and water, movement and gesture. Brook placed the piece in '**found spaces**', not traditional theatres – in Glasgow a disused Victorian tram shed became his 'empty space'.

Brook's more recent productions include ***Hamlet**,* played in French on a carpet against the roughly renovated walls of the Bouffes du Nord, and ***The Man Who**,* which inextricably links the roles of 'author' and director.

Exam practice   15 minutes   answers: page 64

Write supporting notes on the lighting and design for the play you presented for your performance examination. Comment on how Brook's ideas about theatre influence your decisions.

Augusto Boal

Biography

Augusto Boal was born in Brazil in 1931 and trained as a chemical engineer. For 15 years, he ran a theatre in Sao Paulo, Rio de Janeiro, where he began his experiments in **participatory theatre** during the 1950s and 1960s. He went beyond the theatre and organised performances in the streets, factories, unions, churches; wherever he could reach the people of the favelas (slums) of Rio.

He ran **newspaper theatre**, which distilled the news into theatre on a daily basis. In 1971, Boal's work drew the attention of the military dictatorship and he was arrested, tortured and exiled, staying in Argentina, Peru, Portugal and France before returning to his home in Rio.

In Argentina, under another dictatorship, he developed **invisible theatre**, rehearsed in secret and performed in public spaces. Theatrical situations were created in such a way that the public was unaware that a spectacle was being acted out. In Peru, Boal developed a theatre for the people in which bystanders were given power to affect the outcome of the play.

> *'The spectators feel that they can intervene in the action … All can be changed, and at a moment's notice …'*

His **forum theatre** has provided the basis for many Theatre in Education companies.

Boal acknowledged the influence of the practitioner Brecht.

Forum theatre

Boal is most renowned for forum theatre, which bridges the separation between actor (the one who acts) and spectator (the one who observes but is not permitted to intervene in the theatrical situation). Boal's theory developed when a woman in the audience for invisible theatre was so frustrated by an actor who could not understand her suggestions that she came on stage and began to play the role herself. For Boal, this was the birth of the **spect-actor** and his theatre was transformed. *'While some people make theatre,'* said Boal, *'we are all theatre.'*

The audience were renamed 'spect-actors' and Boal developed a process whereby audience members could stop a performance and suggest different actions for the actor, who would then carry out the audience's suggestions. The spectators engage in self-empowering processes of dialogue. A key figure in the forum process was The Joker, a facilitator who formed a link between the audience and the dramatic action. She or he had responsibility for orchestrating the whole event. Boal named his theatre **The Theatre of the Oppressed**, a new and powerful form of political theatre.

Action Point

Read Boal's textbooks *Theatre of the Oppressed* (1979) and *Games for Actors and Non-actors* (1992) for more details of his working methods.

Checkpoint 1

How and why are the people with whom Boal works oppressed?

Boal's current form of forum theatre

The actors (professional or people from oppressed communities) perform a play with a scripted core, in which an **oppression relevant to the audience** is played out.

At the end of the play when the oppressed character(s) have failed to overturn their oppression, the actors begin the production again in a condensed form.

At any point during this second performance, any spect-actor may call out *'stop!'* and take the place of the actor portraying the *oppressed* individual (this actor stays on stage but to the side, giving suggestions to the spect-actor who has replaced him/her).

The **spect-actor** then attempts to overturn the oppression using some argument that the actors have not used. The actors portraying the **oppressors** try to achieve the **original scripted** ending.

If the audience believes that the spect-actor's actions are too unrealistic, they may call out **'magic!'** and the spect-actor must modify their actions accordingly.

If this spect-actor fails in overthrowing the oppression, the actor resumes his/her character and continues the production until another spect-actor calls out 'stop!' and attempts a different method.

If and when the oppression has been overthrown by the spect-actors, the production changes again: the spect-actors now have the opportunity to replace the *oppressors* and find new ways of challenging the oppressed character.

In this way a more realistic depiction of the oppression can be made by the audience, who are often victims of the oppression. The whole process is designed to be **dialectic** rather than **didactic.**

Action point

You might be able to experiment with Boal's invisible or forum theatre by preparing scenes that engage pupils with important issues: bullying, truanting, parental conflict. Present these in a non-theatrical place – the canteen, the foyer, a corridor.

Checkpoint 2

Define **dialectic** and **didactic**. If you are unsure, look in the section on Bertolt Brecht on page 35.

Exam practice   15 minutes   answers: page 64

Select a text you know which examines injustice in some way. Consider how you might perform it in a factory, street, town hall or school, enabling the audience or spect-actors to engage with the issues.

Max Stafford-Clark

Max Stafford-Clark is one of the most significant forces in British theatre in the past 40 years. Stafford-Clark has not only directed but also nurtured the work of many contemporary writers. He is responsible for launching the careers of many leading playwrights, including Caryl Churchill, Mark Ravenhill and Sebastian Barry.

Biography

Max Stafford-Clark began his directing career at **The Traverse Theatre**, Edinburgh, in 1966 and in 1968 he worked for six weeks with the **La Mama Company** in New York. In 1974, Stafford-Clark co-founded **The Joint Stock Theatre Group** with Bill Gaskill; this experimental company was undoubtedly pre-eminent at this time.

From 1979 to 1983 he was Artistic Director of the **Royal Court Theatre**. **Out of Joint**, the company that he established in 1993, is dedicated to the production of new writing.

The development of a process

The early influence of the La Mama Company inspired some experimental work, resonant of the explorations of **Jerzy Grotowski**. In 1969, The Traverse Workshop, freed from performance deadlines, could *'explore the language of theatrical technique'* (William Watson, *The Scotsman* 1970). These experiments began with the physical and spiritual but the emphasis was always on new writing that engaged the audience.

Rehearsal methods

Research ensures authenticity and this approach is used by Stafford-Clark before and during rehearsals. Actors must have a good understanding of the world of the play: its historical period, the environment, the customs and the lives of the characters. During the rehearsal period for *Our Country's Good*, the actors visited Wormwood Scrubs to see a production of a play by the inmates. They also read *The Playmaker*, the Keneally novel on which the play is based, and *The Fatal Shore* by Robert Hughes, which gives a factual account of the convicts' journey.

When Stafford-Clark directed Caryl Churchill's *Serious Money* (a play about the Stock Exchange), the actors got jobs on the floor of the London International Financial Futures Exchange and followed a particular story in the *Financial Times*. Rehearsals for a Joint Stock production of *Epsom Downs* included a day at the Derby, while the actors in *Macbeth*, set in Africa, were coached in possession ceremonies and West African dances in preparation for the 'witches' scene that opens the play.

Collaboration: Joint Stock was established as a 'collective' where all decisions were taken democratically – even casting! Stafford-Clark's work continues to develop new writers and the methods employed in those early days underpin the growth of the play. The playwright, director and actors spend a '**workshop**' period exploring themes, sources or issues.

The workshop **reveals** the essence of the play; the playwright is integral to the rehearsal process. The final version is the result of constant reworking throughout the rehearsal period. *Our Country's Good, Cloud Nine,*

Action Point

Out of Joint tours productions throughout the UK. There is also an **Education Pack** to accompany each play. Try to see the next Out of Joint production at a theatre near you. Download education resources from www.outofjoint.co.uk

Action Point

Read *Taking Stock* by Max Stafford-Clark and Philip Roberts (Nick Hern Books) for a detailed examination of the director's work, told through a series of production case studies.

Grade booster

When you are recording and evaluating **research** it is important to link this research to the text or devised piece, showing how the information was **embedded** into your work. Research for the sake of it has little theatrical value.

Checkpoint 1

Define **collective** and **workshop**.

Grade booster

Think about this process when you are working on **devised** pieces. Try to divide your time evenly between research and exploration, writing and shaping material and rehearsing with fine-tuning. Do not make assumptions about what your piece will say until you have explored the topic fully – you may find something that takes the piece in a different, and more exciting, direction.

T043124

Take note

This technique can also be used for research purposes, where the actor becomes an actor/researcher. Stafford-Clark used this technique to collaborate with the playwrights in creating *The Permanent Way*, *Talking to Terrorists* and *Serious Money*.

Action point

See *Letters to George* by Max Stafford-Clark for an account of this process on *Our Country's Good*.

Watch out!

Many students, and some actors (!), are initially confused when asked to suggest **actions**. They might offer *'quickly'* or *'menacingly'* to describe the way the line is spoken. These words are **adverbs**, not verbs. A test is to add *'you'* to the phrase *'I (action) you'*: if you can't do it to someone, it is not an action.

Grade booster

Using 'actioning' and the playing cards exercises can give performances more depth and conviction.

Epsom Downs and *Serious Money* are examples of plays created in this way.

Actioning is Max Stafford-Clark's 'trademark' technique. The process has some similarity to Stanislavski's *Units and Objectives*. Stafford-Clark devotes up to two weeks of rehearsal to this process; he and the cast divide the text into **units** with **objectives** – similar to Stanislavski. Within the unit, each line has an **action** attached that captures his intention. An action must be expressed as a **transitive verb** – a verb that describes an effect you intend to have on another person. For example, *I reassure you* – 'reassure' is a transitive verb.

The whole text is 'actioned' and Stafford-Clark will refer to actions when giving actors notes in rehearsal. For example, '*You are playing "dismisses" when the action is "belittles"*'. Stafford-Clark cautions against bad acting where an actor plays the *result* of his action not the intention: if the action is **amuses** but the result is **bores**, the actor should play **amuses**. If, during the rehearsal period, the initial actions seem incorrect, they are changed.

Example

Actioning from Stafford-Clark's text for *Macbeth* (2004):

MACBETH	If we should fail?	AWAKENS
LADY M.	We fail?	RIDICULES
	But screw your courage to the sticking-place	URGES
	And we'll not fail. When Duncan is asleep –	ORGANISES

Playing cards are another feature of the rehearsal room, used to determine **status** or level of **emotion**. For example, **how much** does Lady Macbeth want Macbeth to kill Duncan? Answer: 10. How resistant to the idea is Macbeth? In the extract actioned above: 4 – i.e. he can be persuaded. The higher the card given to Macbeth, the harder Lady Macbeth will have to work to persuade him, but ultimately he must be persuaded.

Macbeth was set in modern Africa where Macbeth, a warlord, had overthrown the former leader; in order to examine the levels of **enthusiasm** for the new regime, actors are given random cards. A 10 means they are excited about the opportunities whereas a 2 means that they must flee the country to escape death.

In *Our Country's Good* there is a scene where the officers discuss the merits of theatre; Stafford-Clark issued playing cards to the actors to establish **support** (a red card) or **opposition** (a black card) to the proposed play: the number on the card reflected the degree. Ralph Clark, the director, was a red 10; Ross, vehemently opposed, had a black 10.

Exercises with playing cards explore the different dynamic created when the actors play higher or lower **status** in a scene. In *Our Country's Good* the convict known as Shitty Meg appears in just one scene where she ridicules the officer Ralph Clark, making lewd suggestions about his sexuality. In this scene Meg plays a 10 and Ralph perhaps only 3 or 4, despite the fact that his status in the hierarchy of the colony is the complete reverse.

Verbatim theatre constructs a play from interviews with key figures involved in significant events. Stafford-Clark has frequently taken first-hand experiences as a foundation for character or narrative. During the Joint Stock workshop for Caryl Churchill's *Cloud Nine*, the actors interviewed the caretaker at the Tower Theatre where they were working. Her raw testimony about life in a violent marriage became a prototype for a central character.

In researching *The Permanent Way*, which deals with recent train crashes, the team talked to the survivors, relatives of victims and Railtrack officials. For *Talking to Terrorists*, meetings with terrorist organisations and victims of terrorism provided the material for the play. The play asked, 'What makes ordinary people do extreme things?'

In verbatim theatre, the playwright uses the words from the interviews, juxtaposed to create meaning. The characters' names indicate position but not identity: a Bereaved Mother or an Archbishop's Envoy.

Take note

Students often assume that improvisations and exercises are used only in school drama. Directors like Max Stafford-Clark build improvisation and experiment into their rehearsal schedules.

Checkpoint 2

Max Stafford-Clark worked with **Caryl Churchill** on a number of plays. What do you know about this playwright?

Take note

There is still discomfiture in some theatrical circles about the existence of verbatim theatre, with many writers complaining that its works do not count as proper plays. The playwright David Edgar, however, said: '*Verbatim theatre fills the hole left by the current inadequacy of TV documentary, perished under the tram tracks of reality TV.*'

Exam practice   30 minutes   answers: page 64

For a play that you are preparing for a written or practical examination, select a short scene and 'action' the text.

Katie Mitchell

Katie Mitchell's precise analysis of the text and her detailed approach to character have much in common with Stanislavski. Her pre-rehearsal analysis is infinitely detailed and once the rehearsals begin, the actors engage in a similar process. Every aspect of the character's life history is explored, actors improvise off-stage scenes, questions are asked about every facet of a character's background and the text is trawled for valuable information.

Biography

Katie Mitchell was born in 1964. She first directed at Oxford University where she was a member of a feminist theatre company called **Medusa**. After university, Mitchell gained a considerable reputation for her reinterpretations of classic texts, which she directed for her own company, **Classics on a Shoestring**. She worked as an assistant director at the RSC for two years and subsequently as a director. A number of successful productions followed, including *Ghosts* at the RSC, and in 1996, *The Phoenician Women* for the National, which won the Evening Standard Award for Best Director.

Mitchell studied director training in Russia, Poland, Lithuania and Georgia. '*I decided to go to Eastern Europe because I was looking for a different kind of theatre,*' she says. The acting style she witnessed in Russia was heavily influenced by the later work of Stanislavski and was more fully imagined and free from what Mitchell calls '*theatrical clichés*'.

Mitchell is one of Britain's foremost directors and in recent years has directed *Women of Troy, Three Sisters, Uncle Vanya, The Seagull, The Waves* and *Attempts on Her Life* for the National Theatre and *Forty Winks* and *The City* for the Royal Court Theatre.

Rehearsal methods

Mitchell, like Brook before her, found that the strictures of short rehearsal periods in the UK did not allow for suitable investigation of the text and for the psychological motivation of characters. Her working method has evolved as a way of getting actors to present human behaviour on stage '*with all its lumps and bumps and raw edges*'. It is a Stanislavski-based way of approaching a text and relies heavily on research. '*For me, everything is in the planning ... So you analyse the material very carefully*'.

Links

See Peter Brook, page 50, and Max Stafford-Clark, page 55.

Facts and questions

Mitchell analyses the text before rehearsals. She identifies all the **facts** that the text reveals. These are non-negotiable, for example in *The Seagull*:

→ *It is Russia.*
→ *There is an estate.*
→ *There is a hastily erected stage.*
→ *Masha and Medvedenko have been walking alone.*
→ *Masha is wearing black.*

This list is sub-divided into **immediate circumstance facts** and **back history facts**. Immediate circumstances are the conditions that are specific to the starting action of the play, e.g. *There is a hastily erected stage.* **Back history** is the condition that exists long before the action of the play, e.g. *There is an estate.*

Mitchell then lists all the **questions**, dividing them again into two lists: **immediate circumstances** and **back history**.

→ *Where in Russia is the estate?*
→ *What did an estate typically consist of in 19th-century Russia?*
→ *How long does it take to get from Moscow to the estate?*
→ *How far is the railway station from the estate?*
→ *Was it normal in 19th-century Russia for unmarried men and women to be alone together?*

The entire text is mined for detail in this way. Questions that need researching have an '**R**' placed by them. This structures the research so that only the necessary information is gained.

Mitchell undertakes this herself as a way of investigating the text; it is then repeated with the cast. On the first day of rehearsals, the company reads the text round in a circle, reading one line at a time; no one reads their own part. They are encouraged to read it for sense only. Together they identify the facts and questions; areas for research are divided up among the company. Everyone is involved in creating and researching the world of the play.

Action point

For a text that you are preparing for performance, take two sheets of paper – one for facts and one for questions. Identify the things you need to research with an 'R' and then research them.

Character history

Once there is a list of facts and questions, the actors can begin to construct **character histories**. Mitchell analyses the **back histories** of all the characters from when they were born up to the beginning of the action of the play. The actors continue this process during rehearsal. The facts they have collected about their character are put into linear order.

Initially there are gaps, which are filled as actors start to work with other actors who share a history with their character. A consensus is reached by reading the text, discussing the impression it gives and the historical research. For example, the characters' first meeting and the date of their marriage become crucial to the investigation of relationships

Events and intentions

Katie Mitchell's technique is based on Stanislavski's later work involving the method of physical action, taken on subsequently by Grotowski. She notes that '*Stanislavski was curious to the end and able to throw things away, change and move forward*'. His later work is often neglected, as it seems incongruous with his early 'method' work.

Mitchell divides her text into **events** and **intentions**. An event describes a moment that changes every person in the scene; all entrances and exits are automatically events. Events are often tricky to spot; actors look for the moment of change in a scene.

Checkpoint 1

What was Stanislavski's theory of the **method of physical action**?

Take note

It is important to realise that Stanislavski was always developing and changing his working method.

Example

In the first scene of *The Seagull*, every character has an **intention** leading up to the event, a **reaction** to the event and an **intention** following the event.

Intention:	Masha wants to ease Medvedenko's pain and embarrassment.
	Medvedenko wants to convince Masha that he is OK.
Event:	*Sorin and Konstantin arrive at the makeshift theatre.*
Intention:	Sorin wants to calm Konstantin's nerves before the performance.
	Konstantin wants Sorin to hurry up.
	Masha wants to get Medvedenko to leave the auditorium.
	Medvedenko wants Masha to be quiet.
Event:	*Konstantin sends Medvedenko and Masha away from the theatre.*

Mitchell describes events as 'beads on a necklace' and the intentions as the string that threads them all together.

Place

The work on facts and questions also begins to reveal a sense of place. Mitchell asks the company to draw a map of the area (in *The Seagull*, of the estate) and to list all references to place in the text. In *The Seagull* there are plenty:

→ There is an estate.
→ There is a lake.
→ There are houses on the other side of the lake, only one of which is now occupied.
→ Arkadina arrives by train from Moscow – there is a railway station nearby.

Time

Time is also vital to Katie Mitchell's methodology. This includes historical time – the date when the play takes place, time of day and the amount of time those characters have to complete the action of the scene.

At the beginning of Mitchell's production of *The Seagull* at the National Theatre, the play opened with workmen hurriedly building the stage for Konstantin's performance. At this moment, they are playing **high time pressure**. The fact that the performance is due to start imminently and that Nina is late adds to the pressure. Shamraev has only just released the workers from their farm duties; the sun has set and they must build the stage before the audience arrives. These decisions, although imposed by Mitchell, are supported by the text. She uses time to motivate a particular dramatic effect.

Immediate circumstances

Immediate circumstances are conditions that exist for the characters immediately before the scene. These can include the immediate **back story** of the scene: where they have just been and to whom they have just spoken. In performance, Mitchell has **booths** set up in the **wings** where **simultaneous improvisation** takes place. For example, in *The Seagull* ten minutes before the performance starts, Masha and Medvedenko will start improvising the walk from which they have just returned. Actors are encouraged to decorate the booths with pictures, plants or props to stimulate this improvisation. When Masha and Medvedenko enter, they do so with the immediate recall of that walk and the conversation they had.

Improvisation

Improvisation is also a key part of Katie Mitchell's practice. As well as the simultaneous improvisation above, Mitchell uses it to investigate a character's back history. The improvisation can be about an event that long precedes the action of the play. Mitchell recalls in the rehearsals for *The Oresteia,* '*The first improvisation we did was about the death of the father of Menelaus and Agamemnon, the loss of the kingdom and the war the two sons had to fight to regain the throne.*'

It is crucial to Mitchell that improvisations are set up with the same language as the rest of her rehearsals. Time, place, immediate circumstances, character back history, relationships, events and intentions are all specified to the actors before the improvisation takes place.

Checkpoint 2

What do you understand by **simultaneous improvisation**?

Grade booster

Indicate how you might employ the rehearsal methods of modern directors when discussing techniques in your notes or exam answers.

Exam practice   30 minutes   answers: page 65

Go through a play you are studying and write down all the references to place and then draw a map of any location within the play. This might be one room – think about any references to windows or doors. It might be a whole house. Make informed guesses about the locations of the rooms. How long does it take people to get from the kitchen to the dining room, for example?

Contemporary companies

Nancy Meckler and Shared Experience

Nancy Meckler's company, Shared Experience, has pioneered a distinctive style that unites both text-based and physical theatre. The style goes beyond naturalism into larger-than-life expressionism. Meckler describes her work in the following way: '*I have a strong visual sense and my productions are physically potent.*'

The power and excitement of the performer's **physicality** and the unique **collaboration** between **actor and audience** creates the 'shared experience'. Nancy Meckler's rehearsal process is a genuinely open forum, asking questions and taking risks that redefine the possibilities of performance: '*I want people to feel free to try anything, to be as creative as possible.*'

Action point

Look at the work of other practitioners, such as Grotowski, Brook and Artaud. There are similarities in their approach.

Trestle Theatre Company

Founded by Toby Wilshire in 1981, Trestle Theatre Company developed its own unique style, which combines **mask** and **physical theatre** to create dynamic, devised performances. It presents new work and tours nationally and internationally. Trestle is renowned for its work in education and with young people.

A production of *The Island* in 2000 at the Edinburgh Festival captured the subtlety of Trestle's mask theatre. In February 2000, the two-month-old remains of an old lady were found on a traffic island in the West Midlands. Who was she? Why had nobody reported her missing? Using masks and a large traffic island, the show recreated the final expansive moments of Mildred Thomas.

Checkpoint 1

Why is the **Edinburgh Festival** important to innovative playwrights and performers?

DV8

DV8 is a **contemporary dance** and **physical theatre** company founded in 1986. DV8 aims to take risks, aesthetically and physically, and to break down the barriers between dance, theatre and personal politics. The focus of the creative approach is on reinvesting dance with meaning: DV8's work questions the traditional aesthetic and forms, which permeate both modern and classical dance. Their work asks important questions about key issues in society.

DV8 productions

DV8's 1992 piece *Strange Fish* communicated ideas about loneliness and conflict. Lloyd Newson, choreographer, commented: '*The risk was ... whether dance can deal with complex emotional narrative and whether tragi-comic theatre can in fact be created through dance alone. You can take risks without always being physical.*'

In 2005, *Just for Show* was a mix of corny cabaret, magical illusion, multimedia and dancing that explored the current preoccupation with the cult of personality and the spiritual emptiness it can hide.

Théâtre de Complicité

Founded in 1983 by Simon McBurney, Annabel Arden and Marcello Magni, Théâtre de Complicité, a multicultural company, proceeded to inject a new spirit of **physical** exuberance into the **text-bound** British tradition. It is a constantly evolving ensemble of performers and collaborators. The name *Théâtre de Complicité* is partly in homage to their teachers, Jacques Lecoq and Philippe Gaulier, who encouraged an overt display of 'complicity' between performers.

The Complicité approach

There is no Complicité 'method'; what is essential is collaboration. Their work integrates text, music, image and action to create surprising, **disruptive** theatre. Director Simon McBurney has been described by Stephen Daldry as '*one of the dozen or so most important directors working anywhere in the world*'. The plays use story to examine what it is to be human. They are intellectually daring, yet the adjectives most frequently attached to their work are **physical** and **visual**.

In an interview with the *Daily Telegraph*, McBurney said:
'*The only people who think of me as* visual *are the English and that is because they have an under-developed sense of it, despite a highly developed sense of irony and language. Whereas here we talk of "audiences" – listeners – in France attenders at a play are "les spectateurs" – watchers. I treat the visual with as much respect as the spoken word ... everything begins with a text of some sort.*'

Checkpoint 2

Can you identify similarities between the theories of **Artaud** and the comments made here by McBurney?

Complicité productions

Complicité continues to shake up accepted theatrical assumptions and almost every show is a surprise. At the start of *Mnemonic* (1999) the audience were required to put on blindfolds and imagine what they were doing a few days earlier. A miraculously preserved 5,000-year-old 'iceman' is represented both by a naked McBurney and by an ingenious folding chair.

Productions include *Street of Crocodiles* (1994), *The Three Lives of Lucie Cabrol* (1994*), Mnemonic*, a study of memory (1999) and the multimedia *The Elephant Vanishes* (2004). Complicité's new devised piece takes as its inspiration the heartbreaking story of the collaboration between two of the 20th century's most remarkable pure mathematicians, one British, one Indian. The piece explores the beauty of mathematics and the complexities of modern India.

Exam practice   30 minutes   answers: page 65

See whether you can find any recent reviews of the work of these companies, or see a production if there is one near you. Compare the performances and note the differences and similarities in their styles.

Answers
Key practitioners (2)

Peter Brook

Checkpoints

1 Antonin **Artaud** was a French practitioner who challenged the text-based theatre of Europe and sought to explore physicality, sound and technology. Balinese dancers, who communicated without words, influenced him. Artaud's work gave rise to the term **total theatre**.

2 *Marat/Sade* is a play within a play: the inmates of an asylum enact the murder in his bath, by Charlotte Corday, of Jean-Paul Marat, during the French Revolution in 1793. The Marquis de Sade, after whom 'sadism' is named, is the central character in the play as director of the performance.

Exam practice

The influence of Brook was evident in our staging of Chekhov's *The Cherry Orchard*. We performed on a large carpet in our studio. Brook placed a carpet down to define the acting space in his groundbreaking work in West Africa on *The Conference of the Birds* and in his Bouffes du Nord production of *Hamlet*. Our carpet defined the boundaries of the action and we used only essential pieces of furniture and properties. The back wall of the space had three cherry trees in full blossom silhouetted against it.

In Act 1, a crib draped with white muslin and a white wicker chair suggested the nursery whilst in the outdoor second act we used only a rug and a hamper. Lighting created the warmth of the mid-summer or the cold atmosphere of the house. At the end of the play, the furniture was covered with white sheeting; the packing cases were in sharp focus and the lighting stark and bright. Our costumes were in shades of white or cream.

Augusto Boal

Checkpoints

1 The people of Brazil had very few rights and many were exploited by factory owners. They had no political rights, as they did not live in a democracy.

2 **Didactic:** intended to teach or give moral instruction.
Dialectic: the investigation of the truth of opinions by logical discussion.

Exam practice

The play *Example* (by Belgrade TIE Company) is the true story of the case of Derek Bentley who was hanged for the murder of a policeman in 1953. Bentley was only 19 and of limited intelligence; he was hanged but his accomplice, who actually pulled the trigger, was only 16 so escaped the death penalty. The play is written in short, episodic scenes covering Bentley's life and building to the crime and the trial. I would present this play as a promenade piece with the audience standing around the action without chairs. I want the spectators to feel as though they are complicit in the decisions being made. At the trial, the audience would be allowed chairs; they would be seated as if they were the jury.

Max Stafford-Clark

Checkpoints

1 A **collective** is an enterprise owned or operated cooperatively. All decisions are taken by, and belong to, the members of a group.
A **workshop** is a practical session or period during which actors explore the theme, stimulus or text through improvisation and research.

2 **Caryl Churchill** worked with Joint Stock and Monstrous Regiment in the 1970s and 1980s and was resident dramatist, with Max Stafford-Clark, at the Royal Court, where her work included *Top Girls* (1982) and *Serious Money* (1987). *Blue Heart* for Out of Joint challenged accepted forms of playwriting. Later work includes *Mad Forest*, written after a visit to Romania, and *The Skriker*, produced at the National Theatre in 1994. *Far Away* (2000) and *A Number* (2002) have been produced at the Royal Court, and in 2005 she adapted Strindberg's *A Dream Play*, directed by Katie Mitchell. Playwright Stella Feehily comments that *'If you want a masterclass in writing, you look at Chekhov, and you look at Caryl Churchill.'*

Exam practice

Our Country's Good, Scene 6: The Officers Discuss the Merits of Theatre

Ross: A play! A f ____	**Scorns (Ralph)**
Rev Johnson: Mmmmm.	**Warns (Ross)**
Ross: A frippering frittering play!	**Ridicules (Ralph)**
Campbell: Ach aeh here?	**Encourages (Ross)**
Ralph: To celebrate the King's birthday on June the 4th.	**Charms (Phillip)**
Ross: If a frigating ship doesn't appear soon we'll all be struck with stricturing starvation – and you – you – a play!	**Cautions (Phillip)**
	Humbles (Ralph)
Collins: Not putting on the play won't bring us a supply ship, Robbie.	**Quietens (Ross)**

Note: The **action** refers to the intended effect on a character. Ralph wants Phillip to respect him so his line about the king's birthday can be seen as an attempt to ingratiate himself. **Ingratiates** is not a transitive verb; what he is trying to do is to **charm** Phillip. Ross's final line has two actions: the first part **cautions** Phillip that supplies are running out, while the second part puts Ralph down – **humbles**.

Katie Mitchell

Checkpoints

1 Late in his career Stanislavski became concerned that the system was too rigid and complex and did not allow an actor to explore the role practically. With the **method of physical action** he sought to use improvisation and practical exploration as a stimulus to the actor's discovery of the inner core of the role.

2 **Simultaneous improvisation** is the playing out of an improvised scene during the performance of the play. The improvised scene is played off-stage, spanning the same time as the on-stage action.

Exam practice

Death of a Salesman by Arthur Miller

The Loman house is surrounded by towering apartment buildings, but it used to enjoy country views and open skies. The kitchen has a table and three chairs with a refrigerator in a central position. There is a curtained doorway leading from the kitchen to the stairs. Above the living room is the boys' bedroom and on a lower level is Willy and Linda's bedroom. A trophy, won by Biff, is placed prominently on a shelf. The boys' room is high in the building as it has a skylight window. From the window of Willy and Linda's room the apartment buildings can be seen: these buildings cut out the sunlight. The garden outside the Loman house is in the shadow of the apartment buildings and it is difficult to grow vegetables.

From the boys' bedroom it is possible to hear conversations downstairs. The walls must be quite thin and the house cannot be very large. Next door, the neighbour, Charley, can hear shouting from the Loman house. The houses are obviously built quite close together. Willy parks his car outside the house, a short distance from the door. Linda hears the car start up at the end of the play as Willy drives off.

Contemporary companies

Checkpoints

1 The **Edinburgh Festival** and the thriving **Fringe Festival** are important in the world of theatre as they enable numerous experimental as well as established companies to perform new and exciting work. The whole city is a hive of artistic activity, with plays performed in a multitude of venues. The importance of the Fringe in developing and recognising new talent is enormous. The Festival takes place for four weeks every August.

2 **Artaud** complained that the European audiences of the early 20th century were text bound and appreciated only spoken language; they had little appreciation of the *visual* and the *physical*. McBurney makes similar comments when he compares French and British audiences today.

Revision checklist
Key practitioners (2)

By the end of this chapter you should be able to:

1	Define deadly, rough, holy and immediate theatre.	Confident	Not confident **Revise** page 50
2	Recognise the influences of Artaud and Grotowski on Brook.	Confident	Not confident **Revise** page 51
3	Trace the development of Brook's method through his key productions.	Confident	Not confident **Revise** page 51
4	Explain Brook's key contributions to directing practice	Confident	Not confident **Revise** pages 51–52
5	Understand Boal's Theatre of the Oppressed.	Confident	Not confident **Revise** page 53
6	Define the term 'spect-actors'.	Confident	Not confident **Revise** pages 53–54
7	Explain the use of forum theatre.	Confident	Not confident **Revise** page 53
8	Identify the way research informs the work of playwrights, actors and directors.	Confident	Not confident **Revise** pages 55–57
9	Understand the process of 'actioning' the text.	Confident	Not confident **Revise** page 56
10	Explain the term 'verbatim theatre'.	Confident	Not confident **Revise** page 57
11	Comment on the rehearsal methodology of Max Stafford-Clark.	Confident	Not confident **Revise** pages 55–56
12	Explain how Katie Mitchell uses facts and questions to examine text.	Confident	Not confident **Revise** pages 58–59
13	Understand the technique of events and intentions in preparing a role.	Confident	Not confident **Revise** pages 59–60
14	Comment on the links between Mitchell's work and the later ideas of Stanislavski.	Confident	Not confident **Revise** page 59
15	Define back history, immediate circumstances and the imperatives of place and time	Confident	Not confident **Revise** pages 59–60
16	Understand the working methods of Shared Experience.	Confident	Not confident **Revise** page 62
17	Recognise the distinctive style of DV8 and Trestle Theatre.	Confident	Not confident **Revise** page 62
18	Comment on the contribution of Théâtre de Complicité to modern theatre practice.	Confident	Not confident **Revise** page 63

Exploring the text

The exploration of dramatic text is included in all exam board specifications. With several specifications, there is an emphasis on examining the play in its social context and reflecting on the social or political concerns of the playwright. The importance of the play's form and structure and the analysis of dialogue and character are central to the examination of the text. Your specification may require you to relate your text to the theory and practice of a theatrical practitioner. You should refer to Key practitioners (1) and (2) for additional material.

For this examination, the text must be considered as a piece of theatre. Consequently the visual, aural and spatial elements are essential to the exploration process. You may have to produce exploration notes on your set texts, or a written paper may test your understanding. The early sections of this chapter include the contextualising of plays and an examination of plot and structure. Later sections consider dialogue, character and visual, aural and spatial elements.

Exam themes

- The play in its social, political and historical context
- Plot, form and structure
- Examining dialogue and analysing character
- The nature of audience
- The visual, aural and spatial elements of texts

Topic checklist

	Edexcel		AQA		WJEC	
	AS	A2	AS	A2	AS	A2
Plot and sub-plot	○	●	○	●	○	●
Character	○	●	○	●	○	●
Dialogue	○	●	○	●	○	●
Design: visual, aural and spatial	○	●	○	●	○	●
The playwright and the social and political context	○	●	○	●	○	●

Plot and sub-plot

This section examines the way the story and theme of the play are communicated to an audience. The **plot** is the major storyline of the play while the **sub-plot** is the minor, sometimes parallel, story that is unfolded alongside the main narrative. Some examinations ask you to comment on the plot and sub-plot, examining a **key feature**; others will ask you to show awareness of the dramatist's techniques in revealing the story: the **structure** and **form** of the text.

Plot

The plot is the **narrative** the playwright wishes the audience to follow. Aristotle believed that the plot of a play should have **one unified action** that focuses attention on the predicament of the central character. The plot of *The Crucible* is the story of how Abigail and her followers accuse many women of witchcraft and how John Proctor tries to expose her deceit. In *Oh, What a Lovely War!* by Joan Littlewood's Theatre Workshop, the plot explores the First World War in a Brechtian non-naturalistic style. Sarah Kane's *4.48 Psychosis* charts the psychological journey to suicide whereas in Peter Shaffer's *Equus*, the plot explores the life of Alan Strang, keeping the audience in suspense as it traces the reasons for his horrific crime.

Sub-plot

The sub-plot usually provides a parallel or contrast to the main action; the audience is aware of the comparisons between the narratives. Shakespeare included many sub-plots designed to comment on the main action. In *Hamlet* the plot concerns the protagonist's indecisiveness in revenging his father's murder; the sub-plot engages the audience in the story of Laertes and Fortinbras, whose fathers have also been killed. The sub-plot of *The Crucible* concerns the moral dilemma Proctor faces as he grapples with his own failings and in *Equus* the sub-plot relates to the fragile psyche of the disillusioned psychiatrist, Martin Dysart.

Checkpoint 1

What is the story of the play you are studying? Can you determine what is **plot** and what is **sub-plot**?

Structure

The structure of a play is the way it is put together, the creation of mood and atmosphere, the pace and levels of tension and the exploration of themes. In *The Crucible*, the story is told chronologically, a **linear** narrative, whereas in *Equus*, Peter Shaffer uses an **episodic** structure. This play's narrative is told in a series of **flashbacks** and the play's climax reconstructs Alan's crime. *Oh, What a Lovely War!* is also episodic in structure, using a **montage** of short scenes in a **music-hall** style. Sarah Kane's disturbing *4.48 Psychosis* employs an episodic structure that engages the audience in a psychological journey, piecing together details and creating their own reality.

Dramatic form

Form refers to the way the play is put together – its division into **acts and scenes** and the use of climaxes, moments of tension and conflict.

Shakespeare wrote all his plays in five acts – the convention of the time. **Ibsen** wrote in four acts and modern plays are usually in two acts, an interval normally following Act I. In the early 20th century, plays were often written in three acts, with audiences leaving the auditorium for two intervals during the performance.

Social and cultural developments have determined the change in structure. Playwrights or directors sometimes play the complete text without an interval. This is usually because they feel that the intensity of the play would be diminished by breaking the action and spoiling the dramatic impact.

The form of the play includes the way **key moments** are depicted. In *A Streetcar Named Desire*, Tennessee Williams does not divide the play into acts, merely scenes – each scene ending with a **climax**. The playwright's use of form reveals layers of detail about the central character, Blanche Dubois.

In *Hamlet*, Shakespeare opens Act V with a comic scene with two gravediggers, enabling the audience to laugh and release the tension before the play's tragic climax. The use of monologues enables characters to reveal their thoughts or to convey information: in *Equus*, the psychiatrist, Dysart, talks directly to the audience to tell the story as well as to confide in them about his troubling dreams.

Links

See Drama and theatre in context (pages 10–25) for detailed information about each historical period.

Structure and genre

The **structure** of the play and the playwright's choice of dramatic **form** are determined by the **genre**. The first Greek tragedies had only three actors and epic events happened off-stage; these events were conveyed to the audience by a **chorus** or character, e.g. the servant in Euripides' *Hippolytus*. Contemporary plays frequently employ the convention of characters making **direct address** to the audience to reveal emotion or to communicate unseen events, e.g. David Hare's *The Permanent Way*, directed by Max Stafford-Clark, which traces the tragic impact of recent rail crashes on the lives of survivors and the families of the victims. The genre is **verbatim theatre**, where the plot follows actual events and the actors play the real people whose lives are portrayed.

In comparison, the 19th-century playwright **Anton Chekov** wrote in the genre known as **realism**. The plot unfolds gradually in seemingly insignificant dialogue. In the opening scene of *The Cherry Orchard*, the imminent arrival of Arkadina is commented upon casually but the playwright has prepared the audience for the impact of her entrance as well as signifying themes and issues that will be crucial later in the play.

In **farce**, a comic genre that originated in France in the late 19th century, the plot is revealed through fast-paced verbal and physical comedy and **dramatic irony**. **Feydeau**, **Ben Travers** and **Alan Ayckbourn** are experts in writing farce.

Links

For realism, see page 22 and for Stafford-Clark, see page 55.

Take note

Other examples of verbatim theatre are *The Colour of Justice* (the Stephen Lawrence Inquiry) by Richard Norton Taylor, *Talking to Terrorists* by Robin Soans (Out of Joint) and plays such as *Cruising* by Alecky Blythe (Recorded Delivery). The actors in Blythe's productions wear microphones and hear the actual voices of the people they are portraying as they perform the play.

Take note

The plot of a play can be revealed in many different ways. The structure, dialogue and characterisation all contribute to the audience's understanding of the narrative line.

Checkpoint 2

What is the **genre** of a play? How might the genre influence a play's **structure**?

Exam practice   30 minutes   answers: page 82

Write out the plot of the play you are studying in clear bullet points. Now write the sub-plot in the same way. List the dramatic forms and the elements of the structure that the playwright has used to tell the story.

Character

Characterisation is one element of the structure of a play. The dramatist must keep a delicate balance between the many aspects of a play, character being one of them. Successful dramatists give us the illusion that their characters exist outside the confines of the play. Hamlet is a good example: the character has an emotional depth that engages audiences and actors in detailed psychoanalysis. Conversely, minor characters exist simply to advance the plot or to highlight a key aspect of the meaning. Historically, characters were 'types' such as the Machiavellian villain. In Restoration drama this was indicated by the name, e.g. Lady Fancyfull and John Brute in Vanbrugh's *The Provoked Wife*.

Researching the character

In preparing to perform a role in the theatre an actor undertakes detailed research into the character. If the character was a real person, e.g. in *Our Country's Good* by Timberlake Wertenbaker or *Talking to Terrorists* by Robin Soans, an actor would find out everything possible about the life of the person he was playing.

If you are studying Joan Littlewood's Theatre Workshop *Oh, What a Lovely War!* you would research the First World War, while a study of *Blood Wedding* would clearly be enhanced by investigating the life of the playwright Lorca. Research should include any real events that are referred to in the play and the play's historical and political setting. This would be particularly important for a play such as *Shadow of a Gunman* by Sean O'Casey, which is set in 1920 and centres on the violence in Dublin during this period. This information will give a foundation for performing a role or to write an exam essay about presenting a role on stage.

Character and dialogue

As you have read in the section on dialogue, the language spoken by a character is significant in interpreting the role. Consider not only *what* the character says but also *how* you would speak the dialogue. You need to reflect upon the **volume**, **tone**, **pitch**, **pace**, **intonation**, **accent** and the use of **pause**.

There are notable exceptions, however. In *Mother Courage and her Children*, by Brecht, Kattrin is deaf and unable to speak. In approaching this role, an actor would examine movement, reaction and expression.

Shona, from Caryl Churchill's *Top Girls*, appears in only one scene, in which she is being interviewed. She is a minor character, included to exemplify the desperation women in the 1980s felt to be powerful and successful. Her speech pattern and lexis reveal that her story is fiction.

> 'My present job at present. I have a car. I have a Porsche. I go up the M1 a lot. Burn up the M1 a lot. Straight up the M1 in the fast lane to where the clients are, Staffordshire, Yorkshire, I do a lot in Yorkshire. I'm selling electrical things. Like dishwashers, washing machines, stainless steel tubs are a feature and the reliability of the programme . . .'

Take note

Research and exploration are not merely features of the approach by examination candidates. Professional actors and directors work in this way as a matter of course. See Katie Mitchell and Max Stafford-Clark, pages 55–61. See also Stafford-Clark's *Letters to George* for a detailed account of the rehearsal process.

Checkpoint 1

Define each of these terms.

Action point

Look at a scene or a long speech for the character you are studying. Annotate the text to indicate the use of these vocal terms (right).

Repetition of the immature phrase '*a lot*', her conviction that travelling on the M1 exemplifies success and her lack of complete sentences place her in a different class from the woman who is conducting the interview.

In *The Royal Hunt of the Sun* by Shaffer, Pizarro uses **imperatives** and **declaratives**, to convey power and authority.

> '*Stand firm. Look at you; you could be dead already.*'
> '*If he sees you like that you will be. Make no error, he's watching every step you take.*'

In *The Crucible*, however, Miller indicates Elizabeth Proctor's apprehension in the opening scene of Act 2 with short sentences and the use of **interrogatives**.

> **Elizabeth:** What keeps you so late? It's almost dark.
> **Proctor:** I were planting far out to the forest edge.
> **Elizabeth:** Oh, you're done then?
> **Proctor:** Aye, the farm is seeded . . .

Character and action

Playwrights often indicate the action in a text: in *Death of a Salesman*, Miller gives lengthy directions to the actor, whereas Sarah Kane's *4.48 Psychosis* has no stage directions at all. Shakespeare's plays have few indications of action and those that are printed usually reflect the actions taken by the original actors or stage direction added in later centuries. In *Mother Courage and her Children* the dumb Kattrin's actions are crucial in the communication of character.

> '*Kattrin stands up distractedly . . . Unobserved Kattrin has slipped away to the cart and taken from it something which she hides beneath her apron; then she climbs up the ladder to the stable roof . . . Sitting on the roof Kattrin begins to beat the drum which she has pulled out from under her apron . . . Kattrin stares into the distance towards the town and carries on drumming.*'

The action of a character must be determined by his/her **motivation**. Directors work with actors to find the inner core of the character; this leads to **movement**, **gesture**, **pace** and **pause**. Stanislavski's later work focused on '*the method of physical action*' through which he argued that actors would find '*solidarity and depth*', while Max Stafford-Clark's 'actioning' of the text generates both intonation and movement.

In preparing for your exam you need to consider how, where and when a character moves. The example below is from Shaffer's *Equus*. The central character, Alan Strang, is re-enacting his secret riding of the horse, Nugget, under hypnosis. The actions are prescribed by the playwright.

> *Alan moves upstage and mimes opening the door.*
> *Soft light on the circle.*
> *Humming from the CHORUS: the Equus noise.*
> *The horses enter, raise their masks and put them on all together. They stand around the circle – NUGGET in the mouth of the tunnel.*
> **Dysart:** Quietly as possible. Dalton may still be awake. Sssh . . .

Checkpoint 2

Find examples of **imperatives**, **declaratives** and **interrogatives** in a text that you are studying.

Take note

The delivery of dialogue is also influenced by the director's approach. See Stanislavski, page 30, Katie Mitchell, page 58, and Max Stafford-Clark, page 55.

Take note

If you are answering a question about presenting a role on stage it is important to discuss the *performance* using the language of theatre, *not* to write a literary analysis of character.

Links

See Stanislavski, page 30, and Stafford-Clark, page 55. For Joan Littlewood, see page 25.

Take note

Stillness and **eye contact** are also actions.

Grade booster

If you are writing an exam essay about staging a section of the set text, try to avoid simply indicating the character's movements but rather suggest *why* and *how* this movement is made. What is the effect of your staging on the audience, on other characters in the scene and as a reflection of the theme of the play?

Quietly . . . Good. Now go in.

Alan steps secretly out of the square through the central opening on to the circle, now glowing with a warm light. He looks about him. The horses stamp uneasily; their masks turn towards him.

You are on the inside now. All the horses are staring at you. Can you see them?

Alan: *(excited)* Yes!

Dysart: Which one are you going to take?

Alan: Nugget.

Alan reaches up and mimes leading Nugget carefully round the circle downstage with a rope, past all the horses on the right.

Dysart: What colour is Nugget?

Alan: Chestnut.

The horse picks his way with care. Alan halts him at the corner of the square.

Dysart: What do you do first thing?

Alan: Put on his sandals.

Dysart: Sandals?

He [Alan] kneels downstage centre.

Alan: Sandals of majesty!. . . . Made of sack.

He picks up the invisible sandals and kisses them devoutly.

Tie them round his hooves.

He taps Nugget's right leg; the horse raises it and the boy mimes tying the sack round it.

Dysart: All four hooves?

Alan: Yes.

Dysart: Then?

Alan: Chinkle-chankle.

He mimes picking up the bridle and the bit.

He doesn't like it so late, but he takes it for my sake. He bends for me. He stretches forth his neck to it.

Nugget bends his head down. Alan first ritually puts the bit into his own mouth, then crosses and transfers it into Nugget's. He reaches up and buckles on the bridle. Then he leads him by the invisible reins, across the front of the stage and up round the left side of the circle. Nugget follows obediently.

Alan: Buckle and lead out.

The playwright has given very precise detail of the actions for Alan and for the actors playing horses. As an actor or director you would shape the performance by considering **how** the actions were performed: the pace and energy, the use of pause, facial expression and eye contact.

Exam practice   30 minutes   answers: page 82

Read the section from *Equus* above. Consider the scene from the perspective of the actor playing Alan. How would you perform the action of the scene? Write a paragraph outlining how you would approach the scene and detailing how this might appear in a final performance. Think about research and preparation, the use of movement and gesture and communication with the audience.

Dialogue

Dialogue refers to the words written for the characters to speak. The **genre** of the play determines the specific language the characters speak. The dialogue drives the plot and reveals the emotions and nature of the characters. **Language** can create mood, atmosphere and location as well as creating climax, intrigue and pathos. Dialogue is the raw material that actors have to work with; their individual approach to the role during rehearsal shapes the way dialogue is delivered in performance. Thus every performance and every production of the same text will be unique.

Dialogue and genre

Greek tragedy was written with a formal verse structure. In Gilbert Murray's translation of *Agamemnon*, in *The Oresteia*, Cassandra describes her vision to the Leader:

> 'Ah, ah! What is it? There; it is coming clear
> A net . . . some net of Death:
> A woman: she is in his arms: is she the snare,
> Who blood-guilt with another compasseth?'

Shakespeare writes in **blank verse** and in **prose**; prose was usually used for the lower classes, close friends or humorous characters. *As You Like It* contains many prose scenes, whereas *Macbeth* reserves prose for 'low' characters such as The Porter and Murderers.

Prior to **realism** and **naturalism** playwrights did not try to bring the language of everyday speech onto the stage. **Ibsen**, **Chekov** and **Strindberg** wrote in a style that mirrored normal speech. Reading this today, however, it does not seem natural. In the opening of **Ibsen's** *Hedda Gabler*, the newly wed Hedda and Tesman return from their honeymoon and are greeted by Tesman's maiden aunt:

> **Hedda:** *Good morning, dear Miss Tesman. What an early hour to call. So kind of you.*
> **Miss Tesman:** *And has the young bride slept well in her new home?*

In *Abigail's Party* (1979), Mike Leigh wanted to create genuine conversation; the play was originally created through improvisation.

> **Beverly:** *Actually, Ang, it's going to be really nice, because I've invited Sue from Number 9.*
> **Angela:** *Oh, lovely.*
> **Beverly:** *Yeah, so I thought it'd be nice for you to meet her as well. Yeah, 'cos her daughter's having a party . . .*

Beckett's dialogue in *Waiting for Godot* (1956) reflects the surreal nature of the play:

> **Vladimir:** *But yesterday evening it was all black and bare. And now it's covered with leaves.*
> **Estragon:** *Leaves?*
> **Vladimir:** *In a single night.*
> **Estragon:** *It must be the Spring!*

Links

For more information on realism and naturalism, see page 22.

Checkpoint 1

What does the dialogue in the extract from *Abigail's Party* reveal about the way the play was created?

Take note

The dialogue reflects the **genre** of the play. Many playwrights strive to write dialogue that closely mirrors the everyday speech of the characters. It is not, however, ordinary speech and has been shaped for dramatic purposes.

Links

See Stanislavski, page 30.

Dialogue and character

The **phrasing**, **structure** and **vocabulary** a character employs reveal much about his/her psychological make-up. **Stanislavski** advised his actors to examine the text closely and this close textual analysis continues to underpin the work of actors and directors in shaping roles.

An actor often examines what his character says about himself, about others and what other characters say about him. For example in Timberlake Wertenbaker's *Our Country's Good*, the character Liz Morden is the convict who makes the greatest journey of redemption through her participation in the play. Others say of her, *'How is Lieutenant Clark going to manage Liz Morden?'* and *'You don't have to be able to read the future to know that Liz Morden is going to be hanged.'* Liz herself says, *'Luck? Don't know the word. Shifts its bob when I comes near'* and she says of Ketch (the convict hangman), *'Crapping cull! Switcher!'* Thus we can see that Liz, hard, feared, foul-mouthed and with a fierce temper, has had an appalling childhood.

In David Hare's verbatim piece *The Permanent Way*, the writer has selected and shaped the actual words spoken by the interviewed people in a way that captures the essence of their character. Notice the contrasts in these speeches following the news of the Hatfield train crash:

> **Another Senior Operating Executive:** *All the time I was thinking 'Oh Christ! Is this our crash?' . . . If this is our fault that's the end for GNER . . .* (and after being told they were not responsible) *I thought, 'Thank Christ it's not us.'*
> **Vicar of Hatfield:** *Christianity is a religion of hope. We live in a society obsessed with blame, with blaming each other . . .*

The **lexis** of a character reflects personality and status. In *A Streetcar Named Desire*, Stanley tells Blanche, *'I once went out with a doll who said to me . . .'* The use of the colloquialism 'doll' contrasts with the poetic, educated language of Blanche. The dialogue may be written to reflect a social group (**sociolect**), e.g. the convicts in *Our Country's Good* (switcher, bobcull, prissycove) or the city bankers in *Serious Money* ('Closing out now at 4'; 'Final kerb close 901–2').

Idiolect is the language used by an individual, an inimitable blend of influences on the character. In *Equus*, Alan's father uses the phrases *'if you receive my meaning'* and *'mind your own beeswax'*, which both irritate his son and give him a strong identity which the audience recognises.

Take note

Dialogue is the essential key to unlocking the centre of a character. Actors and directors always examine the text minutely to illuminate the inner core of a role.

Grade booster

When you are preparing a role for the performance exam, make sure that you examine the dialogue for clues to your characterisation. Do not simply think of the lines as something to learn and then recite!

Dialogue creates mood, location and atmosphere

The playwright's fundamental device is the words spoken by the characters. Words also paint verbal pictures for the audience, create tension or humour and add to the mood of the scene. Shakespeare's theatre had none of the technical effects used in modern theatre. Performances took place in full daylight and the words served to create the location for the audience. In *Hamlet*, Horatio's description of the break of day

'But look, the morn, in russet mantle clad,
Walks o'er the dew on yon high eastward hill'

was the playwright's way of indicating a lighting effect. Similarly, Shakespeare creates the atmosphere following the murder of Duncan, not by music or sound effects but through the words spoken by the central characters:

Macbeth: *I have done the deed – Didst thou not hear a noise?*
Lady Macbeth: *I heard the owl scream and the crickets cry.*

Checkpoint 2

Look at a play you are studying. How is the atmosphere created by the dialogue?

In *A Streetcar Named Desire*, Williams establishes the atmosphere of New Orleans with the cries of the street vendors '*Red Hoots!*' and the haunting '*Flores para los muertos*'. Tom Stoppard in *Arcadia* locates the opening scene in 1809, the formality of the period being established in the dialogue:

Septimus: *Well, my answer is that as is my custom and my duty to his lordship I am engaged until a quarter to twelve in the education of his daughter . . .*

The play shifts backwards and forwards in time. Compare the speech above with this from a scene set in 1993:

Chloe: *The best thing is, you wait here, save you tramping around.*

Exam practice   45 minutes

Examine one key scene from a play that you are studying. How does the dialogue create the location, time period, mood and atmosphere? Now select a character, which could be the one that you are playing for your exam. Look at the dialogue. What clues can you find in the lexis and patterns of speech that reveal information about the character? Finally, what conclusions can you form about the playwright's use of language?

Design: visual, aural and spatial (1)

A theatrical production will have a creative team attached to it. This team includes designers who specialise in particular areas, e.g. set and costumes, sound effects, lighting and the writing of the original musical score. The overall concept will be discussed with the director and perhaps the playwright if he/she is still alive. Their shared vision of the play will be at the centre of the creative process. When you are answering questions about design it is important to consider these elements collectively.

Designing the set, costume and properties

Set design

The first consideration is the **historical context** of the play. If the playwright has specified certain features of the set that are essential to the play, then the design must acknowledge these. For example, in *A Doll's House*, the Christmas tree is an important symbol so the designer must consider its position on the stage. The opening stage directions of *A Doll's House* read almost like a novel, giving exact detail of the room. This is a feature of **realism**.

Shakespeare's plays have few indications of set as the plays were presented at The Globe or at Court, with little scenic design. Directors and their designers have located Shakespeare's plays in different times and locations. Peter Brook's landmark production of *A Midsummer Night's Dream* took place in a circus, while Out of Joint's site-specific *Macbeth* was set in Africa.

Some plays require **multiple locations** and the designer's role is to ensure that the set can be changed easily or that locations are suggested with minimum changes of set. David Hare's *Plenty* cuts backwards and forwards in time and requires more than ten locations, ranging from a wood in wartime France to a home in Knightsbridge. The requirements of the play are that it is **naturalistic**, yet the designer must ensure the fluid transition from one location to another.

Summary

Here is a summary of the process of design:

→ What period is the play being set in?
→ What is the theatre space: proscenium arch, thrust, in the round, site-specific, etc?
→ How will the genre influence the design?
→ How will the design reflect the theme and meaning of the play?
→ Is this production set in a historical or cultural context?
→ What is the relationship with the audience?
→ What are the essential features required by the text (e.g. doors/ fireplace)?
→ How many locations must be suggested?
→ What is the mood, shape, texture, colour of the play?
→ What does the costume reveal about class, character and theme?

Take note

Everything that can be seen on the stage is **visual** – light, costume, set, properties. Everything that is heard – sound effects and music – is **aural**. The way the space is designed and used, including the physical relationship with the audience, is **spatial**.

Take note

The set designer often creates a **mood board** – a collage of images, shapes, colours and textures that reflect the play's themes, location, atmosphere and culture. A mood board for *Our Country's Good* might include images of naval uniforms, chains, whips, Australian landscapes, prisons, sand, burned scrubland, sailing ships, Aboriginal art, sail cloth, rags, etc.

Checkpoint 1

Define and give examples of **texture**, **shape**, **colour** and **period** in relation to design.

Watch out!

Do not use numerous blackouts! This disjoints the action and breaks the illusion. It is much more effective to use actors to move furniture smoothly and efficiently in full or dimmed light. In large theatres, sections of set can be wheeled onto the stage on **trucks** or **flown** or a **revolve** can be used.

Checkpoint 2

How are **trucks**, **revolves** and **flying** used in theatre?

Grade booster

Avoid generalisations in your answers about design. The terms **minimalist** and **symbolic**, for example, are often misused. You should also be wary of 'mixing conventions': if your setting is **naturalistic** you would be unlikely to have stylised or symbolic features.

→ What fabrics and textures would the costumes of the period be made from?

→ Will the set and costume be realistic or symbolic?

Costume design

The **style**, **colour**, **texture** and **period** must complement each other. Costume conveys information about **location**, **character** and **historical period**. The costume designer must consider practicalities such as the actor's movement in the costume, the number of changes needed and any specific requirements that might affect choice of material. The costumes must also reflect the climate and season.

Costume reflects social class and status, so it is important when writing about design that you take this into account. In *A Streetcar Named Desire*, Williams describes the poker players in exact detail: *'The poker players . . . wear coloured shirts, solid blues, a purple, a red and white check, a light green . . .'*. The colours signal the atmosphere and status of the men and contrast with Blanche *'daintily dressed in a white suit with a fluffy bodice'*. The exact shape, material, detail and accessorising of the costume are what bring individuality to the design.

If your text is set in a historical period, you need to undertake research into contemporary costume style and into the way clothes were worn by the class of character you are costuming. Should you decide to place the play in a different time, you must ensure that any textual references can be reconciled with the altered setting. Cheek by Jowl's 2006 production of *The Changeling* set the play in a modern asylum with black suits, red plastic chairs and ominous CCTV cameras.

In some plays the costume must essentially follow the playwright's original ideas. One example of this is Joan Littlewood's *Oh! What a Lovely War*, which employs a music-hall style to comment ironically on the follies of the First World War. The characters wear Pierrot costumes, adding items of authentic clothing to signify character. The style of the play is **Brechtian**.

Properties

Properties are the items that are used by the actors during the play. Some playwrights indicate the precise objects they wish to be used in the performance, while other properties are chosen by the actor or director. For example, the suitcases dragged in by Willy Loman in the opening scene of *Death of a Salesman*, the stuffed seagull in Chekhov's play and the picture of Betsy Alicia treasured by Ralph Clark in *Our Country's Good* are all important to the plot and symbolic of the meaning of the play.

Every property must be in keeping with the style of the design; a realistic set and costume design will require properties from the correct period. For example, the cushions, glasses and telephone in *Abigail's Party* must be from the exact era of the 1970s.

Take note

When creating set designs or writing about design you must ensure that the design can be realised in the theatre and that if many locations are needed you have considered the practicalities of showing these settings.

Take note

Nothing that appears on the stage has got there by accident! Every detail of the set, costume and properties has been carefully considered.

Grade booster

Make sure you consider the creative interpretation of design, not simply repeat the information given by the playwright. In answering a question or writing exploration notes about design it is important to comment on how design can contribute to the play's meaning and impact.

Links

For more information about Brecht's theatre, see page 33.

Action point

Make a list of the properties required in one act of a text you are studying. Consider why they are important, for example Loveberg's manuscript in *Hedda Gabler*, which is profoundly symbolic. Suggest what research you would undertake and where you might locate the properties.

Exam practice   30 minutes   answers: pages 82–83

For a text that you are studying, write an analysis of the visual and spatial elements of two key scenes.

Design: visual, aural and spatial (2)

This section is concerned with **lighting**, **sound** and **music**. As with set, costume and properties, the work of the designer is to interpret the text in conjunction with the director and, perhaps, a playwright. Lighting design differs from lighting operation. The designer will create all the effects and oversee the **rigging**; thereafter the stage management team operates them in performance. Likewise the sound designer creates the effects which are operated by technicians.

Lighting design

Theatre lighting has the primary function of enabling the audience to see the action of the play. It also creates **mood**, **atmosphere**, **location** and **temperature**. Lighting can be used to indicate changes in time as well as place and must mirror the style of the production.

In Greek, Elizabethan or Jacobean drama there is no indication of artificial lighting effects; the productions took place outdoors and in daylight, but the playwright's language created the mood and location. Restoration theatres were lit with candles and only in 1817 did gaslight become the first form of theatre lighting that could be focused or changed in intensity. In the late 19th century, electric light was used for the first time.

Lighting a play is a complex and skilled job, requiring artistic flair as well as technical knowledge. Playwrights indicate lighting effects and directors require certain moods to be created through lighting. In *Equus*, Peter Shaffer gives suggestions for lighting effects, especially where tension and heightened atmosphere are indicated. It is, however, the designer's role to interpret this. In some plays the light is from a particular **source** and the designer must make sure that the light appears to be coming from this location.

In *A Streetcar Named Desire*, there is a scene where Blanche lights a candle and carries it to another room. The lighting must subtly follow the candle, be bright enough for the actors to be seen but create the impression that only one candle lights the room. In Shakespeare's plays, characters often appear carrying flaming torches – again the lighting must suggest that this is the source. Where light streams through a window or spills from an open doorway, the designer must position lanterns so as to create the effect.

Lighting shows geographical location and time of day. In *Blood Wedding*, the lighting will be designed to create the temperature by using warm gels from the yellow spectrum, such as straw, and in *The Duchess of Malfi* the lighting will suggest the darkness of the Duchess's prison.

At the end of *The Crucible* the lighting must show the slow rise of the sun signalling the end of John Proctor's life, while the lighting for the *'blasted heath'* in *Macbeth* creates a sinister, haunted mood.

Special effects come under the general umbrella of lighting. An **effects projector** is used to create the impression, for example, that clouds are scudding across the sky. **Back projection** plays images related to the play, as in *Oh! What a Lovely War*, or to depict events that cannot be played on stage. The dramatic train crash and the rolling timetable boards in *The Permanent Way* were created by the designer William Dudley and played as a back projection. This use of video and created images is known as **multimedia**. Examples of **multimedia** productions are *Elsinore*, Robert Lepage's one-man interpretation of *Hamlet* and *Testing the Echo*, by David Edgar, where two large screens are central to the design.

A lighting designer would need to consider the following:

→ Is the lighting naturalistic or symbolic?
→ What is the period? Would there have been electric power?
→ Where is the scene set? Outdoors in sunlight? Inside a modern office?
→ What are the time of day, temperature and weather?
→ Where is the source of the light? The sun? A table lamp? The window? A candle?
→ What is the intensity of the light?
→ Does the lighting effect signify a change of mood or a climax?

Sound design

Sound enhances the **mood** and **atmosphere** of the production and in a similar way to lighting can create the **location** and **period** of the play. In Shaffer's *The Royal Hunt of the Sun*, sound is used symbolically to reflect emotions as well as to create atmosphere. Shaffer was influenced by **Artaud's total theatre** and combines live music with recorded sound.

The effect of heat can be created through the sound of crickets in *Blood Wedding*, while the sound of howling wind could contribute to the atmosphere of *Macbeth*. In *A Streetcar Named Desire*, the piano jazz evokes the atmosphere of New Orleans and the haunting melody of the polka dance, the *Varsouviana*, serves as a symbolic reminder of Blanche's tormented past. Its distorted tones painfully mirror her descent into madness in the final scene.

Most sound effects are created by the sound designer and are played electronically during the performance. Some playwrights specifically require sound to be created by the actors or on-stage musicians. Sound must appear to be coming from the location in which it is created: a radio, a passing train, a dog barking outside, children crying upstairs. In this way it is similar to the source of lighting. In some plays the sound is especially significant. In *A Doll's House*, '*the street door is slammed shut downstairs*' is the final stage direction and has great symbolic weight. The train crash in Hare's *The Permanent Way* has enormous dramatic impact whilst also highlighting the serious political message.

Watch out!

When writing about lighting make sure you know the basic technical terms and use them correctly.

Checkpoint 1

Define the following: **fresnel, gobo, gel, wash, cross-fade, dim, profile spot, barn door, flood, state**.

Links

See page 44.

Examiner's secrets

Avoid numerous blackouts in your performance exam. This disjoints the action and breaks the atmosphere.

Exam practice   30 minutes   answers: page 83

For a play that you are studying, select a section where sound (or music) and light are used to create mood or atmosphere or where they suggest location, weather or time. Write an analysis of how these technical effects contribute to the performance.

The playwright and the social and political context

The cultural landscape

A play reflects the spirit of an age and the audience for whom it is written. In **Greek** theatre, playwrights wrote for a festival in celebration of the god Dionysus; audiences came from the whole social spectrum and theatre was a central feature of life in Athens. Plays featured stories of the gods and of great journeys, mythical characters and epic challenges. If your play is from this period you will need to consider the nature of the audience and the concerns of the playwright.

In Britain, the **medieval mystery plays** appealed to the entire community and drew actors from workers in the town. Religion was central to society and Bible stories were enacted.

Many of **Shakespeare's** plays were concerned with the nature of **kingship** and the state, which was a preoccupation of the era. *Richard III* cannot maintain his unlawful claims and *Macbeth* cannot survive after murdering Duncan. *Richard II*, although weak, is the lawful king and Bolingbroke's descendants pay sorely for his usurpation. The comedies were often set abroad, a reflection of the age of discovery of the new world. When exploring a Shakespearean text you should look at the concurrent historical events, to gain insight into the meaning.

Restoration drama ridiculed the manners and behaviour of the rich who, ironically, made up the audience. Look at the 'stock' characters in a play that you are studying and compare them with real people from the era. The 18th century produced the age of **actor managers** and the drama became less sophisticated. With the exception of **Sheridan** and **Goldsmith**, this era produced few great writers. The 19th century saw the rise of **melodrama**, but plays were seldom original and play writing was in decline. From the era of **realism** and **naturalism** in Europe, **Ibsen** and **Chekhov** commented on life as they saw it. For them, theatre was a vehicle for change. **Piscator** and **Brecht's epic** drama stirred audiences to be politically aware.

In modern British drama, playwrights hit out at social injustice and plays became outspoken in their condemnation of inequality. If you are studying a modern text you should look carefully at the political events surrounding the play and its writer. Mark Ravenhill's *Shopping and F**king*, or Sarah Kane's *4.48 Psychosis* criticise society, while J.T. Rogers' *The Overwhelming* exposes the political inertia in the events leading up to the Rwandan genocide and David's Edgar's *Testing the Echo* examines what it means to be British in today's multi-cultural society.

The nature of audience

Plays are written to tell a story, to reflect the writer's concerns and to appeal to the audience. Audiences are a reflection of society and they have associations with particular theatres; in modern theatre this is known as the **demographic**. The people who make up the audience at *The Lion King* will be very different from those of the Jerwood Theatre Upstairs at the Royal Court. The former attracts theatregoers seeking entertainment with spectacle. The Royal Court audience, however, are likely to be keen to see original and challenging plays by new writers.

Links

Find more detail about the history of the theatre, see Drama and theatre in context, pages 10–25.

Action point

Michael Billington, the theatre critic for *The Guardian*, traces how playwrights reflected the mood of the nation in the modern theatre in *State of the Nation* published by Faber and Faber.

Take note

Significant American playwrights such as Tennessee Williams, Arthur Miller and Eugene O'Neill emerged in the 20th century to challenge the American Dream. Miller's *Death of a Salesman* is the most celebrated indictment of America's failure to deliver 'the dream', while *The Crucible* exposes the witch-hunt of McCarthyism.

Checkpoint 1

Why is the **Royal Court Theatre** important to the emergence of new playwrights?

If you examine the **demographic** of the audience for a play you are studying you will gain significant insight into the playwright's target group. Shakespeare had an audience made up of **groundlings** and more wealthy and educated spectators. If you are studying a play by Shakespeare you should examine the text from an audience perspective. For example, *Macbeth* is tragic with complex imagery but the comic character of The Porter, three witches and ghosts appeals to the groundlings.

A playwright writing for a regional theatre will reflect the demographic and cultural concerns of the audience. **Hull Truck** has a vibrant and loyal audience base and the playwright **John Godber** has written numerous plays that appeal to his audience. **Alan Ayckbourn** writes for his theatre in Scarborough, while **Kneehigh** create theatre for families in locations within their communities in Cornwall.

Checkpoint 2

Who were the **groundlings**?

Take note

Don't forget to take into account the audience for whom the playwright was writing. This will affect the concerns and the style of the play.

The theatre space

The location, shape and structure of the theatre will affect the play. Imposing Greek amphitheatres gave rise to the **chorus**. The townspeople of Chester in the Middle Ages gathered around a pageant wagon to watch the cycle of **mystery plays** and Elizabethan audiences packed into large outdoor theatres. However, attendance at a **masque** in a royal banqueting hall was open only to high-ranking members of society.

Interaction between the men in the **pit** and actors was common in Restoration theatre. Plays written in the **realist** style by **Ibsen** and **Chekov** have intricate stage directions and set detail; these plays were presented on **proscenium arch** stages with an imagined **fourth wall**. Plays written for **theatre in the round** are more intimate and plays first presented in small experimental venues are creative in their use of minimal spaces. Punchdrunk's *Masque of the Red Death*, staged at the Battersea Arts Centre in a unique **promenade** style, was an example of immersive theatre where the audience is both spectator and participant. The first production of a play shapes its final version.

Grade booster

Discuss the relevance of the play for an audience today. Show an understanding of the impact of the original production on its audience and make comparisons with the effect on a modern audience.

Checkpoint 3

What do you understand by the terms **proscenium arch** and **fourth wall**?

Exam practice   30 minutes   answers: page 83

For a play that you are studying, find out **when** and **where** the first production took place. Research historical or contemporary events that might have influenced the playwright and explore the society and politics of the period. Investigate the venue where the first production was staged. What shape is (was) the auditorium? How many does (did) it seat? What conclusions can you draw about how the theatre space might have affected the presentation of the text?

Answers
Exploring the text

Plot and sub-plot

Checkpoints

1 The **plot** of the play is the main story line, involving the central characters. The **sub-plot** is a less significant or parallel story involving minor characters.

2 **Genre** refers to a dramatic form with similar conventions, constructions and characteristics. These features often influence a play's **structure**: farce employs dramatic irony while revenge tragedy involves ghosts, death and madness.

Exam practice

Our Country's Good

Plot: Convicts overcome opposition and rehearse a play

- In 1788 the first convicts are transported to Australia.
- Governor Arthur Phillip asks Ralph Clark to put on a play to civilise the convicts.
- Major Ross disagrees and tries to sabotage the rehearsals and stop the play.
- The convicts hate Ketch Freeman, the convict hangman, and refuse to act with him.
- Ralph Clark works hard with the convicts and begins to see them as real people.
- Food is stolen; Liz Morden is accused and threatened with hanging.
- Against all the odds the play is rehearsed.
- The convicts settle their differences and become a community, civilised by their involvement in the play.
- In the final scene the actor convicts prepare for their performance.

Sub-plot: Love stories

- Wisehammer and Ralph both fall in love with Mary Brenham.
- Mary begins an affair with Ralph.
- Harry Brewer has a convict mistress, Duckling, and struggles to control his jealousy.
- Harry thinks that he sees dead convicts he has hanged.
- He becomes delirious and dies; Duckling realises her love for him.

Form and structure: Two acts, montage of 22 short scenes, titled scenes (Brechtian), juxtaposition, Aboriginal as commentator, doubling, black humour, meta-theatre

Character

Checkpoints

1 **Volume** – how quiet or loud the voice is.
   Tone – the manner in which the words are said.
   Pitch – a high or low voice.
   Pace – the speed of dialogue delivery.
   Intonation – cadence, lilt, modulation or inflection.
   Accent – a regional or national pronunciation.
   Pause – a short silence. A *voiced* pause has 'um', 'er', etc. An *unvoiced* pause has no sound.

2 Text: Doris in *My Mother Said I Never Should* (Scene 2).
   Imperative – DORIS: *Margaret! Come out!*

Declarative – DORIS: *Father will be home soon.*
Interrogative – DORIS: *Have you washed your hands?*

Exam practice

In preparing to play Alan in this scene I would consider his emotional state. My research would include an examination of the events that had led up to this moment, for example his fascination with biblical stories about horses. Reading the relevant section of the Bible story and examining pictures of both Christ in chains and horses would assist me in capturing Alan's mental state. In the opening moments I would react to the horse actors donning their masks with absorption and amazement, my facial expression conveying the awe with which I revered these animals. I would also seek to convey fear; the fear of being so close to a god. My reaction when the horses stamp and turn their heads would communicate panic mixed with anticipation. When leading Nugget my movement would show a mixture of anxiety and excitement, looking around to check I was alone while conveying joy in my face. When Alan kneels in front of the horse I would move into position slowly and reverentially, lifting my eyes towards the mask gradually to create the mood of adoration. The placing of the sacking shoes would also be done with reverence as if in a church. It would aid my performance of this section if I was able to visit a stable and be taught how to put on a bridle; I would need to ensure that I knew the correct procedures to make my mime authentic. The mime must be clear and precise. My aim in performance would be to communicate Alan's worship of the horses by mirroring religious ceremony in preparing the horse for the ride.

Dialogue

Checkpoints

1 The use of 'yeah' and 'cos' show casual conversation and phrases such as 'really nice' sound natural rather than scripted. The play was written following extensive improvisation by the actors.

2 You should consider location, tension, humour and mood.

Design: visual, aural and spatial (1)

Checkpoints

1 **Texture** – sacking, glass, sand, velvet.
   Shape – pointed, angular, circular, rectangular.
   Colour – shades of red, monochrome, yellows and browns.
   Period – Victorian, Second World War, 1960s.

2 **Trucks** have sections of set or whole scenes built onto them and they are rolled into position on tracks in the stage. A **revolve** turns on stage to reveal a new set on the other side. **Flying** refers to items of scenery that are lowered from above the stage and can be removed in the same way. The area above the stage is known in theatre as 'the flies'.

Exam practice

The visual elements in *The Royal Hunt of the Sun* by Peter Shaffer underpin the theme of the play *'ruin and gold'*. The play begins in Spain and then moves to the Inca world of Peru. The first appearance of the Incas is a spectacular moment. They are costumed in wonderful headdresses of vibrant birds' feathers and clothing in rich yellows and ochre. The Incas fill the space and create a powerful impact. When the sun god, Atahuallpa, is first seen he is revealed slowly as a massive medallion that has dominated the stage. It slowly opens like the petals of a flower to reveal the splendid king clad in gold, with a magnificent mask, standing in what has become the rays of the sun. Lighting enhances the moment with a brilliant wash of warm colour reflecting the glow of the sun.

In another key scene from the play the Incas are massacred in the town square; this is symbolised by the drawing of a lurid red cloth from the centre of the sun, which is dragged across the whole stage at the end of the first act. This is accompanied by sensational lighting that washes the stage with shades of red, mirroring the horror of the event.

Design: visual, aural and spatial (2)

Checkpoint

1 **Fresnel** – a spotlight that produces a soft-edged pool of light.
   Gobo – a stencil placed in front of the lamp to project a shape onto the stage.
   Gel – coloured sheets placed in front of the lantern to create mood or temperature.
   Wash – a general covering of the stage space in one colour.
   Cross-fade – changing from one lighting state to another gradually without a blackout.
   Dim – lowering the intensity of the light from bright to low.
   Profile spot – a spotlight that produces a sharply defined edge.
   Barn door – a metal square flap used to prevent light spilling onto unwanted areas.
   Flood – a light with no lens so it cannot be focused and gives a general wash.
   State – the particular arrangement, intensity and colour of lighting on the stage at a specific time.

Exam practice

In Lorca's *Blood Wedding*, sound, music and lighting combine to reflect mood, atmosphere and location. The sound of cicadas invites the audience to feel the heat of the Spanish countryside, while the mood of the location is captured by haunting sounds from a guitar. The lighting uses a mixture of warm straw and salmon to evoke the oppressive heat. In the wedding scene, live musicians accompany the dancing that is taking place in another room while the tense drama is played out on stage. The juxtaposition of lively music and taut dialogue generates an atmosphere of disquiet. Later in the play the surreal forest is created with restrained greens and shadows, the haunting figure of the moon illuminated in an almost translucent light that gives the character symbolic significance. The lighting and sound in *Blood Wedding* echo the themes of passion, revenge and fate.

The playwright and the social and political context

Checkpoints

1 The **Royal Court Theatre** was founded to nurture new writing talent. Playwrights such as Harold Pinter and John Osborne began their writing careers there in the 1950s and 1960s and the Royal Court continues to discover contemporary writers.
2 **Groundlings** paid one penny to stand in the yard area in front of the stage at The Globe.
3 The **proscenium arch** is the 'picture frame' around the stage opening in theatres and the **fourth wall** is a term used by Stanislavski to describe space through which the audience viewed the play. He wanted his actors to imagine that the stage was a real room with four and not three walls.

Exam practice

Antigone, written by Sophocles around 441 BC, would have been presented in an amphitheatre seating thousands of people. Greek dramatists wrote for the festival of Dionysus attended by vast numbers of people. The theatre space was large and the audience a considerable distance from the action, so the actors wore masks. These covered their natural expression and communicated character to the audience without subtlety of physical changes in facial expression. The theatre at Epidaurus near Athens was, perhaps, the venue for a production of *Antigone*. If you drop a matchstick in the centre of the original beaten earth stage it can be heard by people sitting in the highest of the 55 tiers. The awe-inspiring acoustics are attributable to the mathematical precision with which the 14,000-seat theatre was constructed in the 4th century BC. The performance style in this location would be very different from a modern production. Gesture would have been expansive, choral speech slow and measured and there would have been no facial expression or subtle interaction of character.

Revision checklist
Exploring the text

By the end of this chapter you should be able to:

1	Explain the meaning of the terms 'plot' and 'sub-plot' and give examples from the texts you are studying.	Confident	Not confident **Revise** page 68
2	Understand the term 'genre' and explain how it affects the structure of a play.	Confident	Not confident **Revise** page 69
3	Explain the elements of form and structure in your texts.	Confident	Not confident **Revise** pages 68–69
4	Understand why research is important to an actor and a director.	Confident	Not confident **Revise** page 70
5	Explain how character is revealed through dialogue.	Confident	Not confident **Revise** pages 70–71
6	Define volume, tone, pitch, pace, intonation, accent and pause.	Confident	Not confident **Revise** page 70
7	Explain how character is uncovered through movement and action.	Confident	Not confident **Revise** pages 71–72
8	Recognise how dialogue links with genre and how the language of the play reflects character, mood and atmosphere.	Confident	Not confident **Revise** pages 73–75
9	Understand why a designer researches the period of a play.	Confident	Not confident **Revise** page 76
10	Explain the process of a designer's approach.	Confident	Not confident **Revise** pages 76–77
11	Define visual, aural and spatial in relation to design.	Confident	Not confident **Revise** pages 76–80
12	Understand the principles of lighting and use correct terminology when writing about it.	Confident	Not confident **Revise** pages 78–79
13	Understand the principles of sound design.	Confident	Not confident **Revise** page 79
14	Explain why drama reflects the spirit of the age.	Confident	Not confident **Revise** page 80
15	Understand the term 'demographic' as applied to audience.	Confident	Not confident **Revise** pages 80–81
16	Comment on how the shape of the theatre space can impact on the writing of a play.	Confident	Not confident **Revise** page 81

Writing about text

Drama and Theatre Studies examinations in all specifications require you to write about text. Specifications vary in their requirements: some ask you to write about directing, performing or designing in relation to set texts. All specifications set questions on an extract from a text, either prepared or unseen. Certain specifications also require exploration notes on texts that you have studied, forming part of the coursework element of the examination.

This chapter starts with an initial examination of the contextualising of the play. It then explores the role of a director, both in relation to concept and to rehearsal. There is a discussion of approaches to rehearsing and performing a role and a section that prepares you to write about design. The final section equips you to answer the analysis of an extract question. For the AQA and Edexcel specifications the extract will be from a text that you have studied; the WJEC sets an 'unseen' extract.

Exam themes

- Writing about performance, directing and design for set texts
- Contextualising the play
- Analysis of the rehearsal process
- Evaluation of performance
- Creative response to prepared or unseen texts

Topic checklist

	Edexcel		AQA		WJEC	
	AS	A2	AS	A2	AS	A2
Contextualising the play	O	●	O	●	O	●
The director's concept	O	●	O	●	O	●
Writing about rehearsal techniques		●	O	●	O	●
Writing about performing a role	O	●	O	●	O	●
Communicating design concepts	O	●	O	●	O	●
Approaches to unseen and prepared extracts		●		●		●

Contextualising the play

Your exploration notes, portfolio or written exam answer will require you to analyse the background and political or social concerns of the play. Plays are a product of their time and the text will reflect the historical and social context and, sometimes, the playwright's background, experiences and opinions. Events in arts and culture at the time of writing also shape plays.

Contemporary issues

Take note

Contemporary means living or occurring at the same time. Contemporary issues are the concerns, anxieties or problems of society at the time that the play was written.

Playwrights comment on major events that preoccupy society. David Hare's *Stuff Happens* (2003) is a bitter commentary on the Iraq war. The characters are named, including recognisable politicians: Tony Blair, George Bush and Condoleezza Rice. Hare, a formidable political playwright, attacks the decision to invade Iraq and reflects the feelings of the British people who had opposed the invasion. David Edgar's *Testing the Echo (2008)* explores British citizenship in contemporary society. In 1956, *Look Back in Anger* mirrored the emotions of post-war British youth.

Playwrights voice their own concerns and often represent the disquiet of the public. You should research the political climate in which the text you are studying was written. Trace the links between events in society and those in the world of the play.

Checkpoint 1

Why is *Look Back in Anger* important in British theatre?

The playwright's life history

Some plays are openly autobiographical, while others contain people and events shaped by the writer's life experience. Tennessee Williams' *The Glass Menagerie* is wholly autobiographical. The central characters are his mother and sister and Tom (Williams himself), through whose eyes the story is told. If you are studying a play like this you would need to examine the playwright's life story in order to fully understand the connections.

Historical events in the text

A further aspect of contextualising the play involves plays written about, rather than during, a historical period. There are always reasons why the playwright has chosen to set the play in a different time. Peter Shaffer's *Amadeus* examines the life of Mozart, while his epic *The Royal Hunt of the Sun* traces the conquest of Peru. Shaffer's greater purpose, however, was to comment on the nature of worship, drawing subtle comparisons with contemporary values.

Checkpoint 2

Who was **Arthur Miller**? Why was it important for him to attack **McCarthyism**?

When Arthur Miller wrote *The Crucible* he was not free to make a direct attack on the 'witch-hunts' of Senator McCarthy, so he wrote a play about the Salem witch trials of 1792; the audiences drew their own inferences. Timberlake Wertenbaker and Max Stafford-Clark's workshop that led to the creation of *Our Country's Good* took place during the Thatcher era when the Arts were under-funded and under-valued. The resulting play celebrates the redemptive power of theatre; it is set in an Australian convict colony in 1788 where the prisoners are humanised through their involvement in a play.

The cultural context

Theatre connects with other art forms and its plays reflect the changes in style and culture or revolutionary movements. **William Wycherley** wrote 'comedies of manners' during the **Restoration**, which was a frivolous time when society reacted against Puritan self-restraint. The 'manners' are those of society, especially the upper class and courtly circles. The dramatist created the comedy by acute observation and exaggeration and the plots usually included marriage, 'cuckolding' and social indiscretions.

The surrealists, a movement in art and literature between the two World Wars, influenced Beckett's *Waiting for Godot* and the work of Picasso. Beckett's work is also defined as 'absurdist' theatre.

The Norwegian playwright **Ibsen** is associated with **realism**. His plays dealt with serious social issues and were presented in accurately detailed stage settings.

You need to examine your text in its cultural theatrical context.

→ Was it written for a particular space?
→ Was the play commissioned by a theatre?
→ What other plays were written at around the same time? Are there any comparisons?

Links

For more detail on surrealism see Artaud, page 43.

Links

For more detail on realism see page 22.

Themes and issues

What are the playwright's key concerns that lie at the heart of the play? What does he or she want the audience to experience? Is the play aiming to change their perception of events or challenge them to action? **Brecht** sought to politicise his audience and wanted to change their outlook and willingness to act in the face of injustice, whereas **Alan Ayckbourn** draws attention to the idiosyncrasies and social ineptitudes of middle-class people. His comedies might be compared with those of **Wilde** or **Wycherley**, who satirised their own society.

Caryl Churchill's *Top Girls* was a reflection of feminism in the Thatcher years: it examines the political cost of women rising to the top. In *Antigone*, **Sophocles** was concerned with the political vice of **hubris** (shaming a victim in order to make oneself superior) and when **Euripides** perceived Athens becoming aggressive and expansionist, he criticised it in *The Trojan Women*. The radical director Joan Littlewood in the 1960s and John McGrath's 7:84 (a name derived from the statistic asserting that 7 per cent of the nation owned 84 per cent of its wealth) in the 1970s both sought to make political statements through theatrical productions.

The 2006 National Theatre/Out of Joint production of J.T. Rogers' *The Overwhelming* is set in Rwanda on the eve of the Tutsi genocide in which an estimated 800,000 people were slaughtered. The play is deeply provoking and asks profoundly relevant questions that challenge the liberal conscience.

Take note

Playwrights often criticise politics and war. Notice the similarities between Hare's *Stuff Happens* and Euripides' *The Trojan Women*: both criticise invasions that they believed were unjust.

Exam practice   30 minutes   answers: page 102

For one of the texts that you are studying, find out as much as you can about: the playwright's background; significant events at the time the play was written; the themes and issues explored in the play; any historical or political references in the text.

The director's concept

Your examination will probably ask you to consider how you might direct and rehearse the plays that you are studying. The process that a director undertakes prior to the rehearsal period, the casting of the play and the approach taken in the rehearsal room are important. This section and the next will illustrate the way a director might approach a new production and will discuss some of the systems of rehearsal.

Planning the director's concept

Some examinations specifically ask you to plan a director's concept for one of your texts; other examination boards ask you to write about how you might direct or rehearse certain scenes, roles or sections of the play.

The notion of a director's concept has been the subject of negative critical comment. The arguments, mainly by actors, suggested that 20th-century theatre was becoming director's theatre, where the actors had little involvement in the shaping of the play. Nevertheless, the director must have an initial outline of the shape and meaning of the production, although good directors will always include other professionals – actors, designers – in the final form of the production.

The director considers some of the following when formulating a 'concept':

→ What does the play have to say to a modern audience?
→ How do I want the audience to be affected by the performance?
→ Where might the audience's sympathies lie?
→ What are the key moments where you would want to elicit a particular audience response?
→ What was the central concern of the playwright?
→ Where will the play be set (location)?
→ What era will the play be set in (period)?
→ How do I want to portray the relationships in the play?

The director must then prepare the production by considering, in collaboration with designers and producers:

→ design, including costume, and staging
→ casting
→ lighting, sound and music
→ performance style
→ characterisation.

For a contemporary play, the director must have an overview of the central ideas. Brook's 'formless hunch' might sound vague but what he meant was that he would mould his initial instincts during the rehearsal process. If the text was written in a previous period, e.g. by Shakespeare, the director must decide whether it will be set in Elizabethan or Jacobean times or in a different period. This decision is intrinsically related to the concept.

Checkpoint 1

What do you understand by **director's theatre**?

Take note

Peter Brook begins the rehearsal process with what he calls 'a formless hunch' and refers to rehearsals as 'thinking aloud with others'. Directors like **Artaud** and **Grotowski** aimed for a collaborative approach to creating a production.

Links

See Peter Brook, see page 50.

Take note

Read an extract from Brook's *The Shifting Point* entitled 'The Formless Hunch', in *Theatre Directions* by Neelands and Dobson, published by Hodder & Stoughton 2000. This book has many other very useful essays on the craft of directing.

Marianne Elliott's 2006 RSC production of *Much Ado About Nothing* was set in 1950s' Cuba. The production explored passion, corruption and the military. Max Stafford-Clark's Out of Joint *Macbeth* (2004), set in modern Africa, examined the horrors of a country torn apart by a brutal warlord whose reign of terror exploited children as soldiers and saw women raped and murdered.

A concept for a set text

If you are studying a play written in a different era you must decide how you want it to be received by the audience. In Marlowe's *Dr Faustus*, the protagonist 'sells his soul to the devil' in exchange for knowledge and power. You might set the play in the 21st century, exploring the tension in modern society between aspiration and fulfillment. Locating the play in the City of London with Faust as a successful, power-hungry banker would highlight modern society's obsession with wealth and ambition. Your **staging** could include multi-media elements, with screens showing stock markets, adverts for luxury items and images of celebrity. **Sound, light and costume** would also reflect this modern setting.

The director would also decide on the **theatre space** for the performance. If you were creating a concept for Ibsen's *A Doll's House*, written in the 19th century, you might choose to preserve the period but aim to show the claustrophobia and chilly severity of the house. This production might require an intimate space, like the Bush or the Manchester Royal Exchange, rather than a large theatre such as the Olivier at the National Theatre. Your concept, therefore, could focus on the strain and Nora's confinement by staging the play **in the round** with minimal pieces of period furniture. The audience would themselves be part of the entrapment of Nora and their focus would be on the relationships between the characters.

After deciding on your concept, you must then apply it to the whole play. Consider how each **scene** and **character** would tie in with the ruling idea. All aspects of the production must be in line with the overall concept: set, lighting, costume, properties, music and characterisation. **Casting** is an important consideration. If you have decided that Nora is a weak, naïve 'trophy' wife with whom you want the audience to sympathise, you would cast an actor who matched this description physically. **Directing** will naturally follow the concept: if your Nora is submissive, her responses to Helmer's reprimanding of her spending in Act I might be played with coquettish compliance.

Finally, look at the **key scenes** that you have identified as being important to the themes, issues and audience response and decide how they might be presented in relation to your concept.

Checkpoint 2

What is **theatre in the round**? Can you name any other 'in the round' theatre spaces?

Action point

Do some instinctive thinking about your play. Write down the first answer that comes into your head when you read these questions:
→ What **colour** is the play?
→ What **shapes** do you associate with it?
→ What **texture** is it?
→ What is the **word** that you associate with the play?
Now look at your answers and you have the beginnings of your 'formless hunch'. For example, if you have written **red**, **sharp angles**, **rough** and **violent** as your answers, you begin to get a sense of the mood and atmosphere you want to create.

Grade booster

Even if your examination board does not specifically ask you to plan a director's concept, it is a very good idea to do this for each set text. You will then be able to answer questions that require you to suggest approaches to directing or to rehearsal methods.

Exam practice   15 minutes   answers: page 102

Plan the answer to the following: Outline some of the ways a director of (*your set text*) might realise its theatrical effectiveness for an audience today.

Writing about rehearsal techniques

This section focuses on how you might present your ideas for the rehearsal of a set text and how you might write an analysis of the rehearsal techniques you have used when preparing performances. It enhances your answers if you can relate your techniques to what you have learned about professional rehearsals.

What is rehearsal?

Checkpoint 1

What do you understand by the phrase **page to stage**?

Links

See Max Stafford-Clark, page 55.

Rehearsal is the process that takes a text from the 'page' to the 'stage'. How this happens depends very much on the director and on the nature of the company. **Joint Stock**, established in 1974, was a collective whose members worked collaboratively and made joint decisions. **Max Stafford-Clark** (Out of Joint), a Joint Stock director, refers to directing as '*a pragmatic art, it is both an art and a craft*'. **Théâtre de Complicité** explores a text physically, while the playwright/director **Mike Leigh** begins with extended research and improvisation. **Phyllida Lloyd** describes the rehearsal process as '*a voyage of discovery*'. Some directors, however, plan the overall shape of the piece in more detail, leaving less to the actors.

In planning **rehearsal**, it is important to establish an objective, e.g. *to examine the relationship between two characters at their first meeting*. You should then consider techniques that facilitate this aim, e.g. *to use playing cards to experiment with different status levels*.

Checkpoint 2

Write your own definition of **rehearsal**.

Action point

Find definitions of rehearsal from various directors. Compare these approaches to your own idea of what makes a good rehearsal. Look at *Theatre Directions* by Neelands and Dobson; *Letters to George* by Max Stafford-Clark; *On Directing: A Conversation with Katie Mitchell* by Maria Shevtsova; *Directors' Theatre* by Judith Cook; *Taking Stage: Women Directors on Directing* by Helen Manfull.

Example

A rehearsal of the first meeting of Blanche and Stanley in *A Streetcar Named Desire*

Blanche considers herself to be high status (10), refined, well-bred and well-dressed. Stanley also has high status: he is master of the house, a leader in the community, physically strong and dominates his wife (10). If both characters play 10, there is dramatic conflict as both try to dominate the scene. This might be what works best, but what happens when Blanche plays 7 because she is uncertain in this new territory? It will promote **action** – she might 'back away', Stanley might 'advance menacingly'. The rehearsal, therefore, is a process of investigation.

Writing about the rehearsal process

Many students think that rehearsal is about 'blocking' – moving the actors around the stage and indicating how they should deliver the dialogue: this has been described humorously as '*park and bark*' directing! Few modern directors would use this outdated process: today's rehersal practice is more organic and collaborative. When discussing rehearsal ideas for your set text, you should demonstrate how the process might shape the final performance and discuss your aims and methods.

In your writing, you should include:

→ the aims and objectives for the rehearsal
→ the rehearsal in the context of the production concept
→ exercises related to the text
→ references to any practitioners whose techniques you employ
→ specific references to the text

→ comments on the intended performance

→ a discussion of ideas both rejected and included

→ analysis of the effectiveness in performance.

Example for analysing a process

During our practical study of *Our Country's Good* we explored ways of staging the final scene. The mood of the scene reflected the concept, that theatre has the power to redeem and to civilise. We had read Stafford-Clark's account of the original rehearsals in *Taking Stock*, where he mentions the Hogarth picture of 'strolling actors dressing in a barn'; we based our groupings on this. We wanted to create a busy and excited mood so we improvised the scene as if it was back stage at school. Then we discussed the differences between the modern and the 18th century. A box was placed in the space and we filled it with costumes and props; we then improvised the scene again with the convict/actors showing their excitement at discovering fans, shoes or hats to wear.

When we moved on to the text, the objective was to incorporate the activity and busyness from our improvisation but we were also asked to highlight the moment of contemplation when the convicts echo 'tomorrow'. It was important to communicate that the convicts, who had been literally at each other's throats, were now a community. We ensured that the groupings of two or three were static only for a short time, constantly moving and inter-reacting with others. There was an exquisite moment of stillness when Ketch offered Liz her fan as he said 'I couldn't have hanged you'.

Example

A plan for a rehearsal question on the set text *The Recruiting Officer*

As a director, discuss your approach to the first rehearsal of the opening scene of *The Recruiting Officer*. Suggest how you would create the mood and atmosphere of the scene and consider how it would engage the audience.

The aim of the rehearsal is to create a mood of excitement and to give the opening of the play energy.

→ Improvisation: The actor playing Sergeant Kite must 'sell' goods to the rest of the cast as if he were on a market stall. Encourage persuasive language and vocal energy.

→ Discuss what happened, what was effective vocally and physically and replay the scene using the text and with the other actors on stage as Shrewsbury townspeople.

→ Place the cast in the position of the audience; Kite must now address the audience and engage them as if they were the townspeople.

→ The other actors return to the acting space. Give each member of the crowd a specific role and an indication of how they feel about Kite's recruitment message. Replay the scene, allowing the crowd to interject. The actor playing Kite must play to both the on-stage crowd and to the audience.

Exam practice   20 minutes   answers: page 102–103

Analyse a rehearsal of a key scene from your work for the performance exam.

Examiner's secrets

Beware of writing vaguely about rehearsal. Answers that make comments such as *'I would hot seat the characters'* or *'Before rehearsing this scene I would ask the actors to use Stanislavski's emotion memory'* and leave it at that do not **communicate** the rehearsal process. You must analyse and comment on the exercise, showing how it led to the final shape of the scene.

Grade booster

Note how the candidate references the practitioner (Max Stafford-Clark) whose work has underpinned the rehearsal process. The practitioner's ideas are woven into the writing and related to the process, not reiterated as a separate section.

Grade booster

In good examples of writing about rehearsal:
→ the aims are clear
→ the process is detailed
→ analysis is specific.

Writing about performing a role

Both written examinations and **supporting notes** will require you to discuss how you approach and realise the performance of a role. This section will examine ways to analyse character and the skills that enable the effective portrayal of the role in performance. You should also read the section on character in Exploring the text, page 70.

Exploring character

The **playwright's image** of a character is the starting point for your examination of the role. Look at the **physical characteristics** that the playwright suggests, the **actions** the character takes and the way he or she is spoken about by **other characters**. If the character is set in a different **historical** era, you will need to research the appropriate period. After noting all these elements, you should come to your own conclusions about the way you want to play or to direct this role on stage.

Each character makes a **journey** through the play. You should chart this journey, indicating the various emotions experienced and the changes in attitude or objective. Stanislavski called this the **through line**.

Consider these aspects of your character:

Links

See Stanislavski, page 30.

→ appearance
→ position and function in the play
→ vocal qualities
→ physicality and movement
→ relationships
→ actions
→ key moments in the play that reveal character
→ through line and super-objective.

Checkpoint 1

What are the **through line** and the **super-objective**?

Example

Charting the role of Arkadina in *The Seagull* by Anton Chekhov.

→ **Role:** She is a middle-aged actress who is still beautiful but whose beauty and fame have passed their prime. Her views are selfish, hypocritical and self-serving. Ruthless, cruel, sexual, solipsistic but a survivor.
→ **Research:** Chekhov's theatre. The status of actresses in 19th century Russia. Late 19th century Russian social history.
→ **Chart:** Arkadina's journey through her fading career, her fear of the new generation of theatrical talent (embodied in the role of Nina), her complex relationship with her son and her troubled affair with Trigorin. Examine her *relationship* with Trigorin before the play begins and in Act III when she begs Trigorin not to leave her for Nina.
→ **Interpretation:** Arkadina is neurotic, flawed and emotionally vulnerable. She struggles to reconcile her love of her son and her lover with her uncontrollable vanity.
→ **Rehearsals:** Establish her changing relationship with Trigorin and with Konstantin, explore her emotional journey, examine how her vocal tone differs from exaggerated theatrical posturing, to pleading, to harsh and cold. Explore her physical changes from sweeping dramatic affectation to crumpled rejection.

Action point

Create a chart like the one here for a character in a play that you are studying.

Action point

Read *The Year of the King* by Anthony Sher, which charts his creation of the role of Richard III.

→ **Key scenes:** The second part of Act II where she boasts and 'performs'; we also see her cruelty to other women. Her pleading with Trigorin and the bandaging of Konstantin's head in Act III.

Performance

Your analysis of the role will lead to a performance. This might be a performance for your practical examination or a hypothetical production that you outline in the written exam. You need to consider the skills and techniques an actor uses to portray the role on stage:

→ **Voice:** tone, inflection, pace, volume, pitch, pause, intonation, accent.
→ **Movement:** use of space, gesture, stillness, pace, style.
→ **Communication:** eye contact, pause, direct address, aside.
→ **Conviction:** belief in role, emotional engagement, relationships.

Your portfolio or examination answer should consider the following:

→ the role within the overall concept for the play
→ researching the role and period
→ the relationship of this character with others in the play
→ rehearsal methods
→ key scenes that exemplify your ideas.

Checkpoint 2

What is the difference between **pitch**, **intonation** and **accent**?

Structuring an answer

If you are writing an **examination** answer, look carefully at the question to establish exactly what it is asking. When writing **supporting notes**, make sure that you chart the development of the performance, not simply describe the final product. Your answer should follow the plan above with a focus on the main points of the question.

Grade booster

When writing about playing a role, explore the rehearsal process that **led** to the performance, rather than simply describing the outcome.

Example from an examination answer

Arkadina's flawed relationship with her son, Konstantin, is highlighted poignantly in the scene where she bandages his head. There would be a tenderness in the vocal tone when she kisses his head 'You won't be up to any more of these silly tricks again, will you, when I am gone?' I would hold his head in my heads for moment, removing it quickly on 'Your touch is golden'. Arkadina's reply that she has forgotten Konstantin's memories 'entirely' would be delivered sharply, to indicate her refusal to show tenderness. Her tone would remain sharp and her voice clipped as she rejects Konstantin's reservations about her lover. The bandaging would become more brisk as she is challenged about Trigorin's cowardice; I would stop and look directly into Konstantin's eyes on 'You envy him. There is nothing left for people with no talent and mighty pretensions to do but to criticise those who are really gifted.' stressing 'no talent' with biting acidity. I would flounce angrily with a grand theatrical movement on 'I never acted in a play like that in my life' but change the mood suddenly when Konstantin cries. As I asked him to 'forgive your wicked mother' I would be softly kissing his head and holding him closely to show beneath her cold exterior she has a genuine love for her son, which she cannot fully express.

Take note

The candidate has given very precise detail of intentions and backed this up with exact references to voice, movement and emotion. There are also precise references to the text.

Exam practice   20 minutes   answers: page 103

Write a paragraph detailing your ideas for performance of a character from one of your texts in **one** key scene. Include examples of voice, movement and gesture, emotion and intention.

Communicating design concepts

Here we look at how you should approach questions on design. This section examines the decisions you need to make as a designer and the ways that you can communicate and evaluate your ideas in a written examination or in the notes that support your practical examination. You should also read the section on visual, aural and spatial design in the chapter in Exploring the text, page 76.

Design in relation to concept

You must consider the overall director's concept when creating your design. A consistent approach to all design aspects is important, as a clash of conventions would jar in the performance. For example, if you have decided to set *Hamlet* in the 21st century using clean lines in stark white and grey, it would be incongruous to have an ornate 18th-century red velvet chaise longue for the closet scene.

The design will reinforce the concept, creating the mood and atmosphere. Lez Brotherston's design for the RSC's production of *Much Ado About Nothing* captured the colour, passion and atmosphere of Cuba in 1953. A design by Maria Bjornson for *The Cherry Orchard* included a detailed nursery, a reminder that the main characters have never grown up.

Watch out!

Remember that design includes light, costume, sound and music, as well as set.

What are the key functions of design?

→ To create a truthful environment for the actors within a space.
→ To create mood, enhance atmosphere and reflect theme.
→ To reinforce the audience's belief in the play.
→ To create location, time of day and climate.
→ To establish period, social class and culture.

Action point

Create a plan of the different locations, times of day, climate changes and any important action in a text that you are studying. For each one suggest how this might be realised in the design. For example, in Act IV of *The Crucible*, the sun rises slowly – the lighting changes from the blues, used to establish early morning, to straw-filtered light directed through the barred prison window. The effect is set on a timed cross-fade over 25 minutes.

Designing for your set text or production

Your specification may ask you to write about your design *ideas* for a set text that you have studied, or you may be evaluating the effectiveness of the *actual* design for your practical production.

Checkpoint 1

Give examples of four different types of theatre space.

→ You should decide on the **theatre space** that you think would work most effectively for your design concept. This might be an intimate space or a large auditorium. A production of Shaffer's *The Royal Hunt of the Sun* would need a large stage on which to create the epic events, whereas Sartre's *In Camera* is better suited to a small space.
→ You should then consider what you want your design to say about the text: the **mood**, the **atmosphere** and the **themes** all have to be reflected in the design. For example, the heat of Spain is evoked by the sound of cicadas in *Blood Wedding*.
→ Decide on the **shape** of the production: does the concept require sharp angles, curves, the recreation of a real room or multiple locations? A production of *Equus* demands a symbolic set with a square set on a circle; sound and masks contribute to the symbolic design. *A Doll's House* calls for a realistic setting and costumes of the period. However, you may choose to set the play in a more stylised way.

→ What are the dominant **colours** and **textures** that you envisage? You might decide that *Yerma* (meaning 'barren') will use earth colours (brown and yellow) with a cracked, parched texture. Light and sound create climate.

→ What are the requirements of the text, e.g. locations, times of day, events? David Hare's *The Permanent Way* demands numerous locations whereas a farce, such as Orton's *What the Butler Saw*, needs many doors. In *Death of a Salesman* the flashes backwards and forwards in time are conveyed using light and music.

→ What **style** will the design use?

  → Symbolic: reflects the themes rather than creates a location.
  → Realistic: accurate, believable location.
  → Minimalist: an 'empty space' with only absolutely necessary items.
  → Composite: many locations in one setting, avoiding the need for changes.
  → Expressionistic: themes expressed in a physical way.

Links

For a fuller analysis of the 'empty space', see Peter Brook, page 50.

Checkpoint 2

Suggest plays that might be designed in each of the styles listed.

Example

One student designed a setting for *The Changeling* (1622), by English dramatists Thomas Middleton and William Rowley. The Jacobean play is a dark story of lust, murder and adultery, with a comic sub-plot set in a lunatic asylum. The production was set in the round with the 'madhouse' created using large cages that were suspended above the space throughout the performance. The inmates were thus visible during scenes set in other locations. These cages were lowered for the scenes in the asylum. The design skilfully kept the sub-plot and the theme of madness central to the overall production concept.

Structuring an answer

→ Introduce the text and theme.
→ Suggest the theatre space.
→ Indicate the demands of the play – locations, times, weather, entrances, exits, costumes.
→ Outline and justify your design ideas.
→ Refer to shape, colour, texture and material.
→ Indicate how the design would work for some key scenes.
→ Conclude by commenting on the overall effect you seek to achieve.

Action point

Create a **mood board** on one piece of A2 paper. Cut out images from magazines or internet print-outs that you feel reflect the play you are studying. You can also add scraps of material, lighting gels and textures, e.g. sand. Examination questions will ask you to consider **texture, shape, colour** and **period** in your design answers.

Exam practice   30 minutes   answers: page 103

Plan the answer to the following question: Discuss your ideas for the set and lighting design for *(a play that you are studying or performing)* in order to reflect the central themes.

Approaches to unseen and prepared extracts

In all examination specifications, you will be asked to approach a section of a play text from the viewpoint of a director. AQA and Edexcel set questions on a text that you have prepared, whilst WJEC presents an 'unseen' extract. The examination is usually in the **synoptic** module of the course and therefore tests everything you have learned, including practitioners whose work you have studied, texts you have read or performed and productions you have seen. This section will show you how to prepare for the examination and how to approach the questions.

What you have to do

→ **Create** an individual response to the scene or extract.
→ **Discuss** your ideas for rehearsal, design, performance and intended audience response.
→ **Demonstrate** an understanding of the process of creating a production.
→ **Illustrate** what you have learned about theatre practice during the course.

Preparing for this examination

The work that you have done throughout the course forms the foundation for this part of the examination. You should revise the work you did at A/S: practitioners, productions you have seen, visits and workshops you might have attended as well as the work on set texts. Revise **genre** and **style**; make sure you know about the form and structure of plays as well as the theories **practitioners** employ. Re-examine your notes on **dialogue**, **character** and **visual, aural** and **spatial** elements.

Where you are able to prepare your text, you should create your own unique **concept**. Consider everything you want to communicate to an audience, then plan how you will use resources and actors to realise it in the final production. You must imagine that you will be directing the **whole play** and prepare **rehearsal strategies** for every scene; in the examination, you will be asked to write about one scene or section. Your text should be marked up like a director's production script.

It is more difficult to prepare for an unseen text. Practise for the exam by taking a section of a play that you have not read and planning your ideas for the opening scenes. Read the stage directions and any introductory information in order to get the overall picture of the play. You can, and should, practise the skill of reading play texts.

Reading the extract in the examination

→ Balance the time you spend reading and making notes with the time spent writing.
→ Do not go straight to the questions before reading the text thoroughly.

Action point

One of the best ways to prepare for this examination is to read modern plays. Why not form a play-reading group within your A-level class? Each week everyone reads a new play (ask your teacher or lecturer for advice), then share comments. Keep a log of all the plays you have read. This process will also help you to select texts for practical examinations.

Action point

Try to see as many live theatre productions as you can. Select a variety of styles. Do not restrict yourself to the type of theatre that you know well – the best way to learn about concept is to experience a diversity of styles from the viewpoint of the audience.

Checkpoint 1

What is a **production script**?

Checkpoint 2

What information would you expect to gather from reading the **stage directions**?

- → For unseen extracts, consider the mood, genre and style of the play.
- → Highlight important words, phrases or directions that are significant.
- → Read any extra material provided for an unseen piece, such as the playwright's biography or notes about the original production.
- → Think carefully about the choice of question. This is especially important where you have prepared the text: answer the question asked, not the one you have the perfect answer to!
- → For prepared texts, make sure that you refer closely to your concept for the play.

Structuring the answer

- → List the key points you want to make on rough paper. Link them to moments in the text, then plan a logical order.
- → Write in the first person as director, actor or designer 'I would . . .'.
- → Use the correct theatre terms and spell them accurately.
- → Refer to definite sections of the text, with clear, supported examples. Do not be vague or generalise. For example:

> Vague = *'I want to show that Susan is bitter and angry so I would shout at Peter.'*
> Specific = *'Susan is bitter and angry, accusing Peter of being callous following their father's death. I would use a low voice and speak slowly on "I see you have already cleared the wardrobe" to show that I was trying to contain my emotions. I would build to an angry outburst on "How dare you! What gives you the right to make these decisions?"'*

- → Ensure that the reader can picture your ideas. For design questions, you can use fully labelled diagrams. Vague sketches with no labelling are not useful.
- → If the question asks you to 'plan a rehearsal', make sure that you write about directors working with actors. Do not describe the **outcome**.
- → Your ideas should be imaginative but practical in the **theatre**. Remember this is not film or television.
- → Refer to your experience and knowledge of theatre practice.

Action point

Make a list of important theatre terms that you might use in an answer. Learn how to spell them accurately, e.g. cyclorama.

Grade booster

It is not enough for you simply to **describe** the rehearsal techniques without **connecting** their purpose to the question and the extract.

Grade booster

Write about the extract in **theatrical** terms. This is the **synoptic** element of the exam, so you should demonstrate your knowledge of how to bring a text from 'page to stage'.

Exam practice   1 hour 30 minutes   answers: page 104

Read the extract from *Our Country's Good* on pages 98–100. As a director, explain how you would rehearse this scene to heighten the impact of the final moments.

Specimen text

Our Country's Good by Timberlake Wertenbaker is a set text for this unit in the AQA specification. First produced at The Royal Court in 1988, directed by Max Stafford-Clark, the play begins on a convict ship bound for Australia in 1787; the prisoners are rough, hardened and held in contempt by many of the officers. In the Australian prison camp, a young lieutenant, Ralph Clark, directs a play with the convicts. The play demonstrates the power of theatre to unify, redeem and restore humanity to the degraded and embittered criminals.

Characters

Officers
Lieutenant Ralph Clark (the director)
Major Robbie Ross
Captain Campbell

Convicts
Mary Brenham
Robert Sideway
Dabby Bryant
Liz Morden
Wisehammer
Caesar

SCENE FIVE: The Second Rehearsal

Ralph Clark, Mary Brenham and Robert Sideway are waiting. Major Ross and Captain Campbell bring the three Prisoners Caesar, Wisehammer and Liz Morden. They are still in chains. Ross shoves them forward.

Ross	Here is some of your caterwauling cast, Lieutenant.
Campbell	The Governor, chhht, said, release, tssst. Prisoners.
Ross	Unchain Wisehammer and the savage, Captain Campbell. *(Points to Liz.)* She stays in chains. She's being tried tomorrow, we don't want her sloping off.
Ralph	I can't rehearse with one of my players in chains, Major.
Campbell	Eeh. Difficult. Mmmm.
Ross	We'll tell the Governor you didn't need her and take her back to prison.
Ralph	No. We shall manage. Sideway, go over the scene you rehearsed in prison with Melinda, please.
Caesar	I'm in that scene too, Lieutenant.
Ralph	No you're not.
Liz and	
Sideway	Yes he is, Lieutenant.
Sideway	He's my servant.

Ralph nods and Liz, Sideway and Caesar move to the side and stand together, ready to rehearse, but waiting.

Ralph	The rest of us will go from Silvia's entrance as Wilful. Where's Arscott
Ross	We haven't finished with Arscott yet, Lieutenant.
Campbell	Punishment, eeeh, for escape. Fainted. Fifty-three lashes left. Heeeh.
Ross	*(pointing to Caesar)* Caesar's next. After Morden's trial. Caesar cringes.

Ralph	Brenham, are you ready? Wisehammer? I'll play Captain Plume.
Ross	The wee Lieutenant wants to be in the play too. He wants to be promoted to convict. We'll have you in the chain gang soon, Mr. Clark, haha.

(A pause. Ross and Campbell stand, watching. The Convicts are frozen.)

Ralph	Major, we will rehearse now.

Pause. No one moves.

We wish to rehearse.

Ross	No one's stopping you, Lieutenant.

Silence.

Ralph	Major, rehearsals need to take place in the utmost cub — privacy, secrecy you might say. The actors are not yet ready to be seen by the public.
Ross	Not ready to be seen? What were you doing on the beach? You were with him, he told me, you were with Handy Baker.
Ralph	Major, there is a modesty attached to the process of creation which must be respected.
Ross	Modesty? Modesty! Sideway, come here.
Ralph	Major. Sideway — stay —
Ross	Lieutenant. I would not try to countermand the orders of a superior officer,
Campbell	Obedience. Ehh, first ehh, rule.
Ross	Sideway.

Sideway comes up to Ross.

Take your shirt oft'.

Sideway obeys. Ross turns him and shows his scarred back to the company.

One hundred lashes on the Sirius for answering an officer.
Remember, Sideway? Three hundred lashes for trying to strike,
the same officer.
I have seen the white of this animal's bones, his wretched blood
and reeky Convict urine have spilled on my boots and he's
feeling modest? Are you feeling modest, Sideway?

He shoves Sideway aside.

Modesty.
Bryant. Here.

Dabby comes forward.

On all fours.

Dabby goes down on all fours.

Now wag your tail and bark, and I'll throw you a biscuit. What?
You've forgotten? Isn't that how you begged for your food on
the ship? Wag your tail, Bryant, bark! We'll wait.
Brenham.

Mary comes forward.

Where's your tattoo, Brenham? Show us. I can't see it. Show us.

Mary tries to obey, lifting her skirt a little.

If you can't manage, I'll help you. (*Mary lifts her skirt a little higher.*) I can't see it.

But Sideway turns to Liz and starts acting, boldly, across the room, across everyone.)

Sideway   'What pleasures I may receive abroad are indeed uncertain; but this I am sure of, I shall meet with less cruelty among the most barbarous nations than I have found at home.'

Liz   'Come, Sir, you and I have been jangling a great while; I fancy if we made up our accounts, we should the sooner come to an agreement.'

Sideway   'Sure, Madam, you won't dispute your being in my debt — my fears, sighs, vows, promises, assiduities, anxieties, jealousies, have run on for a whole year, without any payment.'

Campbell   Mmhem, good, that. Sighs, vows, promises, hehem, mmm. Anxieties.

Ross   Captain Campbell, start Arscott's punishment.

Campbell goes.

Liz   'A year! Oh Mr Worthy, what you owe to me is not to be paid under a seven years' servitude. How did you use me the year before —'

The shouts of Arscott are heard.

'How did you use me the year before —'

She loses her lines. Sideway tries to prompt her.

Sideway   'When taking advantage —'

Liz   'When taking the advantage of my innocence and necessity —'

But she stops and drops down, defeated.

Silence, except for the beating and Arscott's cries.

Answers
Writing about text

Contextualising the play

Checkpoints

1 *Look Back in Anger* caused a revolution in British theatre at the Royal Court Theatre in May 1956. The play attacked the middle classes, and the setting, a run-down flat, was radically different from the traditional staging expected by theatre audiences. It gave rise to a whole genre of new playwrights known as 'angry young men'.

2 **Arthur Miller**, who died in 2005, was the most distinguished modern American playwright. His plays have been staged all over the world. Miller attacked **McCarthy** because the anti-communist propaganda in America after the war led to the House of Un-American Activities, which accused many artists and actors. Senator McCarthy led this 'witch-hunt'.

Exam practice

Shadow of a Gunman Sean O'Casey

Political biography

1880 Born in Dublin. Family was poor, they lived among Catholics – unusual as most Protestants were well off or members of the landed gentry. Father died age 49 when Sean was 6 years old.

1902–
1911 Joined the Gaelic League. Learnt the Irish language and changed his name to Sean O'Cathasaigh. Later he simplified it to Sean O'Casey.

1911 Met Jim Larkin, the great Irish Labour leader and joined the Irish Transport and General Workers Union and in 1913 joined with Jim and his fellow workers in the Dublin General Strike and LockOut.

1914 Became secretary of The Irish Citizen Army (ICA), and drew up its constitution. O'Casey opposed too close ties with the Irish Volunteers because of their anti-union elements. He resigned soon afterwards over a disagreement.

1916 The Irish Volunteers and the ICA rose in armed rebellion against the British Authorities. The Easter Rising became the background to his play *The Plough and the Stars*.

1920 Ireland divided into the North and South. The Republic of Ireland formed. Life in Dublin was unsettled with the Black and Tans recruited to help the Irish constabulary. This is the background for *The Shadow of a Gunman*.

1922–
1923 Irish Civil war. Background for *Juno and the Paycock*.

1923–
1926 First plays written and produced by the Abbey Theatre, Dublin – *Shadow of a Gunman*, *Juno and the Paycock* and *The Plough and the Stars*. *The Plough and the Stars* provoked a riot.

The play

• The play has the characteristics of a fairly light comedy though with deep political undertones.

• Set at the height of the independence struggle, IRA ruled hearts and minds, hatred for the British Auxiliaries, the Black and Tans.

• The most innocent are drawn into conflict when political feelings are at their highest and there is an occupying army on the streets.

• Explores the romanticising of violence and false heroics.

The director's concept

Checkpoints

1 The **director's concept** refers to the overall view that the director has of the play. The concept may change during rehearsal but the initial ideas give rise to the design, staging and location of the play and underpin the meaning the director wants to convey.

2 **Theatre in the round** is a form of staging where the audience surrounds the action on all sides. Examples of theatre in the round spaces include The Crucible in Sheffield and the Stephen Joseph Theatre in Scarborough.

Exam practice

Production notes for *Antigone* by Sophocles

Themes: state versus individual, conscience versus law, divine law versus human law.

Plot: war has destroyed Antigone's world. Her brothers lie dead on the battlefield. Creon forbids Polynices' burial. She is alone in a world of tyranny.

Design: a war-torn city in a modern world, perhaps Iraq. Skyscrapers redolent of wealth projected onto the cyclorama. The stage floor dusty – hot earth, crumbled cement. Grey, desolate, empty. Costume a mixture of modern, Muslim and military. Lighting evokes heat; sound creates the ongoing war. The plight of Antigone mirrors the daily horrors of women who strive to live according to their religious beliefs in worlds destroyed by tyrants and by their supposed saviours.

Writing about rehearsal techniques

Checkpoints

1 **Page to stage** refers to the whole production process – from the first reading by the director to the first night in front of an audience. During this period the play comes alive and is no longer simply the words in the script.

2 **Rehearsals** are the exploration of the text by actors under the guidance of a director. Together they pursue a mutual objective.

Exam practice

Rehearsal approach to Act III of *The Crucible*: Abigail's 'sighting' of the bird

The atmosphere of threat, panic and chaos creates the dramatic climax to this scene. I would ask each actor to write questions that they want to ask about their characters. Katie Mitchell uses this system in researching roles with the cast. The first rehearsal of this scene would involve physical work where the girls reacted to an imaginary bird. The second exercise would be in pairs where one actor repeated the movements and copied the speech patterns of their partner. It is important to create an instant impact when Abigail screams up to the 'bird', so I would work on a 'primal scream' with the whole company – this exercise is Artaudian: Artaud complained that Europeans had forgotten how to release emotions.

Exploration of the text would then focus on the levels of fear felt by the girls. I would issue playing cards, the level on the card indicating how afraid each girl is of Abigail – Max Stafford-Clark created this rehearsal technique. If Mary Warren is 10 (terrified) and Mercy Lewis is 3 (slightly worried), the dynamic of the scene is affected. Perhaps Abigail has to shoot a look at Mercy to ensure that she joins in. Finally, I would explore the choral climax to the scene by building the volume, pitch and tone of the voices to a crescendo when Mary runs screaming to Abigail. I would aim to have a sudden change of mood, to very quiet and still as Abigail draws Mary towards her and the girls form a tight circle around their leader. In the silence, Abigail looks triumphantly at Danforth.

Writing about performing a role

Checkpoints

1 The **through line** is the actor's journey through the play as he works to achieve his/her overall aim. This is his/her individual **super-objective**, e.g. Hamlet's super-objective is to avenge the murder of his father, it is what propels him through the action of the play.
2 **Pitch:** a high or low level in the voice, similar to a musical note.
   Intonation: the rise and fall of the voice that affects the meaning of what is said.
   Accent: pronunciation and the way people in a particular area or group speak.

Exam practice

Sideway from *Our Country's Good*. Act 1, Scene 11 – The first rehearsal

Sideway is a sympathetic character in this scene, he is also a source of humour. In this section, Sideway's objective is to impress Ralph with his acting ability. Sideway's physicality is the key to the comedy; he exaggerates his movement and gesture when he is emulating Garrick, for example when he adds literal gestures to every line *'Arms across, Worthy'* and *'safe and sound returned'*. In playing this scene, I would show a clear distinction between Sideway's own movements and his theatrical flourishes. When accusing the other convicts of stealing the handkerchief I would move swiftly, making eye contact with the others, especially an accusing stare at Liz Morden. When he is *'establishing [his] melancholy'* or greeting Worthy, the gestures would be deliberate, measured and flamboyant.

Researching Garrick's performance style would give an insight into Sideway's ideas. Sideway's natural voice will have a cockney accent and reflect his innate confidence and bluster; he speaks with a fast pace and lilting inflection, showing that he is cheerful. As Sideway the actor, I would play the section where he is sobbing to build his melancholy with a lower tone of voice, showing that he is copying Garrick. The key to

Sideway's comedy will be the timing, ensuring appropriate pauses before amusing lines.

Communicating design concepts

Checkpoints

1 Thrust stage, theatre in the round, promenade theatre, street theatre, end-on staging, traverse staging or proscenium arch theatre.
2 Symbolic: Strindberg *A Dream Play*
   Realistic: Ibsen *A Doll's House*
   Minimalist: Kane *4.48 Psychosis*
   Composite: Miller *Death of a Salesman*
   Expressionistic: Wedekind *Spring Awakening*

Exam practice

A Dream Play is a symbolic play with surreal qualities. In his preface, Strindberg wrote that he wanted *'to imitate the disjointed yet seemingly logical shape of a dream'*. I have considered the nature of dreams: in dreams, there are often doors and most people dream in black and white. In Strindberg's text a locked door is a recurrent image. I want to create a sense of the disorientation of the dream world but the play requires almost 40 scenes. The set will be an uncluttered, composite room, allowing the focus to be on the stage action and enabling multiple locations as scenes are set in many different places. The walls of the set will be on trucks so they can move backwards and forwards and the stage space can become a small, claustrophobic domestic setting or a large public space. This strange movement of the walls suggests the illusory world of a dream.

I will have a simple, claustrophobic setting with a wooden floor and wood-panelled walls. At the back of the stage, there will be double doors, like the oversized doors in dreams. The grey wooden panels hint at being enclosed in a box, yet their style reminds the audience of a wood-panelled drawing room. The colour will be from the black and white spectrum, with many shades of grey to evoke the atmosphere of a dream. The walls will be without pictures or other adornments. Lighting will create the atmosphere and will be rigged so that light appears to come from the source – overhead lights, moonlight or table lamps. Lighting will also create dramatic changes of mood by flickering, dazzling or blacking out suddenly. Subtle changes of light will create the dream-like quality and I will use an effects projector to produce drifting grey clouds on the cyclorama.

My design ideas for *A Dream Play* aim to capture the surreal style while ensuring that the stage space works for the action of the play. The doors will facilitate the entrances and exits of actors as well as enabling symbolic items of furniture to move easily on and off the stage.

Checkpoints

1 The **production script** is the director's copy in which he/she has detailed every action, inference, sound effect, music cue and lighting effect. The director might also note rehearsal ideas or research questions in this script. It is the complete working document for the production.

2 **Stage directions** are the playwright's method of communicating information about the characters' actions, the setting and the music or lighting effects. You gain insight into the way the playwright saw the production, as stage directions are usually visual. You do not have to obey them all!

Exam practice

(The first section of an exam answer)

My aim for the performance of this scene is to create dramatic tension that builds to its terrible climax, Arscott's brutal punishment. This scene encapsulates the meaning of the play: theatre has the power to redeem. The convicts have made a journey from disparate and confrontational prisoners, who have no self worth to a united and dignified company standing against the cruelty meted out to them by Major Ross.

I would begin the rehearsal of this scene by actioning the text: this technique is a used by the original director, Max Stafford-Clark, to engage the actors in the intentions of their dialogue. Actions reveal the emotional intention of the lines and determine movement, gesture and intonation. For example the action on Ross's line '*We'll tell the Governor you didn't need her and take her back to prison*' is 'confronts (Ralph)'; the actor playing Ross might move to Ralph and speak in a sarcastic, low tone. When Ralph offers to read Arscott's part Ross 'belittles' him with '*The wee Lieutenant wants to be in the play too. He wants to be promoted to convict*'. Later in the scene, when Ross has made Dabby kneel on the floor his action on the line '*Now wag your tail and bark, and I'll throw you a biscuit*' is 'debases'; Ross wants to reduce the convicts to the level of animals.

Dramatic tension is heightened in this scene by the use of pauses and silence and through the reactions of the convicts and Ralph Clark to Ross and Campbell's callousness. During rehearsals, I would explore the pauses by examining with the actors the emotional truth within them. One exercise is to ask each actor to speak aloud their internal thoughts during the pauses. When Ralph tells Ross that '. . . *we wish to rehearse now.*' The convicts are '*frozen*'. The tension in the air must be palpable. The actor playing Caesar, who is very afraid, might be thinking '*If Ross is annoyed by this I might be the scapegoat*' whereas Sideway, who is altogether more confident and optimistic might think '*You tell him Lieutenant, don't let him stop our rehearsal*'. These thoughts will then influence the physicality of the convicts and their 'frozen' picture will have an emotional energy. I would explore the emotional reactions to the humiliation of Sideway, Dabby and Mary in a similar way; my aim would be to build the physical responses through emotional engagement. When Ross intimidates Mary, Wisehammer might feel that he wants to protect her and move towards Ross but Sideway, fearful for Wisehammer's safety, pulls him back. It is vital to the dramatic impact of this scene that the convict's reactions are truthful.

The use of pause is also important in creating the power of the officers and the apprehension of the convicts. The officers' dialogue often begins with a key impact word; '*Punishment*' or '*Modesty*'. I would want the actors to allow these words to 'drop' into the tense atmosphere with a sense of their weight and importance. The scene turns on the word 'modesty' and it is after this point that Ross seeks to degrade and to humiliate the convicts thus asserting his status over Ralph.

The convict actors create the dramatic impact at the end of the scene through the change in mood. Exercise elsewhere in the rehearsal period will explore the convict's level of competency as actors. In this scene, the impact is achieved through the juxtaposition of brutality, the cries and beating of Arcott, and the proud and controlled performance of Sideway and Liz. Rehearsals would explore the sudden vocal and physical changes: Liz is in chains so one rehearsal might involve playing the scene with her hands tied together, attempting to use gesture whilst ensuring that her head was held high and her body exuded pride. Another exercise would involve the actors playing Liz and Sideway playing the dialogue over a number of other members of the cast crying out in agony as if being beaten. The actors must retain their control and dignity whilst registering their anguish.

Revision checklist
Writing about text

By the end of this chapter you should be able to:

1	Understand how contemporary issues influence playwrights.	Confident	Not confident **Revise** page 86
2	Know how to recognise the influence of the playwright's life history on the text and recognise the political concerns of the playwright.	Confident	Not confident **Revise** page 86
3	Identify and research real historical events in a play.	Confident	Not confident **Revise** page 86
4	Understand the cultural context of a play.	Confident	Not confident **Revise** page 87
5	Assess the historical and social background in a play.	Confident	Not confident **Revise** page 87
6	Connect the themes and issues to the political and social climate and to the wider social agenda.	Confident	Not confident **Revise** page 87
7	Understand the theory of 'director's concept'.	Confident	Not confident **Revise** page 88
8	Appreciate how to create your own concept for a set text.	Confident	Not confident **Revise** pages 88–89
9	Understand how the concept decisions will affect the choice of space and cast.	Confident	Not confident **Revise** page 89
10	Discuss different approaches to rehearsal.	Confident	Not confident **Revise** page 89
11	Write clearly about your own rehearsal process.	Confident	Not confident **Revise** pages 90–91
12	Understand how to create a design concept for a play.	Confident	Not confident **Revise** page 91
13	Write clearly about the process of creating a role.	Confident	Not confident **Revise** page 92
14	Structure an answer about your creation of a role or your ideas for a performance.	Confident	Not confident **Revise** page 93
15	Appreciate the function of the design elements.	Confident	Not confident **Revise** page 94
16	Know how to use shape, colour and texture in your own designs.	Confident	Not confident **Revise** pages 94–95
17	Structure an answer on design.	Confident	Not confident **Revise** page 95
18	Structure an answer on an unseen or prepared text.	Confident	Not confident **Revise** pages 96–97

Devised theatre

Your Drama and Theatre Studies specification will require you to devise and evaluate original theatre. This can be a demanding task and this chapter will examine approaches to the process taken by professional companies and then go on to suggest how you could structure your own devising practice. Teachers/lecturers usually assess the devising process and this contributes to the final unit mark. All specifications require a written evaluation of the process, charting and analysing your work from the initial stimulus to the final performance. The final part of this chapter will consider written evaluations and records.

Exam themes

- Responding creatively to a stimulus or theme
- Working as a group on a devised theatre project
- Performing original theatre to an audience
- Documenting the process of the devised work
- Written analysis and evaluation

Topic checklist

	Edexcel		AQA		WJEC	
	AS	A2	AS	A2	AS	A2
Creating theatre: a professional perspective		●		●	○	●
Stimulus and themes		●		●	○	●
The audience: communication and response		●		●	○	●
Managing group work		●		●	○	●
Planning and shaping		●		●	○	●
Building to performance		●		●	○	●
Recording and evaluating		●		●	○	●

Creating theatre: a professional perspective

This section outlines the work of professional theatre groups whose practice uses devising techniques. Some companies begin with improvisation and exploration, which leads to a final text; other groups continue to experiment during performance.

The art of devising

Links

See page 15.

Checkpoint 1

Who was **Joan Littlewood**?

Commedia dell'arte combines many of the important features of modern devised theatre and the roots of improvised performance can be traced to this genre. Stock characters, scenarios and improvisation are found in the work of companies like **Théâtre de Complicité** and **DV8**.

Elsewhere in this guide, we have referenced the work of practitioners such as **Brecht**, **Littlewood** and **Stafford-Clark**, whose creative process does not begun with a scripted text. Observers frequently mention the **ensemble** nature of devising; it is essential to recognise the importance of group dynamics when devising work. Professional approaches communicate significant features of the process and before embarking on your own devising programme, you should try to see or read about professional devised work.

Joint Stock

Founded in 1974 by Max Stafford-Clark, William Gaskill and David Hare, this collective of actors, writers and directors spent ten weeks creating a play. The aim was to create a new form of **ensemble** theatre. The result continues to influence working methods today. For six weeks they undertook physical work, improvisation and games in addition to researching themes and issues. There were lectures from experts, visits to key venues for research purposes and examinations of background material.

For *Cloud Nine* (Caryl Churchill) the material came from the sexual history of the actors. The collective was an ensemble who shared all decisions and whose trust enabled them to produce plays with depth and passion. Following the workshop phase, there was a gap while the playwright wrote the text; a four-week rehearsal period then followed. David Hare's *Fanshen* is a key example of the process – the play, based on William Hinton's book, deals with the effects of the Communist Revolution on rural China.

Joint Stock enshrined the policy of equality into every aspect of their collective. The work of this company had a lasting influence on the many experimental companies which followed in the 1970s and 1980s.

Action point

Read Caryl Churchill's *Cloud Nine* or David Hare's *Fanshen* as examples of Joint Stock's work.

Checkpoint 2

What do you understand by **ensemble**? Why do you think it is so important to devising?

How you might use this method

You could use similar methods by interviewing people whose work or experiences could contribute to your theme. Research and reading were key elements of Joint Stock's approach and this is very important to your devising process.

Improbable Theatre

This company has an international reputation for inventive, even shocking, work. The actors rarely have a defined script prior to performance and improvise in front of the audience. Their 2006 production of *Theatre of Blood* for the National Theatre was one of the few productions where a script existed, but they were encouraged to experiment with it, change it and be inventive throughout the rehearsal process. Frightening and funny, this play was in the horror tradition of Grand Guignol and Victorian melodrama.

Phelim McDermott, director of Improbable Theatre, is committed to working spontaneously with actors. His method developed from **Instant Acting**; it removes 'line learning' from the process. In *Shockhead Peter*, the actors were not allowed to learn their lines! In *Animo*, the company created an hour of improvised theatre from a collection of everyday objects, Words like 'strange' and 'ingenious' are frequently used to describe Improbable's work.

Action point

Read some very useful reports on Improbable's creative process on their website, www.improbable.co.uk.

How you might use this method

You might explore a stimulus or text in this innovative way, using spontaneous improvisation and physical theatre before settling on a final script.

Kneehigh Theatre

From its home in Cornwall, Kneehigh Theatre has built a reputation for creating popular theatre for audiences throughout the UK and beyond. Kneehigh creates theatre for families in locations within their communities. The company is celebrated as one of Britain's most exciting touring theatre companies.

Kneehigh uses a wide range of art forms and media as a 'tool kit' to make new and accessible forms of theatre. A spontaneous sense of risk and adventure produces extraordinary dramatic results. Themes are universal and local, epic and domestic. There is no formula to the way Kneehigh makes theatre; however, it always starts with the **story**. The process develops through the creation of **character**. The play builds from a shared creative imagination and the process keeps returning to the story. It is told and retold and thoughts are scribbled on huge pieces of paper. Characters are created by looking to serve and to subvert the story. Music and sound create the world of the play and can spark an idea as much as improvisation or the creation of a character. One of the most used phrases at Kneehigh is 'hold your nerve' – devising can be a terrifying process.

How you might use this method

If your stimulus is a story, examine the narrative using a similar method. Try storyboarding your narrative line or writing everyone's ideas on huge pieces of paper to use during the devising period.

Exam practice   15 minutes

Consider your own devised work. Which company or companies do you think reflect your practice?

Stimulus and themes

The examination specification or your teacher may determine your topic or starting point, or you may have an open option. The correct selection of the stimulus or theme can ensure that the process of creating your own theatre is productive. This section will look at effective ways of making that decision and will examine factors that can influence the choice. The case study details how a theme can be used as a springboard for the devising process.

Factors affecting choice

If you are not given a topic, you will need to choose one with your group. There are various things to consider – the gender balance in the group, the skills and interests of the individuals, plays, practitioners and topics covered during your course, work that you have seen professionally, the space and the audience. Any one of these may spark a debate or suggest a starting point. Remember that once the topic has been agreed you will all be working on it for a significant period. It is very important to get it right!

Avoid:

→ allowing the dominant character in your group to pressurise the decision
→ making a choice based on a vague connection with a practitioner
→ choosing a theme that is clichéd or over-exposed
→ trying to recreate a version of a play that you know well
→ attempting something that is technically too demanding for your venue
→ selecting a genre or style of which your group has little experience.

Features of a well-chosen stimulus

→ The whole group is inspired by the topic.
→ There is a wide skill base in the group that will ensure that the topic is treated effectively.
→ Research material is easily accessible.
→ The theatre space or studio can accommodate the treatment of the topic.
→ All students have an opportunity to demonstrate their abilities through the theme.
→ The theme is unlikely to be seen in other examinations and the treatment of it is original.
→ The theme inspires creativity and experimentation.

Successful stimuli

→ Historical event: the Suffragettes
→ Art: Picasso's *La Guernica*
→ Current event: the 7/7 bombings
→ Audience given: theatre in education
→ Site and audience given: care home for the elderly
→ Poem: Peter Porter's 'Your Attention Please'

- → Theme: seven deadly sins
- → Issue: human cloning
- → Adaptation of a novel: Aldous Huxley's *Brave New World*
- → Song: Paul Simon's 'A Most Peculiar Man'
- → A visit: St Fagans Museum, Wales
- → Newspaper article: 'What is Celebrity?'

Case study: the King's Cross fire

The group had seen Out of Joint's production of David Hare's *The Permanent Way*, a verbatim piece about recent rail crashes. Their chosen stimulus was the King's Cross fire of 1987, in which 31 people died. A newspaper report in 2004 told of the body of Alexander Fallon, unidentified since the tragedy and known only by his tag number, 115. His daughters approached police to suggest the final victim might be their father, who, aged 72, was living rough on the streets of London at the time of the fire. This modern link provided the structure for this work.

The group undertook specific research using archives and the internet. Although they were not able to interview the real people, using the verbatim technique they each found out about one person involved in the story. Following the creation of individual character studies, students interviewed each 'actor' in role. From this starting point, the characters for the devised piece were created. Research also revealed key facts, times and sequences of events. The structure of the piece began to take shape.

The opening scene, based on the first scene in *The Permanent Way*, involved travellers reading newspapers and shouting headlines from 1987 and 2004 reports.

The final piece used a montage technique to juxtapose events from the 1987 fire with the Fallon family's quest to find their father.

Action point

Make a list of other topics in each of the genres suggested here.

Take note

The process undertaken for this piece included:
- → research
- → theatre style that mirrored the stimulus production
- → detailed character development
- → a clear production style.

Grade booster

Devised drama should be presented with complete production values. The best work has a clear narrative or theme and is completely ready for performance.

Exam practice   15 minutes

Choose one of the suggested topics and brainstorm your initial ideas for creative interpretation.

The audience: communication and response

Your devised piece will be assessed by your teacher or by a visiting examiner or moderator. Effective communication with the target audience will be considered and supporting notes and records will require an evaluation of your planning in relation to audience. This section will examine the choice of audience and suggest ways that you can structure the piece for them.

Target audience

The style of your devised piece may determine your audience, for example theatre in education or a play for pre-school children. Normally, however, the audience consists of friends and family of the participants. Nevertheless, you should consider the material in relation to the target audience. The following questions are a guide to your planning:

→ Is the age or gender of your audience specific?
→ What are the audience's expectations?
→ Have they any prior knowledge of your topic?
→ What type of theatre do your audience normally see?
→ What are their primary concerns?
→ Will your audience be offended by the topic?
→ Do you want to shock, instruct, amuse or enlighten your audience?
→ Will the venue have an effect on the reception of your piece?

Links

For an analysis of Artaud's theories, see page 44.

Answers to the above questions relating to an AS level play on the Holocaust using Artaud's techniques for a mixed audience of peers and family include:

→ Mixed age and gender.
→ Students might anticipate a challenging piece but parents will not know what to expect.
→ Some of the students have heard of Artaud but parents may not have any experience of his work.
→ Most parents are more familiar with conventional plays and musical theatre; students are more used to going to the theatre but few have experienced Artaud.
→ Parents are concerned about jobs, money, politics and the environment; students with relationships, exams and entertainment.
→ Parents could be shocked by violence or strong language; students are less likely to be upset by it.
→ We want to use 'total theatre' to explore the Holocaust; our aim is to shock and to enlighten.
→ Our performance will take place in a small studio; we will be able to create a claustrophobic effect.

Action point

Make a list of answers for *your* proposed audience. Are there any additional questions you might ask yourself?

The final play made the audience confront some harsh realities. Light, sound and physical theatre played an important role in the production. The material was 'shocking' but not overtly violent or sexual and there was no offensive language.

Planning for an audience response

You should consider your aims for the devised piece. If your play wants to **shock** the audience or to **awaken** their interest in a key issue, you will need to structure the drama to create this response. Remember that swearing and shouting are not in themselves shocking – you must think about the dramatic impact. Many practitioners, such as **Brecht** and **Artaud**, sought to provoke their audience. This comment from a candidate's supporting written evidence encapsulates the aims for the audience response:

> *'In addition to our aim to educate, we wanted to entertain and to engage our audience . . . we did not allow the audience to be passive, but forced them to form their own opinions and, perhaps, question the actions and decisions made by the characters.'*

Communicating your ideas to the audience

One of the key problems examiners encounter when watching devised work is that the **participants** are very clear about the meaning but the **audience** is not. This occurs for a number of reasons:

→ The devising group is not precise in defining the aims at the start of the process.
→ The structure of the play is confusing.
→ Characters are not introduced specifically.
→ Multiple roles are not differentiated clearly.

It is usually apparent that these groups have worked closely with the piece for so long that *they* are in tune with the nuances of text and character but there is incomplete communication with the audience.

The structure of the play should ensure that there is effective communication with the target audience. This might involve simple devices such as introducing and repeating a character's name or more complex staging or technical techniques, such as back projection, that establish location.

The style and structure must also communicate to the audience. **Montage** is a popular and effective construction, yet it must be arranged so that each episode is unambiguous and the audience can follow the narrative. Try to link the choice of dramatic technique to the desired outcome. During the process, you should ask *'What do we want to say? What reaction do we want to evoke?'* rather than *'Why don't we use montage/sound collage/narration, etc. because we haven't used it yet'*!

Action point

Read the sections on Key Practitioners, pages 30–63, then reflect on how your group wishes the audience to react.

Checkpoint 1

How did **Brecht** and **Artaud** aim to affect their audiences?

Checkpoint 2

List the ways in which multiple roles can be clearly and simply defined in a devised piece.

Example

This section from a candidate's supporting notes highlights the point: *'Initially the office setting proved difficult. <u>We</u> knew that we were in an office; however, we felt that this might not be clear to the audience. We decided that each character would perform a mime that they would replicate to open every office scene. These mimes were typical tasks – photocopying, phone answering or working on a keyboard. Although we had no scenery, the six chairs were placed in exactly the same configuration for the office.'*

Exam practice   30 minutes   answers: page 122

How did your group plan for a range of responses from the audience?

Managing group work

The importance of effective group work cannot be over-estimated. The dynamic of the group can affect both the success of the piece and the experience of the participants. This section will consider approaches to group work, discuss potential pitfalls and suggest positive strategies that can be employed to avoid conflict.

Successful group dynamics

If your class is large enough for there to be more than one group, you should consider carefully how it is divided. Working with your friends might not be the most successful approach. Taking the **Belbin Test**, a management strategy for analysing team roles, can reveal characteristics that individuals are not aware they possess. The key to Belbin's assessment is that each team needs a range of skills. Belbin categorises personality traits, pointing out both the positive and the negative aspects of each 'type'. The test itself can be found online and resembles a magazine quiz, with points allocated to each answer; the highest totals indicate the **two** dominant personality features.

Belbin's roles	Positive and negative traits
Shaper	+ task leader, drive, passion
	– irritable, over-sensitive, dominant
Coordinator	+ listener, focused, disciplined
	– uncreative, stubborn, restrictive
Plant	+ original, questioning, intelligent
	– resents criticism, preoccupied
Implementer	+ reliable, efficient, practical
	– lacks communication, unimaginative
Resource investigator	+ extrovert, enthusiast, opportunist
	– over-optimistic, loses interest easily
Monitor evaluator	+ strategist, discerning, judges well
	– not inspirational, lacks drive
Team worker	+ mild, perceptive, diplomatic
	– indecisive, hesitant, wants to please
Completer finisher	+ conscientious, delivers on time, painstaking
	– anxious, worrier, reluctant to delegate

Belbin's premise was that every team needs the different skills outlined but should be aware of the strengths and the weaknesses of its members. If you relate the roles above to your drama group, you will probably find a number of **shapers** and **resource investigators**. Further examination of the strengths and weaknesses will show you that too many of this personality type in one group can lead to argument.

Example

We found [The Belbin Test] very useful in understanding how each of us, individually, worked in a group. It was important to determine each individual's strengths and weaknesses so that we were able to work on the weaker points and use the strengths effectively in our production. The support of the group and the shared understanding of the dynamic enabled us to avoid arguments.

Defining responsibilities

It is a very good idea to be clear from the outset what each person's responsibility will be. Try to list all the possible roles at the start of the process – you will inevitably discover forgotten tasks as you progress, but an equitable division of responsibility early on prevents resentment. Where possible, link the tasks to skills. If some members of your group study Art and Design, for example, it makes sense for them to undertake the design aspects of the piece. Discuss the jobs that no one wants to do and distribute those fairly.

Checkpoint 1

List the roles that you consider important to an early discussion of responsibilities.

Formal agreements and contracts

Drama groups, by their very nature, have a strong identity and feel a close bond. Devising is challenging and can test even the healthiest of relationships. Some groups find that a clear 'contract' or agreed procedure can avert conflict.

Contracts have included the following:

→ Each discussion will be chaired by a different member of the group.
→ We agree to be punctual to every lesson and not miss a session unless ill.
→ In the event of unavoidable absence we will phone/text (name).
→ No suggestion will be rejected without discussion and consideration.
→ Every voice will be heard.
→ Ownership of ideas is held by the group, not the individual.
→ If we cannot make a decision, the majority vote will decide.
→ We will aim to allocate roles equally.
→ Each session will begin with warm-up and trust exercises.
→ No dispute will carry over to the next day.
→ Allocated responsibilities will be completed by the agreed deadline.

Action point

Write a contract for your own devising group. What do you think are the essential points that should be included?

Managing discussion

Links

See page 150.

Elsewhere in this guide we discuss Edward de Bono's **Six Thinking Hats**. De Bono's system was designed for business and management discussions and it can be very effective in structuring decision making. For example, **yellow hat thinking** will ensure that everybody finds positives about the work; a change to **black hat thinking** allows the raising of all negative points. However, when the discussion changes to another type of thinking, there must be no more negative comments. This system prevents a domination of negativity and encourages reflection on constructive achievement. Another strategy for managing discussion is to elect a new 'chair' for each discussion.

Reading the background to companies such as **Joint Stock**, who worked collectively, reveals that at a professional level there has to be an agreement and a structure. It is even more important at A level, when there are many other pressures and demands on your time.

Action point

See *Taking Stock* by Stafford-Clark and Roberts for a case study detailing Joint Stock's approach.

Checkpoint 2

Can you name two other companies working in **devised theatre**?

Exam practice   30 minutes answers: pages 122–123

Write an analysis of the group work for your devised piece. If you are embarking on the process, it may cover only the early stages; if you have completed your work, it will be a reflection of the whole experience.

Planning and shaping

This is the most crucial period of the process: the theme has been chosen, the groups organised and the responsibilities assigned, but the most significant part of the work remains to be done. This section will examine the schedule, consider time management and suggest approaches to research and to structure.

Managing time

In her excellent guide *Devising: A Handbook for Drama and Theatre Students* (published by Hodder & Stoughton in 2000), Gill Lamden suggests an eight-week plan that works backwards from the examination or performance date. This plan assigns **Week 8** to the first week of the process and **Week 1** becomes the final week. This 'countdown' method adds an imperative to the schedule as the time diminishes.

Management of the time within each session is also crucial. You should have an agreed structure to each lesson – for a 2-hour session, 10 minutes might be used for **warm-up** activities and 15 minutes for **discussion** of ideas. The **objectives** for the session are then set and the remaining time used to achieve them. The 10 minutes at the end of the session are used to **evaluate** and to set the **agenda** for the next session. You should always build in time to set the objectives for the next session and to agree what each individual will do before you next meet.

At key points during the devising period, you should take an **audit** of progress to determine what needs to be done, e.g. technical needs, an evaluation of the way the piece is being shaped, a revisiting of the aims or a consideration of the target audience.

Checkpoint 1

What do you understand by the term **audit**?

Research

Devising seeks out the **truth** about the theme, ensuring that **facts** are correct, but it should also involve **deeper exploration** of the issues. The ability to undertake relevant research and to use it effectively is one of the keys to success. Research can be used to transform ideas into precise pieces of theatre. Although the internet is useful, there is the potential for superficiality. The 'Google-print' style of internet research reveals little – team members arrive at the rehearsal with sheaves of paper that have not been read or filtered, much of which will be irrelevant. Effective research is discerning and analytical.

Directors and playwrights use research as a fundamental tool in the creative process. Interviews with real people, reading historical texts, examining archives and finding newspaper reports are all practical approaches to discovering information. Remember that research material can include photographs, artworks, music or taped voices. Research can also include an investigation of **style** or **genre** that you have selected for your piece.

Some questions to ask about research material are as follows:

→ Is this material unbiased?
→ Are there other accounts of the event(s)?
→ How have other writers treated this theme?
→ Are these the true facts?

Links

For a discussion of how Max Stafford-Clark uses research as a starting point for the creative process, see page 55.

Action point

Make a list of all the possible sources of information on your topic.

→ Does this piece of research lead me to another useful source?

→ Have I discovered something that will take our work in a different direction?

→ Does this material have dramatic potential?

Style, form and structure

By now you will have a clear idea of the theme, topic and aims. The next decision is to agree a **style** for the piece. You may decide on a **realist** or **non-realist** style, or you may be following the ideas of a practitioner or playwright.

Define the style at the start – it will be the cornerstone of your creative decisions. If, for example, you have chosen to examine the issue of human embryo research in a **Brechtian** style, presenting the audience with a dilemma that they must **judge**, you might use **representational characters**, **a narrator**, **montage** and **back projection**. Whatever your choice of style or genre you must ensure that it is applied consistently throughout the play.

The **structure** of the devised piece will reflect the style and genre but will emerge as your group's experiment with **form**. Do not be afraid to experiment, as this will reveal what works and what does not. Your sessions should involve 75 per cent practical activity and no more than 25 per cent discussion. As research material is gathered, treat each piece as a stimulus for practical work.

Record each piece of work in a central place. You should also record your **personal journey** in a log, as all specifications require an evaluative commentary. Continue to create, explore and experiment, then revisit what you have created. This prevents you spending too long polishing a particular section.

Development of **character** is important – you will receive a significant number of marks for your own performance. Your characterisation must be in the same style as the piece. Consider how people such as your character speak and how they move; examine their emotional journey, beliefs and values. If the person you are playing actually existed, research him or her in detail. Consider the use of **voice**, **movement** and **gesture** in depicting the role(s).

The group must consider the **overall shape** of the piece. How will it start? Where are the moments of climax? Are there any important sections that anchor the piece? What will happen at the end? To gain an objective observation of your 'first draft', invite friends to an after-school session or share your work with other sub-groups within the class. It is quite common for devised work to be ambiguous for people who have not been involved. Your neutral observer will be able to point out any areas of confusion and to comment on the impact. You can then relate their comments to your aims and intentions and rework any unclear sections.

Links

For a discussion of the King's Cross fire piece, see page 111.

Take note

Other possibilities include:

→ total theatre

→ naturalism

→ pantomime

→ physical theatre

→ expressionism

→ verbatim theatre.

Checkpoint 2

Define **total theatre** and **verbatim theatre**. Comment on their suitability as genres for your devised piece.

Links

For a detailed exploration of techniques that build a truthful role, see Stanislavski, page 30.

Exam practice   15 minutes

Make a list of the roles and scenes in which you appear during the devised piece. Opposite each item, indicate the skills that you will display in the examination performance, e.g. *Opening dance sequence – **movement skills**.*

Building to performance

This section will trace the development of the final stages of your work, leading to the performance. We will consider the final rehearsals, technical rehearsals, touring and planning for your audience.

Devising or rehearsal?

Is there a point where devising stops and rehearsing begins? At what stage do you finish the creative experiment and begin to shape the product for the audience/examination? Arguably, no theatrical production is ever perfect. Indeed, professional companies continue to make changes, even to the script of a new play, right up to 'press night'. However, there must come a time when you **consolidate** your devised pieces and begin to **polish** the play. Your group should agree when the devising ends and the new phase of rehearsing your creation begins.

There are equally controversial arguments about the production of a **text** or **script**. It is never a good idea for someone to try to write the scene in advance of the improvisation or exploration, but it is sometimes useful to **record** and **shape** the material following the session. It is better to refer to the **performance text** rather than the **script**. The text can include elements such as movement sequences, music or physical theatre, whereas a script implies only dialogue. Remember that the text represents everything that the audience experiences during the performance – before you can rehearse it must be consolidated and agreed.

Checkpoint 1

Define **devise**, **rehearse** and **consolidate**. In what ways are they different?

Final rehearsals

The text now becomes the blueprint for your work and you will approach it in the same way as you might a play written by a playwright. Your concern should be **communication**, both with your audience and with each other. The rehearsals at this stage must focus on the **energy** and **pace** of the production and on the exact technical details. You must agree on the exact features of the design and the properties. Where will furniture, blocks or props be positioned? How will they get on and off the space? Who will operate the sound, lighting and music?

Grade booster

It is important to ensure that you address these points and rehearse carefully – very effective devised plays can be spoiled by slapdash technical work or a lack of thought about properties, costume changes or sound cues.

Technical rehearsal

The technical rehearsal is very important: it is likely that you will have limited technical support or that you will be operating everything from within the group. Plan the technical elements carefully. The notes of one student read:

> 'During the devising period we referred frequently to "the storm" that was to be created by sound effects and music. As the examination approached, we realised that we had not done anything to achieve this effect. We used vital time to find and record the effect, resulting in fewer final rehearsals.'

Plan your technical rehearsal:

→ Run the play from **cue** to **cue**; you do not need to perform every scene.

Checkpoint 2

What is a **cue**?

→ For each cue (light/sound/music, etc.), check that the **level** or **volume** is correct and note these levels or programme them into the board.

→ Run every section that includes a **costume** or **set** change. Time these changes to ensure that they are quick. An audience/examiner loses concentration if there are endless blackouts where students fumble about not knowing where things are placed.

→ Make sure that **props** are positioned correctly and returned to the same place. Time any **changes** to props, e.g. if table lamps have to be switched on or wine glasses emptied to suggest passage of time.

Dress rehearsal

Always plan a full dress rehearsal into your schedule. This should be a performance as if to the real audience, where everything is as it will be for the exam. Some teachers mark this rehearsal as a 'mock exam' and give feedback. The important thing to remember is that you should **never stop**, even if you forget a section or an item of the set is in the wrong place. Carry on as you would in the performance, then rectify the problem and re-rehearse the scene afterwards. At the dress rehearsal all the technical crew, if you have any, must be there to perform the roles that they will undertake for the exam.

Touring

A number of groups tour their devised plays to schools, prisons or senior citizens' homes. If you are planning to tour, you must rehearse practical aspects, such as packing the minibus. Will the blocks or set fit into it? How long will it take to load, therefore what time must you arrive in advance of the exam? You should also try to **mark up** the performance space with **gaffer tape** on the floor of your drama studio, as it is unlikely that you will have an opportunity to rehearse in the space.

If you are touring or performing in an unknown venue, you should check practical details. How many power sockets are there? Will you need extension leads? Is there an area for 'back stage'? It is advisable to keep technical elements to a minimum when taking your show on the road!

Performance

This is the culmination of all your work – sadly, some students present the piece only once, which is a shame. Ensure that the group **checks** all technical elements in advance. You should plan for a cast warm-up and relaxation exercises. It is also worth spending some time as a group recapping your aims and objectives.

You have discussed your target audience and your intentions – now is the time when you will finally present those ideas. Enjoy the performance and be proud of what you have achieved.

Exam practice   15 minutes   answers: page 123

Write bullet points for a planned answer analysing how the rehearsals and the production process contribute to the final performance.

Recording and evaluating

Every specification requires some form of recording and evaluation of the work. This section will outline effective methods of recording and structuring your notes and suggest an approach to writing supporting written evidence, supporting notes or journals.

Keeping records

There is no substitute for keeping a **personal journal** throughout the devising period. Professional actors, designers and directors keep journals or notebooks in which they reflect on the process and note important issues. Your record should include personal comments, newspaper cuttings, sketches and accounts of workshop sessions.

Remember that it is for your own use, so the style will reflect your personality and you can choose a format that will be helpful for your final written document.

Your record might include:

→ an evaluation of the initial decision-making process
→ a statement of the theme and objectives
→ your response to the Belbin Test results
→ discussion of the target audience
→ newspaper cuttings or other research materials
→ sketches of costume or set ideas
→ experimental jottings
→ analysis of workshops
→ accounts of scenes created, with details of your role within them
→ research into your own role(s)
→ a mood board for the design or for the concept
→ lists of technical requirements
→ notes from rehearsals
→ lists of things to do or find.

Try to keep your record like a diary. Take it with you to every lesson or lecture and add something during or after each session.

Analysis and evaluation

A summative piece of work on your devised piece will include some of the following:

→ a rationale for the choice of theme or inspiration
→ aims and objectives
→ target audience and desired audience response
→ research
→ group work and group dynamics
→ development of roles or designs
→ analysis of process, workshops and shaping
→ analysis of acting techniques, form and style
→ communication with the audience
→ evaluation of the performance
→ consideration of health and safety
→ social, cultural and historical context.

Grade booster

It is easy to identify a set of notes or records written at the last minute in different coloured pens! Good evaluative documents can trace the journey and development of the piece with precise and genuine reflections on exact moments. There is a sense of progression and shaping as opposed to simple description.

Example

'Today we worked on a difficult scene. Our aim was to affect the audience emotionally and to leave them feeling moved and helpless. David had found the scene challenging and slightly embarrassing. We dimmed the lights in the studio and recounted sad moments from our lives. One or two were close to tears. David then improvised his monologue and we all closed our eyes. He seemed to lose his embarrassment and the speech was very moving. After this we all wrote down the line or phrase that we had found the most emotional and gave them to David. He created his final speech from our list.'

Take note

Check your own specification for exact details of the requirements for the written evaluation of your work.

Remember that the final document should be **analytical** and **evaluative**, not descriptive (see the notes following each example below). You should choose examples for detailed discussion rather than make vague or sweeping statements.

Checkpoint 1

What is the difference between **analysis** and **evaluation**?

Examples

Version 1 *'My monologue at the end was very effective as it communicated the key ideas to the audience. I varied my vocal tone throughout in order to create various effects and the final performance had the desired impact.'*
[This lacks detail and precise analysis.]

Version 2 *'My final monologue encapsulated the key ideas in our play. I used a variety of vocal techniques to produce the desired impact.*
There are people in Africa who need your help *[Low measured tone]*
I asked you to send them aid, food, medicines and bandages
[Increased volume and intensity]
You filled it with junk *[Loud and forceful]*
You wanted to show what you had so you put useless junk in this
box *[Stressed 'useless', low tone]*
Your possessions are swallowing you *[Angry, strident]*
Now, release your soul! *[Pause after 'now', calm, quiet]*'
[The detail in the second version gives a real sense of the moment and shows the candidate's intentions.]

Make sure that you use the correct **terminology** when discussing aspects of your work. For some specifications the journal or record is part of the **synoptic** component of the examination – you are expected to demonstrate your learning from all areas of the course.

Links

See Exploring the text, pages 68–83.

Health and safety

Consideration of health and safety is important throughout the process. Some specifications require you to document your appreciation of the importance of health and safety issues in relation to your devised piece.

Each production will have its own special concerns, but here are some ideas to consider:

→ appropriate clothing
→ safe use of lighting towers and ladders
→ fire exits and evacuation procedures
→ correct laying of cables
→ electrical safety procedures, especially regarding plug sockets and lighting rigs
→ lifting correctly
→ fights or physical theatre sequences
→ flames, especially candles.

Checkpoint 2

What is the health and safety rule with regard to running **cables** across the audience space?

Exam practice   20 minutes   answers: page 123

Write a paragraph detailing the creation of your role, or your designs, for the devised production.

Answers
Devised theatre

Creating theatre: a professional perspective

Checkpoints

1 **Joan Littlewood** (1914–2002) was a controversial and outspoken English director who founded the Theatre Workshop at Stratford East. Her most celebrated production was *Oh! What a Lovely War* and she launched the careers of many playwrights and actors, including Barbara Windsor and Brendan Behan.
2 An **ensemble** is a company or group of people who work closely together. Brecht's company was known as the Berliner Ensemble. Ensemble work is important in devising, as this requires sharing, equality and trust.

The audience: communication and response

Checkpoints

1 **Brecht** wanted his audience to judge the events and to become politically engaged in the issues. **Artaud** sought to shock his audience by assaulting their senses.
2 Multiple roles can be defined by costume items, through vocal tone or accent, style of movement or specific gesture. The role might be defined by introducing the character in the dialogue or by using direct address.

Exam practice

Our twin aims were to educate and to entertain our audience, who were from Year 6, so we used various dramatic devices to ensure that we captured their attention. Our opening scene was both visually and aurally intense, with a choreographed rain dance by the tribe. We realised that the naturalistic scenes might lose their interest, thus we interspersed these sections with tribal scenes that were visually exciting. The business people in our play sought to engage the audience's attention by creating exaggerated characters with whom the children could identify.

We were committed to forming a strong rapport with our audience. We used direct address to involve them in the issues and created the impression that we were confiding in them. At one point members of the tribe sat among the audience; their surprise and enjoyment were evident. We performed the next scene in a stylised whisper and our position within the audience heightened the busy, fast-paced atmosphere. A scene where overheard information is passed on continued the 'whisper' technique; we used the style of Chinese Whispers, with which the children could identify.

Another aspect that we had to consider during the devising process was our use of language. Much of the vocabulary in the office scenes was unfamiliar – for example, 'profit', 'turnover' and 'revenue'. We interspersed words like 'money' instead of 'profit' with the more sophisticated terms.

We wove a number of comic elements into our piece. Not only did this entertain but it also had the power to convey the message: Brecht's 'Spaß' had a similar purpose. This comedy sprang principally from the business people. One character, Deidre, was dim-witted and hard of hearing – her comic voice and movement proved a particular favourite with our audiences. One scene included a whoopee cushion, which caused much hilarity.

The business people were archetypes whose characters were quite exaggerated; the audience were able to relate to them easily. Some of these characters had recognisable catchphrases that made them memorable.

To ensure that the audience were left to think about the drama, we ended by posing a question in the final cliffhanger. We did not allow the audience to be passive, but forced them to form their own opinions.

Managing group work

Checkpoints

1 Recorder or scribe, designer for set, costume, lighting and properties, a liaison officer [if touring], administrator who books rehearsal space and types up schedules, research coordinator.
2 DV8, Frantic Assembly, Kneehigh, Théâtre de Complicité, Improbable Theatre, Trestle.

Exam practice

At the beginning of the process, we wrote a devising contract. This included agreements regarding attendance at lessons, meeting deadlines and sharing responsibilities equally. Additionally the contract covered the methods for settling disputes, the chairing of discussions and the shaping of materials. This contract did not eradicate argument or heated discussion, but it did provide a clear framework for resolution.

In order to strengthen the group we participated in many exercises and activities outside the rehearsal time. For example, we went to South Wales to visit a museum for our research. This involved a long journey and an overnight stay in the youth hostel. We became a very close group and this helped us to create a strong piece. I felt that establishing group unity prior to the devising period meant that we began the process with a clear work ethos.

Following the selection of the theme, we discussed the aims and objectives; the results were recorded in our group logbook. A different team member chaired each discussion and this ensured equality and meant that everyone was heard. We used the skills of group members effectively – a song was composed by a musician and the dance choreographed by a student studying Dance A level. One group member took responsibility for shaping our improvised dialogue into text, which we read and evaluated at the next session. There were people in the group who had lively and original ideas and they often led the improvisations, others were excellent researchers who would undertake to find exact details or check facts. We shared the technical elements evenly, but we were all involved in the mechanical tasks such as painting the blocks and moving the lights from Studio 1 to the Hall.

During the later rehearsals, we tested our ideas by choosing one person to observe the scene; their feedback and constructive criticism enabled us to see the piece objectively. Our group work was not without its low points, but overall I feel that we worked very effectively. Our final piece was very powerful and there was a sense of great achievement. Perhaps most importantly, we were all still talking to each other at the end!

Planning and shaping

Checkpoints

1 An **audit** is a stock-taking or appraisal exercise. It establishes where you are at any specific moment. The term is often applied to the scrutiny of accounts.

2 **Total theatre** originates in the work of Artaud and refers to the use of many non-verbal forms of communication. This genre would enable the group to use movement, mime, dance, masks, rituals and technical effects to create a powerful piece of theatre.
   Verbatim theatre takes the actual words of people who have been involved in an event/tragedy/accident and shapes them into a play. This genre would be interesting if there was a local story that could be the stimulus for the drama.

Building to performance

Checkpoints

1 **Devise** suggests the formative, creative, inventive period of the process. **Rehearse** implies a shaping and structuring, while still allowing for changes. **Consolidate** means to strengthen, confirm and make secure, implying the final stages when the piece will not change.

2 A **cue** in the theatre is a signal, reminder or indication for an effect or a line of dialogue. A cue can be verbal, visual or aural.

Exam practice

- Analysis of group skills.
- Research and its use in rehearsals.
- Development and shaping of ideas.

- Establishment of clear aims for each rehearsal.
- Style and genre: how these affected rehearsal.
- Structure and form: production process.
- Practitioners: Brecht and Grotowski. Techniques used in rehearsal.
- Technical elements: production process.
- Evaluation of the performance.

Recording and evaluating

Checkpoints

1 **Analysis** is a dissection of the work to expose the aims, clarify the intentions and investigate the methods. It implies an objective, even clinical approach.
   Evaluation is an appraisal or judgement, an assessment of the outcome and a critical review of the piece.

2 If you need to run a **cable** across the audience area, you must tape it down with white gaffer tape, ensuring that it can be seen. You must not run a cable across an aisle or walkway.

Exam practice

The stimulus for our play was a National Youth Theatre production of *2.18 Underground*, which we saw at the Edinburgh Festival. Our setting was on the London Underground and each character was making a journey, which unknown to them would be their last. The characters were named after stations: I was 'Angel', my father's pet name for me.

The history of the characters, revealed through a series of flashbacks of significant moments from the past, emerged gradually. My role was a character making a journey to see her father whom she had not spoken to since she was 16; her father was ill and Angel planned to be reconciled with him now that she was a mother herself. I developed my role in two ways: the girl on the train was thoughtful, quiet and considerate in sharp contrast to her teenage self who was abusive, arrogant and uncouth. I established a different vocal tone and movement quality for the two time zones. My relationship with the other passengers contrasted with the teenage attitude to my father. The function of my role was to convey the poignancy of the moment when I leave my father and to evoke a sympathetic response from the audience for the actor playing my father.

Revision checklist
Devised theatre

1	Name the main devised theatre companies in the UK.	Confident	Not confident **Revise** pages 108–109
2	Explain why ensemble work is an important element of devised theatre.	Confident	Not confident **Revise** page 108
3	Understand how to select a productive stimulus.	Confident	Not confident **Revise** page 110
4	Understand how to develop the devised work in relation to the target audience.	Confident	Not confident **Revise** page 112
5	Recognise how the structure of the piece can elicit an audience response.	Confident	Not confident **Revise** page 113
6	Know how to use the Belbin Test and de Bono's Six Thinking Hats to structure group work.	Confident	Not confident **Revise** pages 114–115
7	Recognise the value of group contracts and sharing of responsibility in minimising conflict.	Confident	Not confident **Revise** page 115
8	Understand the strategies for managing time.	Confident	Not confident **Revise** page 116
9	Know how to shape research material into effective theatre.	Confident	Not confident **Revise** pages 116–117
10	Understand how to use form and genre in structuring the devised piece.	Confident	Not confident **Revise** page 117
11	Understand the organisation and running of technical and dress rehearsals.	Confident	Not confident **Revise** pages 118–119
12	Know how to keep appropriate records of the devising process.	Confident	Not confident **Revise** page 120
13	Explain the subtle difference between analysis and evaluation.	Confident	Not confident **Revise** pages 120–121
14	List the key health and safety requirements.	Confident	Not confident **Revise** page 121

Performing scripted plays

The essence of theatre is the process of taking a play from 'page to stage'; your exam specification places great value on your ability to present a text to an audience. You may choose to be examined as an actor, a designer of set, costume, masks and make-up, lighting or sound. In one specification you will present either a monologue or duologue as well as a group performance.

This chapter traces the creative journey. The early sections advise you on selection of text and approaches to rehearsal, while later sections cover the specific skills of performing and designing. There is a section that guides you through the process of selecting and rehearsing a monologue or duologue. All examination boards require a final analysis through concept notes, process journals or evaluative records; some boards ask designers and directors to make a presentation to the examiner/moderator. The final section covers the written evaluation and documentation of the process and the oral presentation of your design ideas.

Exam themes

- Selecting and editing text for performance
- Rehearsing the play: 'page to stage'
- Creating and performing a role or an audience
- Creating and realising a design for a performance
- Documenting and evaluating the process
- Written analysis and evaluation

Topic checklist

	Edexcel		AQA		WJEC	
	AS	A2	AS	A2	AS	A2
Choosing the play	O		O		O	
Directing decisions	O		O		O	
Exploration, development and rehearsal	O		O		O	
Creating a role	O		O		O	
Working as a designer	O		O		O	
Notes, journals and presentations	O		O		O	

Choosing the play

Every specification requires the performance of a scripted play. This may entail a free choice of text, a text selected from a set list, or your teacher may make the decision. This section will look at the choice of text.

First, choose the play

It is important to remember that the production is for **assessment** and therefore must enable all candidates to demonstrate their ability. This is advanced level work, therefore your choice of play should be appropriately **challenging**.

There are some key questions to ask when choosing a text for this examination:

→ What type of play interests the group? Have you studied or seen similar plays during the course?
→ How many actors will be in the group? What are the examination board's limits?
→ Will any candidates be examined as technicians? Does the text provide suitable opportunities?
→ What type of performance space is available to you? Can the text be staged in this space?
→ Do you need to cut the text to meet time limits? Will this be possible without weakening the structure?
→ Is there a correlation between the level of challenge in the play and the level of skill in the group?
→ Will this play provide equal opportunities for achievement by all candidates?

The optimum method for choosing the right play is through regular reading throughout the course. Elsewhere in this guide, it is suggested that group play-reading sessions improve knowledge of drama texts. Do not choose a play without reading it! Seeing the play in performance or reading the cast list and the plot outline are no substitute for a complete reading of the text.

Choosing monologues or duologues

→ Avoid selecting from books of audition pieces without reading the whole play. Remember that you will be required to produce an outline of your concept for the examiner.
→ Know the whole play well. You are presenting a section for examination but this should appear as if in a production of the full text.
→ Research the **social, cultural and historical context** of the play. This will be important for your **concept notes** and will ensure that your performance style is appropriate.
→ Consider the rehearsal techniques of practitioners that you have studied when working on the speech or dialogue.
→ Adhere very carefully to the **time limit**. Select your scene or speech so that it has a clear start and end, but with a watchful eye on the timing.

Watch out!

All specifications allow **cross-sex casting**. Make sure that you make decisions that are in the spirit of the text. For example, plays with multiple roles might lend themselves to such casting choices, whereas in plays that are more naturalistic this may be less effective.

Terminology

Cross-sex casting means that women play male roles or vice versa. This is sometimes written into the text, e.g. Caryl Churchill's *Cloud Nine*, or is a common feature of the genre, e.g. Brechtian representation. Brecht sought to 'distance' the audience from emotional involvement in the story. He used many devices to achieve this aim, one of which was that roles were represented rather than embodied by an actor. It is less common for naturalistic plays such as *A Doll's House*.

→ Do not create a monologue or duologue by piecing together fragments of dialogue from across the scene or play. This is a performance of a **short extract** in the context of the whole play. Imagine that your examiner has just 'dropped in' to your production and is seeing this moment.

Will the choice of play enable you to meet the exam criteria?

Examiners and moderators are awarding marks for your skill as a performer or a designer. When selecting the text you should bear in mind the criteria for your specification and ensure that the play chosen gives you a range of opportunities.

Marking criteria include the following sections:

Performer

Voice: The voice should be clear, audible and the tone used appropriate to the role(s). A variation in pitch should convey mood or emotion. Effective use of pause will show control of the drama and there should be modifications of inflection. The voice will augment the characterisation.

Movement: Movement will be completely in keeping with the role(s). At times, moments of stillness will show control. The use of gesture should be appropriate to the character.

Characterisation: The character should be believable and the performance consistent. Characterisation should be in accordance with the style and context of the play.

Communication: The performance should communicate with the audience; there will be an awareness of the audience response. Performers should connect with others members of the cast and make a positive contribution throughout the performance.

Designer

Materials: There should be an inventive and appropriate choice of equipment, techniques and materials, which are employed to create meaning and impact.

Final design: This should be completed with accuracy and detail with a high level of finish. Designs should demonstrate an absolute understanding of the demands of the production.

Communication: Designs should communicate with an audience and reflect the overall concept of the production.

Checkpoint 1

Give an example of an actor using a **pause** to create impact in a performance.

Examiner's secrets

Try not to run over the suggested time; examiners will not award marks for work performed after the time limit. Over-long pieces are often self-penalising and they will take you longer to create and to rehearse. Quality not quantity is important.

Checkpoint 2

Give some examples of **materials** used in set design, costume design and lighting design.

Grade booster

As a performer, aim to embody the role. Your performance skills should be used to create a convincing character. As a designer, use your resources creatively, ensuring that your design enhances the performance and reflects the concept.

Exam practice   20 minutes

Make a list of possible texts for your performance exam. Opposite each title, write the points in favour and points against this choice. Compare your list with the others in your group.

Directing decisions

You need to consider the question of a director for the performance of your chosen scripted play. Specifications vary: your teacher or lecturer could direct you, the directing might be a collaborative process or one student might choose to be examined as a director. This section will look at approaches to directing for the practical examination.

The question of directing

Three options exist: teacher director, group directing and student director.

Teacher director

If your teacher is directing your play, it is important to remember to take note of directing techniques, exercises or practitioner's ideas employed. Your supporting notes will require an evaluation of the process of the work. Keep a **reflective journal** or diary, documenting rehearsals and noting any rehearsal methods. You could ask your director to make explicit how the rehearsal was **structured**, the rehearsal **aims** and any **influences** on the strategy used. Look at this example from a student's journal

> 'Blue Remembered Hills by *Dennis Potter.*
>
> *Today we worked on the scenes where the children chase the squirrel. The rehearsal aim was to recreate believable childlike movement and vocal tone, whilst retaining the idea of underlying cruelty. We began with a warm-up, a children's chasing game, and, before we played the scene, the director asked us to reflect on the **events** and **intentions**. This technique, based on the work of the director Katie Mitchell, has links to Stanislavski. One of my main intentions was to frighten Willie and to retain power over him. I spoke the line "They got sharp tith, mind. Like red-hot needles. And once they get hold of you they never let go, squirrels don't" in a low, menacing tone, with my face very close to Willie's.'*

During the rehearsal process, be alert to possibilities for the role and carry out research. Do not simply rely on the director to tell you where to move or what you are feeling – the performance will have greater depth and credibility if you have engaged fully in the creative process.

Group directing

This can be the most difficult option and requires a clearly agreed strategy. Read the section on group dynamics in Devised theatre, page 114. You should decide on the **concept** for the production and agree a rehearsal methodology.

Your approach could include the following:

→ One student leads a warm-up at the start of every session.
→ Each student will direct a scene; these will be chosen in advance.
→ Rehearsals will be prepared by this student before the session.
→ One student will take responsibility for the production script.
→ All decisions will be recorded in the production script.

Take note

AQA Unit 2 can be directed by the group or one student can be examined as a director.

Edexcel Unit 2 is directed by the teacher/lecturer.

WJEC DA1 is directed by the group.

Links

See Katie Mitchell, page 58.

Links

See The director's concept, page 88.

- → There is a chairperson for every discussion or debate.
- → An objective view will be sought where we cannot agree on a decision (e.g. a teacher or student from outside the group).
- → A rehearsal schedule will be drawn up in advance.
- → Technical responsibilities will be agreed and shared evenly.

It is vital to channel the energy of the group into the creative process and not into disputes or arguments. The more you can agree in advance, the less likely it is that petty disagreements will spoil your work.

Checkpoint 1

What is a **rehearsal schedule** and why is it necessary to have one?

Student director

The student director must have the trust of the group, who must remember that the director will be marked on his/her work. The student director must take into account that the students in the cast are also working for an exam. Directing is exciting but demanding; it is not an option for a candidate who chooses it by default as an alternative to acting.

It is the director's job to **provoke interest** in the text and to **stimulate exploration** of themes and character. You should consider the following:

- → You must know the play thoroughly; read it at least three times before rehearsals begin.
- → Casting decisions are important. Will you cast the play or will the group or the teacher cast it?
- → Plan every rehearsal fully. Define your aims and share them with the cast.
- → Do not 'block' every move in advance. This will stifle creativity and can lead to a stilted performance.
- → Read widely about professional directors. Use their ideas for exploration of text and for rehearsal techniques.
- → Select carefully those techniques that will open up the play for you and your cast rather than going through a 'shopping list' of ideas, which can fragment the process.
- → Consider how you will deal with your peers if they do not want to accept your direction. It is better to allow individuals to try their own ideas and to evaluate them constructively. Make it clear *why* you have made a choice and be able to support your decision.
- → Keep a detailed log of the whole process. This will be a useful point of reflection and form the basis for your presentation to the examiner.

Checkpoint 2

What is **blocking** and why might it stifle creativity?

Exam practice   30 minutes   answers: page 142

For the text that you have selected, produce a bullet-pointed list under the following headings: Themes, Concepts, Characters, Rehearsal ideas and Dramatic intentions.

Exploration, development and rehearsal

This section will help you through the rehearsal process. There can be no definitive approach to developing the concept or rehearsing the play and this section is not intended to give prescriptive rules. It will outline ways of working and suggest methods that have proved effective in producing strong performances of scripted text.

Exploring the text

Research is important to this element of the exam. Once you have chosen the play, you should read about the playwright, the theme and the social and cultural context of the play and the period of writing. Look at the **style** of the play: is it naturalistic, expressionist or was the playwright influenced by a practitioner? Answers to these questions will inform your directing, characterisation and design decisions.

Explore the text for **theme** and playwright's **meaning**. Note significant scenes, as they will become focal points in the shape and rhythm of the performance. Decide on the **climaxes** and moments of **tension** and discuss the intended **impact** on the audience. Look for evidence of **characterisation** and agree how each character will be portrayed in relation to the overall concept. This scrutinising of the text uncovers what director Annie Castledine terms the 'architecture' of the play.

Action point

Buy a scrapbook and keep all research material in it. You will find this early material very useful when you are making decisions about set, costume or properties.

Checkpoint 1

Define **impact**, **tension** and **climax** in relation to performance.

Example from early notes

'My Mother Said I Never Should.
Dramatic impact – key scenes:
1 Jackie gives away Rosie. 2 Margaret's death. 3 Rosie tells Jackie that she has discovered the secret.'

Systems of rehearsal

There is a detailed discussion of rehearsal work in Key practitioners, pages 30–63 and Writing about text, pages 86–97. You should read these chapters before embarking on your work for this element of the exam. Your group or director should plan each rehearsal with reference to the concept and the aims for performance.

Warm-up exercises

These exercises are relevant only where they enhance the quality of the rehearsal. They have two purposes: to relax the actors, release tension and encourage trust or to create the mood required for the rehearsal. Therefore, if your rehearsal aim is to create a mood of menace, there is little point in playing a game of tag as a warm-up. If your group has found agreement difficult in the previous session, you might begin with a trust exercise. Match the warm-up to the purpose or you will just waste time.

Action point

Devise a warm-up exercise and try it out with your group. Make sure that it has some link with the rehearsal aim.

Rehearsal aim

Always decide what you are trying to achieve during a rehearsal and then agree how you will do it. The decision will be influenced by the concept, the prior work and the stage of the rehearsal period. Early rehearsals will focus on the staging and development of character whereas a later session may concentrate on achieving pace by sharpening links between scenes. It a good idea to agree the focus of the next rehearsal before leaving the studio – everyone can prepare appropriately and arrive at the next session ready to begin.

Checkpoint 2

What do you understand by **staging**?

Experiment

Use the ideas you have learned during the study of practitioners, analysis of live performance and practical exploration of text. Do not feel trapped into simply staging the play and learning the lines. The most exciting work comes from focused experiment – try out ideas, then review them. Never dismiss an approach without trying it first.

Manageable sections

Do not aim to rehearse too much of the play in any one session, especially early in the process. In Max Stafford-Clark's account of the rehearsals for *Our Country's Good,* he describes a rehearsal period of three hours on the scene *The Question of Liz.* This scene is only three pages long! You will not have the luxury of this amount of time, but if you aim to cover too much you will end up merely running through the scene rather than exploring the opportunities.

Action point

Read as much as you can about directors' rehearsal methods. Make notes of suggested techniques that you might use during your own rehearsal work.

Recording

Once a decision is reached on a section of the play, you should record the results in the production script and in your own script. This ensures that everybody is clear and that there is no ambiguity when you return to the scene later.

Grade booster

Ensure that all rehearsal time is used effectively. The final performance will then have a good degree of polish and you will feel confident and secure.

Exam practice   30 minutes

Choose one section of your text and create a rehearsal plan. State the aim of the rehearsal and say how this links to the concept. Suggest appropriate warm-up exercises. Select a technique, either from a practitioner or one you have used during your course. Plan how you will use this with actors. Finally, outline how the scene will look after this rehearsal.

Creating a role

This section gives advice on approaching a role. You may be playing more than one character in your piece and you should approach each one separately. This will enable you to present well-defined and different characters. The section directs you to the work of practitioners whose methods can help you in creating believable characters and gives specific information about voice, movement and gesture.

Preparation and research

Your supporting notes will document and analyse your personal journey. In addition to the group work during rehearsals, you should undertake personal work on the role that you will play. You will have used this approach when studying the set text.

Academic analysis will not reveal the **depth** of a character – you will need to find your own **relationship** with the role. You must examine the text to discover what fires your imagination, then piece together a character history from the information in the text.

Ask yourself about the character's social world, relationships, past life, ambitions, wealth, occupation and beliefs. Look at the **language** your character uses – this is an indication of status, education, energy and age. You should also trace your character's emotional journey through the play.

Vocal and physical development

The examination criteria refer to key skills such as voice, movement, gesture and communication. Your individual work on the role must pay attention to the development of these skills.

Vocal skills

Make sure that you understand every word that you are saying. This is particularly important if you are playing a role from a period play, which may be written in verse or in an unfamiliar style. Explore the **vocal texture** of the dialogue. Does the character speak in short, sharp sentences? Does he/she use long pauses or are the speech patterns in flowery imagery? The way you deliver the dialogue is affected by its style.

Consider your **breathing**. A common fault is the 'rainbow voice', which becomes faint at the end of phrases. This is because insufficient breath is taken or there is a lack of control of its release. You must breathe correctly so that you can **project** your voice within the theatre space.

Does the character have an **accent** or different vocal style from you? Research the accent in the same way as you would the character's background. Listen to recordings of people or of actors speaking in this way. Make sure that the delivery of dialogue is **clear** and vary the **pace** of the dialogue. Consider appropriate use of inflection, pause and intonation.

Learning lines

You may have had experience of learning lines but it could be the first time you have worked on text as opposed to devised drama. Actors have their individual methods and line learning is linked to the type of learning style that you prefer:

Links

See Exploring the text, pages 68–75.

Links

See Stanislavski, page 30 and Katie Mitchell, page 58.

Action point

Create a chart of the play from your character's viewpoint. Show the high and low points and moments of emotional intensity, elation or despair.

Action point

If you are rehearsing a monologue try to pair up with another student to share your work. This use of a 'critical partner' will help you to explore ideas and receive practical advice.

Take note

There is an essential difference between 'performing' and 'acting'. Performing implies *putting on* a particular voice and physicality, e.g. a croaky voice and bent back to play an elderly person. Acting implies a transformation of the 'self' into the character, which is why practitioners like Stanislavski ask actors to 'work on themselves'. This ability is what defines great actors.

Checkpoint 1

What do you understand by **vocal texture**?

- → Highlight your lines in the text.
- → Read the lines aloud, trying to hear the rhythm of the words.
- → Ask a friend or relative to read the other roles aloud, then stop for you to speak your lines.
- → Make aural links between the cue line and your line.
- → Think about *why* you say your line – your *intention*. This will help you to recall the emotion as well as the words.
- → Record the play, leaving a space for your lines. Play this back and speak your lines in the spaces. You can also record the play with your lines and listen to the recording in your room or in the car.
- → Look at the shape of the lines on the page – a visual learner can often recall a picture of the words.
- → Test yourself on long speeches by writing them out after you have learned them.

Action point

Try one of these methods and compare it with the technique that you would normally use.

Physical skills

The creation of a well-rounded character requires **physicalisation** of the role. You should consider the **centre of energy** of your character. Does he move from the head, the chest or somewhere else? An over-confident and bumptious official, such as Dogberry in *Much Ado About Nothing*, may move from the chest whereas a sharp, prickly female manager, such as Marlene in *Top Girls*, could lead from the chin.

The practitioner **Michael Chekhov**, a descendant of the playwright Chekhov, who was familiar with Stanislavski's work, created an exercise where the actor moved as if his character was an animal. Stanley in *A Streetcar Named Desire* might be a lion and Mother Courage a carthorse.

Entrances and exits give vital information about your character. Do you sweep into the room as a confident character or enter timidly? What has happened to you before your entrance? Katie Mitchell has her actors improvise the off-stage scenes during every performance.

Consider how the character **moves** and what he does in moments of **stillness. Eye contact** is also important. Remember that you are in role throughout the play, not simply when you are speaking. How might your character **sit**? How would he handle **objects**? **Gesture** must always be appropriate but never distracting. Finally, you should take into account the costume and shoes: how will they affect or enhance the movement? You must rehearse in any period costume for a few weeks before the exam – long skirts or 'mock-ups' of the real thing will suffice if costumes are going to be hired.

Action point

Find out more about Michael Chekhov's physical exercises.

Links

See page 61.

Checkpoint 2

How can **eye contact** reflect mood, emotion and attitude?

Exam practice   30 minutes   answers: page 142

Write a detailed profile of the main role that you are preparing for the practical exam. Include your ideas for the physical and vocal treatment of the role with examples of specific moments in the play.

Working as a designer (1)

All specifications offer design and technical skills as a practical option. Preparing for this role requires the same degree of detailed research and planning as for a performance. This section and the next two will outline the stages of the design candidate's process, and recommend ways to create original ideas and realise them in the performance. They will also suggest research methods, recommend resources and discuss the portfolio or supporting notes and presentation.

Set design

Take note

The Manchester Royal Exchange is a theatre in the round.

The role of the designer links inextricably to the **concept**, so your first discussion should be with the director. Simon Higlett's design for the Manchester Royal Exchange's 2002 production of *Yerma* embodied a central theme in the design of the floor:

> *'The round of the theatre gave a strong metaphor for realising this sense of the earth as a planet. Mixed in with this was the exploration of a series of paintings of women and Simon was struck by the rounded, almost sculpted form of a belly. As he and the director looked at the photograph, there was a revelation about the relationship of the earth surface that was to be the stage floor and the belly of a woman. Here was the possibility of saying something about Yerma's sterility.'*

Ian MacNeil designed a landmark production of J.B. Priestley's *An Inspector Calls* at the National Theatre in 1993. The design placed the house of the smug, complacent, middle-class family on stilts set on a cobbled, darkened road, where tramps and beggars wandered. The audience looked into their lives as if peering into a doll's house. When the family is brought down at the end of the play, the house on stilts collapsed, vividly exemplifying the central theme of the play.

In professional theatre, the same person usually designs the set and the costumes. They will discuss the play's overall look with the director and other key design and technical staff such as make-up, set and lighting designers.

Links

See pages 76 and 95.

Following the initial discussion, create a **mood board** that encapsulates your ideas. Professional designers use this technique to focus ideas and to explore textures and colours.

Research is closely connected with the mood board, as it is from the research that you will find material. The designer must know the text in as much depth as the cast and director. Research could include:

→ the historical and social context of the play
→ the themes and meanings intended by the playwright
→ location implied or explicit in the production
→ talking to people who have lived in or visited the location/country
→ furniture, interior design and architecture of the period from books or a museum visit
→ visual research, e.g. postcards and pictures
→ the setting and period for your production.

You will also need to audit the available **resources**. Will you be required to create the set from materials that are available at your school or college or will you have a budget? You must look carefully at the **space**. Is yours the only play or will another group perform on the same day? How much space will the action of the play require?

Remember that the primary function of the set is to enable the actors to perform the text. Where are the entrances and exits? Does the play require any important features – a window, a fireplace? Consider the actor/audience relationship at this point. You should record all your early ideas, sketches and research for your **portfolio** or **supporting notes**, which must show the **development** of the design.

Making the model

The designer will normally make a model of the set and you are required to do this for the examination. The model has two purposes: it provides the actors with a clear image of how the set will look and it is a blueprint for the construction. The model must use the standard scale 1:25: 1cm = 25cm and each 4cm = 1m. Before you begin, measure the space accurately, including door and entrance widths, then create a **ground plan** to this scale. The **materials** might include balsa wood, masking tape, thick black card, plywood or MDF for the basic structure, plus a knife. Make the model carefully and to scale.

Colour, texture and proportion

Colour creates mood and emotion but it can also create optical effects. A space can seem larger in lighter shades. You should also avoid flat colour blocks on large areas as this lacks **texture**. Remember that colour must work well with the **costumes**.

Texture gives a visual message – rough, broken stone can imply decay, marble columns suggest splendour. Using PVA glue or car bodywork padding can give a textured effect to scenery. Painting can also add texture by using rags or stippling.

The **proportions** of the set design have implications for meaning: oversized items create the illusion that actors are small, e.g. giant leaves and flowers for the forest scenes in *A Midsummer Night's Dream*.

The construction of the set may involve other, non-examination candidates. This is acceptable; the designer in the theatre would not have to build the set. Make sure that you allow sufficient time for this and have pre-arranged your team.

Watch out!

Do not decide that your design will be minimalist – a tree and black drapes may be appropriate for *Waiting for Godot*, but you will be unable to demonstrate your skill as a designer.

Action point

Make a list of all the available resources, including a budget figure if you have one. Make a scaled ground plan of the space, then experiment with your ideas. Measure carefully so that when you come to build the set you know that it will fit. Look at this **practical** plan in conjunction with the ideas in the **mood board**. You will start to see an early picture of the design.

Checkpoint 1

What is a **ground plan**?

Exam practice   20 minutes

For your chosen skill, research the work of professionals who work in this area. Look at examples of their designs and evaluate them in terms of visual impact, suitability for the period and evocation of mood. Note down what the design says to you in terms of concept.

Working as a designer (2)

This section will outline the approach to costume design, masks and make-up.

Costume design

The costume designer will research costume styles, fabrics and designs to suit the production's time period or setting and create costume ideas to fit in with the production's concept and budget.

Follow the process of research and discussion outlined in the previous section for set-design candidates. Creating a **mood board** is equally important for costume design: you will also include colour swatches and snippets of material. Costumes reflect the period, the mood and atmosphere, suggest temperature or time of day and signify character. Consider all these elements in your design. You must also ascertain the speed of any costume changes and ensure that they are accomplished in the time allowed: many small buttons will slow down a change, so you might need to add Velcro.

You must also ensure that the costumes look effective when seen together: a costume designer will produce the designs in a linear format, so that they can be seen side by side.

Some specifications require the costume-design candidate to create one complete costume, while others ask candidates to design, locate and oversee the costumes, with no requirement for the designer to construct them.

Process
→ Research period, character and concept.
→ Create a mood board or scrapbook.
→ Look carefully through the play for specific requirements and changes.
→ Sketch initial ideas: consider shape, line, colour and texture.
→ Measure all actors accurately.
→ Select materials or locate hire outlets.
→ Organise the making of costumes to a set deadline.
→ Arrange fittings, leaving time for alterations.
→ Look at the costumes under the lighting.

Your portfolio or supporting notes will include notes, designs, photographs, material samples and measurements designed to show the development of your thinking that led to the final product.

Masks

Masks were traditionally worn in Greek and Roman theatre, medieval actors wore masks to portray devils and monsters, while the most significant genre in the history of masks is Commedia dell'arte.

In modern theatre **Brecht** used half masks, mask theatre companies like **Trestle** and **Trading Faces** work exclusively in masks, and playwrights, for example Peter Shaffer, write masked characters into their work. If you have chosen this option, you will obviously be working on a text where masks are integral to the design and concept of the piece. As a mask or make-up designer, you will liaise with the costume designer very closely.

Checkpoint 1

What do you understand by the term **costume plot**?

Take note

Check your specification for the exact requirements. Do not choose costume design if your exam requires you to **make** a costume unless you are skilled in this area. However, where this is not a requirement, someone with enthusiasm for costume design but no construction skills can still achieve highly.

Links

See page 13.

Process

→ Collect illustrations of masks and discuss ideas with the director.
→ Research the play and characters who wear the masks.
→ Sketch design ideas and experiment with materials.
→ Decide on the construction and materials.
→ Decide whether the masks will be whole face, half face or above the face.
→ Measure and fit the masks carefully to the actors, ensuring they can speak clearly while wearing them.
→ Create the masks using your chosen process.
→ Decorate or paint the masks according to the design.
→ Check the masks under the lighting and with the costumes.

Your portfolio or supporting notes will detail the research and design process, evaluate the decisions made about materials and construction, outline character profiles and analyse the impact of the masks in performance.

Make-up

Theatrical make-up has changed significantly in modern theatre. Improved and sophisticated lighting has reduced the need for make-up, which is now much more natural. Materials have developed appreciably, enabling realistic simulations of scars, wounds and skin texture.

If you have chosen make-up as your design skill, you should ensure that suitable opportunities exist for creative design and application. A play requiring fantasy make-up, for example *The Insect Play*, a play set in a historical period, such as April de Angelis's *Playhouse Creatures* and *A Laughing Matter*, or a text that entails construction of scars or wounds will give you opportunities to demonstrate skills. Some specifications require you to produce designs for the make-up for the whole play and to oversee the application, while others entail the application of make-up as part of the exam.

You should research the period – make-up has trends similar to fashion. Decide on the materials you will need and plan your designs in detail. Practise applying the make-up to the actors in advance of the exam date: each individual's skin will react differently to the make-up. You should also see the make-up under stage lighting to ensure that the tones and details are correct. Ideally, you should apply the make-up in strong light – this is why dressing room mirrors are traditionally surrounded by lights.

Take note

Make-up should reflect the concept and have an impact on the production. Colin Richmond's designs for Headlong's production of Bond's *Restoration* used absurd wigs and deathly make-up, to give the performance a nightmarish quality.

Exam practice   20 minutes

For your chosen skill, research the work of professionals who work in this area. Look at examples of their designs and evaluate them in terms of visual impact, suitability for the period and evocation of mood. Note down what the design says to you in terms of concept.

Working as a designer (3)

This section will outline the approach to lighting and sound design.

Lighting and sound design

You can choose to be examined as a designer of both sound and lighting, or you can opt to concentrate on one of them. If you have selected this option, ensure that the play provides opportunities for you to demonstrate your skills. Ideally, the play should require at least four lighting **states** or sound effects and opportunities to demonstrate the operation of equipment. This includes **dimming** and **cross-fading** lights, bringing in sound effects accurately and creating mood, atmosphere or location through sound or light.

Lighting

Watch out!

The primary function of lighting design must be to enable the audience to **see** the action. Do not ignore this when creating effects or moods. Washing the entire stage in deep red will reduce actors to shadowy figures and, unless this is your intention, you will lose marks.

Lighting design ensures that the action can be **seen**, creates the **illusion** of natural light that determines time of day or temperature, creates special effects and augments **themes** identified in the **concept**. Work closely with any students responsible for set and costume design. A good lighting designer will simulate natural light sources. Alternatively, effective lighting can create abstract effects – grotesque shadows cast from low-level lighting.

If you have chosen this option, you will be familiar with the different types of lantern and with polycarbonate colour filters known as 'gels', gobos and effects projectors. Following your research, audit and experiment, you should plan the lighting rig and decide on how you will use colour. Never use a single flat **colour**; many different shades of blue appear in a normal sky. Reserve **primary colours** for pantomime or symbolic effects; never try to show the **emotion** of a character through lighting.

Attending rehearsals will ensure that you are familiar with the requirements of the production and know the key positions on the stage. You must ensure that you light the whole space. Rig the lights at an appropriate **angle**, 45 degrees above and 45 degrees to the side of the performers, dividing the space into sections and lighting each section to provide a **general cover** of light. When rigging lights you should have an assistant walking and standing in the space. The light should always light the face, even if they stand on a table or block. Never light the floor!

Checkpoint 1

What is **general cover**?

Process

→ Study the text for information regarding time, weather, location and effects and sources of light.

→ Discuss the concept with the director and other technical candidates/students.

→ Create a **mood board** or scrapbook with pictures that encapsulate your early ideas.

→ Audit the resources at your centre and see whether any special lanterns need to be hired.

→ Check the electrical safety and maximum wattage of your system.

→ Draw a scaled plan of the rigging, indicating where each lantern will be hung.

- → Before deciding on colour, experiment with different gels.
- → Rig the lights observing health and safety requirements. Never rig alone. Patch the dimmer board.
- → Plot the lighting cues on a cue sheet and note them in the text.
- → Go through the lighting plot with the director before the technical rehearsal, noting the levels, speed of changes and exact timing of cues.
- → At the technical rehearsal, work from cue to cue with the actors. At this rehearsal, you will mark any exact spots where actors must stand.
- → Only after everything is agreed should you programme the lighting board. Make sure you know how to override a programmed cue if something should go wrong.

Action point

Make sure you understand the following terms: lanterns, electrical safety, gel, patch, dimmer board, cue sheet.

Sound design

Sound design can enhance the mood and atmosphere of the production or create dramatic impact. A sound designer should undertake the research, audit and experiment process outlined above. Sound can be divided into two categories: **acoustic** sound, produced live, such as a door slam, and **pre-recorded** sound. Make sure that if the sound is pre-recorded it is believable. You may choose to record some sounds yourself, indeed your specification may require you to create several original effects.

The play *Masterpieces* has a climatic scene set on a London Underground platform. A student designing sound for this play visited London to record tube trains from the platform to achieve a more authentic result. You could also sample sounds and create a disk or computer file, which you can play to the directors or group before making a final decision.

Your study of the text will reveal the necessary effects arising from the text, e.g. a dog barking or screeching brakes. **Ambient** sounds create background and atmosphere, distant thunder echoing the impending tragedy or birdsong to suggest early morning.

You will need to write a **cue sheet** detailing exactly when a sound begins, its volume and duration, as well as the equipment on which it is played. Remember that the audience should hear sounds referenced in the text before the actors mention them. If the line is, '*It sounds as though we are in for a major air raid tonight*', the sound of distant planes must begin well before the line is spoken. Consider the source of the sound and its distance from the stage action.

In *The Cherry Orchard*, the early stage direction is '*Closer, though still distant, a train whistles its approach*'. The speakers must be located to suggest the direction of the station and the volume must create the impression that the train is in the distance. Sound effects should **fade** up and down seamlessly with no audible click or hiss from the equipment. It is often necessary to synchronise sound and lighting.

Your portfoilio or supporting notes should include the research materials, initial ideas, analysis of the textual requirements, a source sheet, a cue sheet, justification of design ideas and an evaluation of the product.

Action point

Check that you can define the difference between acoustic and ambient sound.

Checkpoint 2

How do you mark up a script to indicate **sound** and **light cues**?

Exam practice 20 minutes

For your chosen skill, research the work of professionals in this area. Look at examples of their designs and evaluate them in terms of visual impact, suitability for the period and evocation of mood. Note down what the design says to you in terms of concept.

Notes, journals and presentations

A written analysis of your preparation and performance may be part of the final examination. This can involve the concept notes, supporting notes or journals detailing your progress from initial ideas to final performance or a presentation about your work to a visiting examiner.

The journal/diary

To succeed with this element of the exam you should keep a diary throughout. The importance of process documentation is stressed elsewhere in this guide.

When writing your notes you will need to show **personal insight**. Your response will be richer and more accurate if you have a reflective journal from which to draw. The journal could include:

→ research: website addresses, titles of books or records of conversations, details of visits
→ rationale and decision making
→ photographs and sketches
→ design plans and audits of resources
→ discussions with directors, professionals or teachers
→ rehearsal plans and analysis of rehearsals
→ character development and personal exercises, e.g. on voice or movement
→ health and safety considerations and problem solving.

Writing supporting notes

There must be a clear **rationale** for the choice of text or extract that makes reference to the **whole play**.

You should analyse your extract and casting or design choices. There should be a detailed account of the **research** undertaken, showing an understanding of style, genre, cultural and social context and political influences. The document must detail and analyse the **rehearsal process** or development of the **design element**. It should contain **evaluative** comments and a sense of the **journey** of the piece. There should be a comprehensive analysis of the development of your **skill**, as either an actor or designer. If your supporting notes are to be submitted prior to the performance, evaluate the **potential** of the performance; if the evaluation follows the performance, your comments should refer to the **actual** production.

Example from supporting notes

*'My character, Linda Loman [*Miller's* Death of a Salesman], has an emotional scene at the end of the play. Her husband has committed suicide and the impact of the Epilogue is phenomenal. I was struggling to capture the emotion truthfully so I used Stanislavski's "emotion memory". I needed to find an analogous emotion, as I had obviously not suffered the loss of a husband. I recalled the death of my grandmother, who was very close to me. I collected photographs of her and made a collage of them and I then recalled the moment when my mother broke the news of her death and the emotion I felt at her funeral. This enabled me to find the emotion in performance when I was able to cry real tears, rather than making a false "crying" sound.'*

Links

See Devised theatre, pages 108–121.

Getting the top grade

The diary is important, regardless of the assessment method. If your specification requires supporting notes or a portfolio, you will draw the final document from your ongoing record. There must be a sense of the **personal journey** in your analysis.

Checkpoint 1

What do you understand by **rationale**?

Take note

AQA Unit 2 requires the application of the methods of an **influential practitioner**. This student has given precise detail of her problem, the practitioner whose work she studied and the precise method she employed. There is also a clear evaluation of the performance.

Presentations

Plan your presentation, rehearse it and time it. You should have your portfolio or supporting notes, model box or costume ready and ensure that the moderator/examiner has a clear view of the work. On the day of the exam, make sure that any electrical equipment, computers, lighting boards, etc. are working to avoid any last-minute panic. You should select the presentation method with which you are most comfortable. If you have other people involved in your presentation, you should rehearse with them in advance. The aim is to give the listener a sense of the process of your work and to highlight any key aspects of your design that you want them to note in the performance.

Writing a performance concept

Unit 2A for Edexcel requires a performance concept from candidates. Approaches to this may include:

Research	period, political climate, playwright, character, setting, accent, history
Rehearsal	practitioners, aims, exercises, improvisations
Acting/Role	voice, accent, movement, emotion, relationships
Audience	intended dramatic impact, moments of shock, laughter or tension
Concept	themes, interpretation, intended meaning
Design	research, meaning, colour, texture, line, character, impact
Space	movement, set, design, staging, audience, proxemics

Extract from a performance concept

'Susan from Plenty *by David Hare sc.7*

"Plenty" (1978) tells the story of post-war British decline through the life of one woman, Susan Traherne. The theme of the play is that someone who has had a "good" war finds it impossible to be satisfied in the peace. When Susan was 17, she served as a courier with the French Resistance. The memories of excitement and the bravery haunt her during the rest of her wearying and psychologically debilitating life with a diplomat in the post-war years. Some critics have made comparisons between Susan and Ibsens's Hedda Gabler. Much of Hare's work asserts the power of romantic love to change lives: Susan pines for "code name Lazar", with whom she had a brief and passionate affair in France. In this scene Susan speaks out against the lies and hypocrisies of Suez, and in so doing helps to ruin her husband's diplomatic career.' (141 words)

Watch out!

The performance concept must be a maximum of **500 words**. You will need to plan this carefully to ensure that you include the required elements.

Grade booster

When you are referencing practitioners, it is important to discuss exactly *how* you used their technique. Give a clear example of the approach you took, why you chose this approach and how it improved your performance.

Checkpoint 2

Can you explain what is meant by the **context** of the monologue?

Take note

The candidate references the social, political and historical context of the play, linking this with the character. There is clear evidence that she has researched the playwright and understands the context of the monologue in relation to the play's central themes.

Exam practice   20 minutes   answers: page 143

Supporting notes: Analyse the decisions you have made about the use of space in relation to audience in your production. (You can write from the perspective of an actor or designer.)

Answers
Performing scripted plays

Choosing the play

Checkpoints

1 The actor playing Elizabeth Proctor in *The Crucible* might **pause** during her interrogation in Act III, when Danforth asks whether her husband has ever been unfaithful. An agonised pause before she says *'No, sir'* reflects her emotional turmoil and creates dramatic tension.

2 Set designer: canvas, paint, wood, perspex, cloth, furniture, carpet
Costume designer: fabric, dye, feathers, beads, flowers, fabric paint
Lighting designer: lanterns, gels, stands, dimmers, colour wheels, gobo

Directing decisions

Checkpoints

1 A **rehearsal schedule** is an overall plan for the rehearsal period. It specifies dates, times and location of rehearsals and, ideally, indicates which scenes or sections will be rehearsed. It is important as it enables group members to plan their diaries and reduces confusion.

2 **Blocking** refers to the pre-planned movement of the actors in the space. Some directors prefer to organise the exact movements of the characters in advance and while this gives a clear structure, it can prevent an individual creative response.

Exam practice

Hamlet
Themes: revenge, corruption, insanity
Concept: Hamlet has been driven mad by his father's death and his mother's hasty marriage. He hears voices and imagines events. He is incarcerated in a hospital where the play is enacted by inmates. The concept is based on Peter Weiss's *Marat/Sade*.
Characters: Hamlet – patient; Ensemble – voices and images in his mind; Claudius – psychiatrist and actor of King; Ophelia – nurse and actor of girlfriend; Gertrude – therapist and actor of mother; Horatio – fellow patient and actor of friend.
Rehearsal ideas: research and reading about Artaud, Brook and Weiss. Reading and manic depression and schizophrenia. Physical work using animal characteristics. Re-ordering of 'to be or not to be' speech to create an 'imagined voices' soundscape.
Dramatic intentions: To assault the audience's senses. To use light, sound, physicality and music to highlight themes. To use multiple-role technique for all characters, except Hamlet. To reorder the text, juxtaposing scenes and reallocating dialogue.

Exploration, development and rehearsal

Checkpoints

1 **Impact** refers to the effect of the play on an audience. **Tension** is a build-up of atmosphere or strain in a scene, often leading to a release, outburst or climax. **Climax** is a high point or dramatic moment created through performance or technical techniques.

2 **Staging** refers to the use of the stage space: the relationships and distance between characters, the flow of movement around the space, entrances and exits, moments of stillness to heighten tension, the proxemics and the use of furniture and setting.

Creating a role

Checkpoints

1 **Vocal texture** refers to the variety of vocal tones and volume in a scene, creating diversity and interest.

2 **Eye contact** shows the character's feelings: avoiding eye contact reflects fear or dislike, holding eye contact for a long time can show control or intimidation, eye contact across a space can indicate attraction, flirting or a shared secret. The eyes are very important in performance.

Exam practice

John Proctor in *The Crucible* by Arthur Miller

Proctor is an honest farmer whose one sin haunts him. The play explores the question, 'how can a man live in the face of evil?', that evil being the vindictive witch hunt in Salem. Proctor's character embodies the central premise of the play and his journey covers his relationships with Elizabeth, his wife, and Abigail, his servant/mistress. Proctor is essentially honest and God-fearing; he is also outspoken, suspicious and resentful.

Vocally, Proctor is strong with a rough accent, resonant of English the West Country where his ancestors lived. His voice is cold and suspicious in Act 2 with Elizabeth, and harsh and angry when reprimanding Mary Warren. In Act 3, Proctor's rage erupts and he creates a dramatic climax with his outpouring of anger. In Act 4, in the prison, the anguish, guilt and emotional turmoil must be evoked vocally.

Physically, Proctor begins as confident, upright and strong, yet by Act 4 he is crumpled, broken and has aged disproportionately during his imprisonment. He strides in Act 1, but shuffles in chains in Act 4.

Working as a designer (1)

Checkpoints

1 A **ground plan** is a scaled map of the performance space detailing the entrances and exits and the positions of set and furniture. A ground plan can be used by a lighting designer to indicate lantern positions and lit areas.

Working as a designer (2)

Checkpoints

1 The **costume plot** is a list or chart that shows which characters appear in each scene, what they are wearing and their overall movement throughout the play. This helps track the specific costume needs of every character. It can also identify any potential costume challenges, such as very quick changes between scenes.

Working as a designer (3)

Checkpoints

1 **General cover** is the basic lighting of the whole space, ensuring that the lighting is even and that it lights every part of the set.
2 The accepted shorthand for 'the book' is SFX for a sound effect and LFX for a lighting effect. Each cue is numbered alongside the cue line, e.g. SFX 1 *Don't leave me* – door bangs off stage right. LFX 3 *Go, bid the soldiers shoot* – slow fade to BO 10 seconds.

Notes, journals and presentations

Checkpoints

1 The **rationale** is the justification, reasoning and validation of your decisions.
2 The **context** of the monologue refers to the events in the play before and after the section that highlight the relevance and significance of the speech. Contextualising the speech might also involve comments about the key themes of the play or the playwright's main concerns

Exam practice

Road by Jim Cartwright

We have divided our stage space into sections. Scaffolding will create three high and three low living spaces and in front of this, at floor level, is the road. We have sectioned and defined this by painting the floor. The fact that the road is on the floor level will help the audience to feel included in the play. We are seeking to enhance the relationship with the audience by the use of direct address and this Brechtian technique will be continued by having the actors move among the audience. For example, in Skin-Lad's monologue, he runs down the centre aisle, speaking to the audience from within their space.

We want the living spaces to seem cramped and claustrophobic and to suggest the working-class background by using scaffolding. Poverty is communicated by using the harsh, stark structure and by dressing the rooms with functional and shabby furniture. The cramped space reflects the living conditions of the working classes in Thatcher's Northern England. Each room will be separately lit and this focuses the audience's attention while creating a sense of the community.

Our audience will be students from Years 10 and 11 and we want them to feel involved in the play from the outset. We aim to make effective use of space in the opening sequence; the characters will enter from behind the audience and from the sides. The characters then build parts of the set on the road, leaving trolleys, cones and dustbins behind them. Our intention is to make the audience feel as though the characters are part of their group and to relate the issues of the play to themselves.

The audience will be involved at another key point when Scullery holds out his hand and touches an audience member in the front row on the line *'Watch the kerb, missus!'*. We aim to connect with our audience and to encourage them to empathise with the characters; the close proximity of the audience will enable us to make this connection using eye contact and direct address.

The overall intention for our use of space is to make the audience feel trapped in the community with the characters. The meaning we are seeking to communicate is to encourage the audience to strive for their dreams and not to allow themselves to be confined by their situation.

Revision checklist
Performing scripted plays

By the end of this chapter you should be able to:

1	Understand how to choose a suitably challenging text.	Confident	Not confident **Revise** pages 126–127
2	Recognise the key elements of the directing process.	Confident	Not confident **Revise** pages 128–129
3	Know how to scrutinise a text for meanings and themes.	Confident	Not confident **Revise** page 130
4	Plan a rehearsal with clear aims and techniques.	Confident	Not confident **Revise** pages 130–131
5	List approaches to creating a role.	Confident	Not confident **Revise** pages 132-133
6	Employ appropriate strategies for learning lines.	Confident	Not confident **Revise** pages 132-133
7	Understand the terms 'centre of energy' and 'vocal texture'.	Confident	Not confident **Revise** pages 132-133
8	Understand the role of the designer in the theatre.	Confident	Not confident **Revise** page 134
9	Understand how a designer uses research.	Confident	Not confident **Revise** page 134
10	Know how to create a set design and model box.	Confident	Not confident **Revise** pages 134–135
11	Recognise the importance of colour, texture and proportion in design	Confident	Not confident **Revise** page 135
12	Understand how to create effective masks and make-up.	Confident	Not confident **Revise** pages 136–137
13	Understand how lighting and sound create mood, atmosphere and location.	Confident	Not confident **Revise** pages 138–139
14	Know how to rig lights, create sound effects and write cue sheets.	Confident	Not confident **Revise** pages 138–139
15	List the essential elements of effective suporting notes or portfolio.	Confident	Not confident **Revise** page 140
16	Plan a presentation.	Confident	Not confident **Revise** page 141
17	Plan and write a performance concept for a monolgue or duologue.	Confident	Not confident **Revise** page 141

Responding to live theatre

This chapter focuses on the live theatre production. All specifications include an evaluation of a performance; some exam boards test this at both AS and in the synoptic module at A2. Your ability to reflect critically on the performance of a play demonstrates your knowledge of every aspect of theatre, from the director's concept to the actors' performances and the designers' creative contribution. Some specifications link the analysis of the production at A2 to your understanding of the theories of a practitioner (see pages 30–66) or a study of theatre history (see page 10–25).

This chapter begins by suggesting activities to prepare you for a theatre visit and discusses the semiotics of performance analysis. Further sections cover the taking of notes and early responses to the productions. The chapter concludes with an outline of how to analyse a production in depth. It is important to use the correct terminology when writing about performance (see the Glossary, pages 173–175).

Exam themes

- Understanding of the director's concept
- Reading the signs in performance
- Critical evaluation of acting and design decisions
- Discussion of a production in its social, cultural and political context
- Analysis of a production with reference to a practitioner's theory

Topic checklist

	Edexcel		AQA		WJEC	
	AS	A2	AS	A2	AS	A2
Preparing for the theatre visit	○	●	○		○	
Semiotics: signs and systems	○	●	○		○	
Taking notes and initial responses	○	●	○		○	
Reading the director's concept	○	●	○		○	
Analysing the production	○	●	○		○	

Preparing for the theatre visit

Your ability to respond with clarity and insight is enhanced if you prepare fully for the theatre visit. This section will suggest approaches to the visit that will enable you to appreciate the production fully. Remember that you will probably see the performance only once, so you need to be able to appreciate and evaluate the detail.

The theatre space

Research the location of the performance. It might be a theatre with a history, such as **Drury Lane**. Theatres built at this time were very large and the audience are often a long way from the stage; this will affect your reception of the production. Other theatres have a particular culture or style – the **Royal Court Theatre** is renowned for its new, and frequently controversial, writing.

The stage could have a specific design – **The Crucible** in Sheffield and the **Manchester Royal Exchange** are examples of '**theatre in the round**', while the **Swan Theatre** at Stratford-upon-Avon and **The Globe**, on London's South Bank, are constructed as Elizabethan thrust stages.

The production may not be in a traditional theatre. Street theatre, promenade productions and site-specific productions – in warehouses, mill buildings and disused factories – all have their own unique ambience. The shape of the auditorium and the actor/audience proxemics will shape your response.

Action point

Find the websites for some of the theatres mentioned here. Many of them are interactive, giving you a view of the stage space and a concise history.

Example

Out of Joint's 2004 production of *Macbeth* was set in Africa. The play toured both in the UK and worldwide. Performances took place in various locations, including an old mill in Batley, Yorkshire and a castle in Wales. The production was promenade and some scenes were staged outdoors.

Read the play and research the playwright

It could be argued that reading the play before the performance might spoil your enjoyment. This is a powerful argument. Nevertheless, as the theatre visit is for examination purposes, pre-reading will enable you to consider your expectations prior to seeing the performance. You will be in a position to consider the **director's concept** and to measure this against your own interpretation. The text of a new play, however, may not be published and street theatre, or other improvised performances, will have no published text.

Read as much as you can about the **playwright**. He or she may have a particular style, plays may treat similar subjects or be intrinsically linked to personal experience. **David Hare** is known as a political playwright whereas **Alan Ayckbourn** is synonymous with comedy. **Arthur Miller's** *After the Fall* is based on his marriage to Marilyn Monroe, while **Berkoff's** *East* draws on his personal experience. Other playwrights, for example Caryl Churchill, cannot be assigned to a particular genre or perspective.

Checkpoint 1

What is **promenade theatre**? What is an **auditorium**?

Checkpoint 2

Can you name three plays that have **political arguments**?

Critical reviews

Critics generally review theatre productions, especially in London. It is the critic's job to comment on the play after seeing an early performance at 'press night'. These articles can have a significant effect on the success or failure of the play.

Prior to your visit, read a variety of reviews online – this will give you an idea about what the critics felt. Of course, you must judge the play for yourself, but reading the views of others can stimulate your thinking and provide a benchmark for your opinions.

Programmes and education notes

Programmes vary in their value as a student resource – some, especially in the West End, are expensive yet have little more than cast biographies and numerous adverts. The National Theatre and the RSC produce programmes with a wealth of information about the text and the production, while other companies, for example Out of Joint, the National Theatre and the Manchester Royal Exchange, produce excellent education materials that give a real insight into the production process.

Try to buy a programme or obtain an education pack where the materials are helpful. Most theatres will print a cast list, which is free; make sure you get one of these, as it is important to name actors, designers and directors correctly in your answer.

Action point

Read the review pages of newspapers such as *The Guardian* (Michel Billington), *The Times* (Benedict Nightingale), or the *Evening Standard* (Nicholas de Jongh) every week. This will give you an insight into the way critics write about theatre. It does not matter whether you know the play or not. You can read these in the paper or online.

Watch out!

In your exam answer, do not simply reiterate the critics' comments. The examiner is interested in your own analysis. You could, however, refer to a line from a review as a counterpoint to your own view.

Grade booster

Know the names of actors, designers and directors. Spell them correctly. When referring to an individual on a second occasion, use the surname, e.g. '*Hytner's production*', '*McKellen's performance*'.

Exam practice   30 minutes
answers: page 160

Carry out research into a play that you have seen or are going to see. When was it written and first performed? Is the play typical of the period? What can you discover about the playwright? What else has he/she written? What is the design and capacity of the theatre? Read any reviews that have been published. What are/were your expectations?

Semiotics: signs and systems

The art of analysing performance relies on reading 'signs': this is known as **semiotics**. This section will explain the background and uses of semiotics and show you how to relate them to live theatre productions.

Signs and meaning

The earliest semiotician was **Saussure**, a Frenchman whose theory was based on the assertion that meaning in society is linked to a common understanding of signs. The most obvious of these are letters and writing. The combination of shapes that make up Chinese or Greek writing is understood by people from those countries, but not necessarily by others. A sign, in a language, is a combination of the **word** (*signifier*) and the **image** (*signified*). For example, if you read the combination of the letters f-i-s-h you conjure up a picture in your head of a **fish** – not a cat or a spoon!

In the 1960s, **Barthes** developed semiology to include signs other than language, '*any system of signs . . . images, gestures, musical sounds, objects, and the complex associations of all of these, which form the content of ritual, convention or public entertainment*'. This reading of **multiple signs** in performance enables audiences to interpret the production.

Take note

The Czech, **Kowzan**, identified 13 sign systems for performance analysis. Eight were about acting and five about technical elements.

What are the signs in a performance?

Words	what is said
Intonation	how the words are delivered
Movement	of the actors in the space
Proxemics	staging, positioning, spatial relationships
Gesture	detailed, small movements
Setting	design, décor, furniture
Properties	objects on the set or used by the characters, their positioning
Lighting	colour, angle, intensity, changes, darkness, light
Costume	shape, colour, period, texture
Sound	effects, background noise
Music	creation of mood and atmosphere, implicit in the text

When watching a play you are reading these signs all the time. These signs can be further categorised as **iconic** and **symbolic**. An **iconic** sign is a literal picture of the concept, e.g. the envelope that indicates a new message on your mobile. A **symbolic** sign has no obvious connection but is understood by everyone, e.g. the tick on Nike products.

Checkpoint 1

List three **iconic** and three **symbolic** signs in everyday use.

→ In theatre, iconic signs usually indicate realism: period furniture or costume, doorbells ringing, food and drink.
→ Symbolic signs in the theatre **suggest** rather than **indicate**: lighting changes to reflect mood, a ladder to represent climbing a mountain, dramatic music to herald the entrance of a villain in melodrama.

Often there will be signs that are both iconic and symbolic.

→ In Miller's *Death of a Salesman,* a refrigerator has a central position in the kitchen and in one sense it is **iconic** – literally a kitchen appliance that locates the scene. However, it can also be seen as **symbolic**, representing the aspirations of Willy Loman to achieve the material possessions associated with the American Dream.

→ In a production of *The Overwhelming,* at the National Theatre, a single skull, positioned on a high shelf, although never referred to, served as a visual reminder of the images of Rwandan genocide. A table of stacked cabbages similarly evoked this image: in a climatic 'coup de théâtre', the cabbages are hacked with machetes and simultaneously a shutter drops to reveal shelves of bleached skulls.

Mise-en-scène

This phrase means 'put in the scene'. Interpretation of the performance involves 'reading' these signs. The director, designers and actors have made decisions about every image that you see. Everything from the positioning of a fruit bowl to off-stage battle sounds has been planned so that an audience will understand the intended meaning.

Checkpoint 2

What is a **coup de théâtre**? Can you analyse the sign systems in this example?

Links

See Stanislavski, page 30.

Grade booster

In your notes on the live performance, record the iconic and symbolic signs employed by the director. These can be linked to the overall concept.

Exam practice   15 minutes

Consider a production that you have seen or been involved in. Make a list of how signs were used to shape the understanding of the director's interpretation.

Taking notes and initial responses

Here we look at ways that you might record your thoughts about a production. This section will suggest approaches to 'reading' the performance as you watch it and methods that enable you to formulate your opinions in a general sense. Later sections will look at more specific analysis and structuring answers.

During the performance

It is tempting to scribble frantically throughout the productions, noting every nuance of acting, directing or design. This is distracting to both actors and other audience members and it means that you are not **involved** in the theatrical experience. It is impossible to be emotionally engaged or politically affected if only half your mind is on the stage action.

You should, nevertheless, focus on the **signs** of the performance – notice the set design, the lighting rig and the costume plot and be aware of the director's concept and intended meaning. If there is an interval, you could note down key points briefly; the journey home on the train or coach is another good opportunity for discussion and note-making.

Checkpoint 1

What do you understand by **set design**, **lighting rig** and **costume plot**?

Initial responses

This response should take place as soon as possible after the performance – ideally the next day. You may have seen the production alone or with family members, but most students visit the theatre with their A-level group. Prepare for the discussion thoroughly; you will get more from the group analysis if you have considered your opinions meticulously. Below are three different approaches to organising your first thoughts.

1 De Bono's Six Thinking Hats
This framework focuses thinking into categories and it helps to compartmentalise your first impressions of the performance.

White hat:	**Pure facts** such as the date, the name of the theatre, the company, the director, play title, the plot and the genre.
Red hat:	**Feelings** such as laughter, tears, anger, frustration, boredom or empathy.
Black hat:	**Negatives**, critical comments on the production.
Yellow hat:	**Positives**, aspects of the production that impressed you.
Green hat:	**Alternatives**, how could this have been done differently?
Blue hat:	**Planning**, having completed the 'thinking', use the material to plan your notes.

Links

See www.debonothinkingsystems.com for more information.

2 Visual, emotional and thematic moments
Consider the production and select three moments that had an effect on you and which you recall vividly.

→ One **visual** moment, when something you saw had an impact (e.g. a dramatic lighting effect).

→ One **emotional** moment, when *you* felt an emotional response (e.g. you were moved to tears or laughter).

→ One **thematic** moment, when something on the stage reflected an important theme in the play (e.g. a symbolic sequence of movements that mirrors a key theme).

Analyse these moments by considering **why** they made an impact, **how** the impact was created theatrically and the **meaning** that can be understood. This exercise is most effective if the whole group carries it out. The sharing of the three selected moments highlights many significant sections of the performance.

3 Mind map

Many students are visual learners and prefer to record their ideas in charts and pictures. Mind maps are very effective ways of setting out thoughts and shaping jumbled information. Write the name of the play in the centre of a large sheet of blank paper (A3), draw branches from the title and write **along the line** the aspect of the performance. Now, from each line you draw further branches to describe each thought. To make the map visual you can add coloured images that jog your memory.

Checkpoint 2

How would you define **impact** in this context?

Action point

Try this exercise for a play that you saw some time ago, perhaps a production that you are not studying for the exam. The moments that you remember in detail will be the ones that made a significant impact.

Grade booster

Analyse your response to the production in detail. Note specific examples. This will enable you to support your comments concisely in the exam or exploration notes.

Exam practice   15 minutes

Create a mind map for the most recent production that you have seen. See how much detail you can include and add some colour and symbols to help you to remember details.

Reading the director's concept

This section will look at how you can understand the overall concept and the director's interpretation. It is not always immediately obvious – a skilled director will weave themes and concepts into the production with subtlety. Your purpose as a member of the audience is to **receive** the production and **read** signs.

Reception and production

Checkpoint 1

What do the words **reception** and **production** mean?

The play **text** exists as a written document. The director shapes an interpretation of the dialogue, plot and actions indicated by the playwright: this is the **production**. An audience experience the performance: this is the **reception**. As a receiver of the play, you should be open to the interpretation yet you should be critically evaluative. Your prior reading of the text will establish what the writer provides and what the director has created. This is the key to the **concept**. For example, the text of Sarah Kane's *4.48 Psychosis* has no stage directions, no suggestion of locations or design and even the dialogue is not assigned to a specific character. Therefore, any production of the play will be truly the director's interpretation.

Conversely, in *A Doll's House*, Ibsen is highly specific about the physical environment and the stage action is explicit in the directions. This does not mean that every production of the play will be the same – nothing could be further from the truth. Each production represents the director's interpretation of the playwright's work.

As **receivers**, each audience member interprets the play according to their emotional and personal experience.

Meaning, message, concept

We have established elsewhere in this guide that there is a difference between **meaning** and **message**. Playwrights create works that have complex and subtle meanings. Even political playwrights like **Brecht** rarely deliver a **message** but rather lead the audience to an understanding of the situation, inviting **judgement**. We have also explored the perception of the **director's concept** (pages 88–89) and you will have discussed the concept for your practical examination.

Checkpoint 2

Can you name three contemporary directors who have not been discussed in this guide?

Terminology

Auteur is French for **author**. The term suggests that the director has become a 'co-author'.

A director approaches the text from a particular standpoint, which he/she shapes through the work with actors and designers. The concept is a combination of the meaning intended by the writer and the contemporary relevance of the text to the intended audience. Some directors are described as **auteur directors**, who produce versions of the play that are so far away from the original intention that they are almost rewritten, while others are more '**playwright's directors**', who faithfully produce the text to make clear the writer's intentions. The director will test the concept during rehearsal, ensuring that it is viable.

Examples

Robert Lepage's *Elsinore* is a good example of the work of an **auteur director**. The original text, *Hamlet*, was reshaped dramatically. Peter Hall could be described as a **playwright's director**, with his recent seasons at Bath presenting classics in a fresh yet authentic style.

Reading the concept and revealing the intention

Ask yourself the following questions:

→ What does the setting and staging say to me?

→ What is the focus of the relationships?

→ How are characters represented? Where is my sympathy?

→ Which key moments evoked an emotional response? What did they tell me about the interpretation?

→ Did any technical effects focus my attention on specific aspects of the play?

→ What was my immediate emotional response at the end of the performance?

Answers to these questions will focus your thinking and give you an initial impression of how *you* **received** the production.

Adapter Ben Power speaks of the very contemporary value of Headlong's 2004 production of *Faustus* in which Marlowe's characters and the world of contemporary art occupy the same hellish landscape.

'We didn't want to position Dr Faustus alongside a modern narrative of someone literally selling their soul to the devil, that would have been too straight-forward, too pat … We wanted a modern situation which had the controversy, the whiff of danger, which necromancy had to an Elizabethan audience, but which also had a heightened quality, a certain poetry. It is these qualities which attracted us to the world of modern art and to the Chapman Brothers in particular.

'Our aim was to tell a story which engaged the audience emotionlly and intellectually, which provoked, which was theatrical, modern and metaphorical; a story which examined the irrevocable act, the deed which cannot be undone. In short, we aimed to create a rough modern equivalent of the Marlowe, to harness it to the original and to sit back and see what connections and collisions occured for the audience.'

Action point

Consider a play that you have studied or read but have not seen in performance. Note your ideas for a re-interpretation of the text. What might it say to a modern audience? Where could it be set? Will this concept be viable for the whole text?

Exam practice   20 minutes   answers: page 161

Write a concise paragraph outlining the director's interpretation of the play you have seen in performance. Give a clear indication of how and why you came to this reading of the production.

Analysing the production (1)

The next two sections will outline the facets of performance analysis. Earlier sections have prepared you for the theatre visit and examined methods of reading the signs and the director's intentions. We will now look closely at the design and technical elements and at the precise evaluation of production values and of performance skills.

Design and technical elements

The performance space

Each space has its own ambience; this will influence how the audience receive the production. Spaces can be formal or informal – either seated in a large theatre facing towards a stage, positioned in the round or as a promenade audience. If there is no barrier, such as a raised stage, a curtain or proscenium arch, the audience are not separated from the action.

Actors might appear to speak directly to you as an individual in an informal space whereas in a large auditorium you will be unlikely to observe the fine detail of facial expression. You should record your feelings about the space in your notes.

Set design

The primary function of the set design is to create the environment for the play. It does this in two ways: it reflects the themes and the director's concept and it provides the necessary functions for the text. If there is no curtain you will be able to see the set before the play begins. Think about what it says to you. What are the features that strike you?

Consider the following in your analysis:

→ Is the set **symbolic**, **expressionistic**, **naturalistic** or **composite**?
→ Does it reflect a particular **period**?
→ What is on the **floor**? (Many students ignore the floor of the stage.)
→ What is implied about the **off-stage world**?
→ How does the set underpin the **concept** and **style** of the play?
→ What key features of the set create **theatrical impact**?
→ What meanings do **colour**, **texture** and **shape** convey?

Lighting

Lighting has various functions, according to the type of performance. Lighting design, like set design, is integrated with the overall concept. Light is particularly important in creating or enhancing the mood and atmosphere, but it also indicates elements of the narrative, for example time of day or climate. It is important to refer to lighting terms and equipment correctly at this level.

Lights will have been positioned (rigged) to illuminate the space and to support textual references. The source of the light is important –

Take note

Edexcel Unit 4 involves analysis of a live production of a play written between 525BC and AD65 **or** 1564 and 1720 **or** 1828 and 1914. Researching the original performance conditions is part of the study for this unit. Examination questions require an evaluation of the live production with reference to the original performance conditions. Students studying this unit should refer to the chapter on Drama and theatre in context, pages 10–28, when revising for this examination.

Action point

If you have access to the internet, look for photographs of previous productions of the play. You will be able to compare and analyse different designers' interpretations of the setting.

Links

For some useful terminology and a discussion of lighting design, see page 138.

whether the sun is streaming through a window or a single candle lights the room, the light must appear to be coming from that source. **Naturalistic** lighting will be a subtle recreation of sunlight, moonlight or indoor lamps whereas **expressionistic** lighting will reflect the play's themes in a more obvious way.

Consider the following in your analysis:

→ How did the lighting reflect the **style** and **concept**?
→ Where were the light **sources**?
→ How did the lighting design enhance the **mood** and **atmosphere**?
→ What did lighting reveal about **location**, **time** and **climate**?
→ How and why did the lighting **states** change?
→ When and how did the lighting make an **impact** on you?

Costume

Costume reflects character, period, social class and theme. Like all other design elements, the costume relates to the theme. Some designers costume every character in shades of the same colour: this will undoubtedly reflect the director's view of the play. A production of *The Seagull* at the RSC used whites, creams and beiges in a range of tones and textures throughout the costume plot. Costume shows age and rank; changes of costume may signal to the audience that a character has lost status or grown old.

Make sure that you note the finer details of costume, shoes, accessories and wigs. Be aware that costume decisions have been made about each item of clothing, even in a modern-dress production.

Consider the following in your analysis:

→ How did the costumes relate to the overall **concept** for the production?
→ How did costume indicate **character**, **social class** or **rank**?
→ Did the costume create a **period** or was the design timeless or modern?
→ How were **colour**, **style** and **texture** (materials) used to create the meaning?
→ How did the costumes **relate** to each other?
→ Was there any aspect of the costume plot that made a particular **impact** on you?

Checkpoint 1

List some terms that can be used when writing about lighting design.

Terminology

A lighting state refers to the colour, intensity and areas that are lit in any one lighting cue. When the lights change in any way this is a new **state**.

Watch out!

Avoid simplistic statements about colour. Designers rarely costume a character in red because they are angry or in green because they exhibit jealousy.

Examiner's secrets

Take care when writing about modern productions. Students will often suggest that the costumes are 'normal' or 'everyday'. This implies that the actors have simply turned up in their own clothes! A designer will have made a decision about every item and it is your job to analyse why and to judge the effectiveness of the choice.

Checkpoint 2

How can **material** and **texture** signal a specific meaning?

Sound and music

Sound relates to on-stage effects – e.g. a telephone ringing, cars arriving or thunderstorms – and to the creation of mood or expectation. Music is often composed specifically for the production and many theatres have an area where musicians play live, even if the audience do not see them. Music creates atmosphere and relates to the theme in the same way as light and set design. Felix Cross's haunting choral climax to *Talking to Terrorists* at the Royal Court took the Western hymn 'O little town of Bethlehem' and gave it spine-tingling Middle Eastern musical inflections.

Consider the following in your analysis:

→ What was the **purpose** of the sound effects?

→ Did the effects arise from the **text** or were they **additional**?

→ Were any sound effects abstract, created to augment the **mood**?

→ What did sound communicate about the world **beyond the stage**?

→ Was any of the sound or music **live**? Did actors create it? How effective was this?

→ How did music create **atmosphere** or reflect the **themes**?

→ Did the sound or music have an **impact** on you at any point?

Exam practice 30 minutes   answers: page 161

Make a list of the answers to the questions on sound and music. For each answer, indicate in note form exactly what you observed and whether it was effective.

Analysing the production (2)

This section considers the analysis of the actor's performance; many students find this quite difficult. Initially we will reflect on the impact made by a specific actor and then we will focus on the language of analysis and the assessment of skills.

Creating the role

The practitioner Stanislavski broke new ground in his approach to the science of acting. Today we go to the theatre expecting the actor to be convincing in his/her characterisation. It is possible to see many productions of the same play, yet each performance is unique; the writer of this guide has seen *Hamlet* over 30 times!

The actor creates a role using a complex and, at times, indefinable range of skills and techniques. What singles out the truly exceptional performers is a distinctive quality that engages the audience. Each actor's performance should be consistent with the concept and in tune with the style or genre. There are occasions when you might feel that an individual actor's performance style jarred in some way. For example, in a naturalistic production of *The Seagull*, if the role of elderly Sorin is performed in a grandiose style, more appropriate to melodrama, the performance disrupts the natural rhythm of the piece.

When you are evaluating a performance, your first consideration should be how effectively the role is created.

Checkpoint 1

What style of acting would you expect to see in **melodrama**? How would this be different from **naturalism**?

The actor and the text

If you know the play well you will have your own idea of how it could be presented. The text is the actor's primary means of communication; the actor mediates between the playwright and the audience when performing the text. There will be scenes or speeches that have particular importance and you should consider these moments when assessing the actor's performance.

If you were analysing a production of *The Crucible* you might take particular note of the way Abigail performs in the trial scene in Act III. Your critical response to the performance of Liz Morden in *Our Country's Good* could take account of her speech in the prison that opens Act II. The actor will have considered his/her interpretation of the text, in collaboration with the director. This may be very different from your own ideas but nevertheless valid and exciting.

Physical and vocal skills

The actor inhabits the role physically and vocally. Your analysis will judge how these elements of the performance combine to create the role.

Physical skills include:

→ walking
→ sitting or standing
→ posture
→ stillness
→ gesture
→ fast-paced comic movement, e.g. in farce
→ fight scenes
→ physical theatre.

Vocal skills cover:

→ pace, tone, pitch
→ volume and silence
→ accent
→ modulation and intonation
→ pause.

When you are analysing a performance it is important to link these skills to specific moments from the production and to reflect on the meaning created. It is particularly interesting to comment on vocal and physical skills if you are discussing an actor who plays more than one role.

Example from exam answer

'For each role, Monica Pearce created a different posture and tone of voice. The transformation from confident executive to abused victim was incredible. In the first role, she moved with an assured swagger and had upright posture at the desk; her impatient drumming of fingernails belittled Peter. Her voice was deep, with a precise and clipped delivery. As Mary, the battered wife, she shuffled across the space, glancing furtively around and rubbing her hands in a repetitive nervous gesture. The vocal tone was high-pitched and insecure, almost whispered, yet audible. She looked downwards, avoiding eye contact with other characters; the moment when she slowly took the baby's rattle from her pocket was filled with pathos.'

Relationships

The actor's on-stage relationships relate to the concept and are communicated in a variety of ways. Actors will use a range of techniques to convey relationships, the relative positioning in the space, eye contact, or lack of it, facial expression, vocal tone, physical contact or the avoidance of contact. Every nuance of the performance builds the picture of the characters' relationships.

When you are considering the presentation of character, you should look for these exact details. In a production of *Hedda Gabler*, Hedda brushed away her husband's attempts to touch her; this gives an immediate insight into the relationship. Sustained eye contact can suggest love but can signal disgust or hatred with different accompanying facial expression.

Example from an exam answer

'Although the actor's face was often gaunt and completely emotionless, when he made eye contact with Sarah he seemed to glow inwardly, his face brightened and a wry smile filtered across his lips. This showed how he was suppressing his love for her.'

The actor will also form a relationship with the audience; this is affected by the stage space. Actors may narrate parts of the story, making direct eye contact with the audience. There may be sections when a character confides in the audience, perhaps a tragic **monologue** or a **comic aside**. At other times, a performer connects with the audience through comic timing or emotional engagement. When you are analysing the audience response you should comment on your personal response and the collective reaction.

Checkpoint 2

What are **monologues** and **asides**?

The live performance with reference to original conditions

→ Research the physical shape of the theatre, the social conditions of the audience and the concerns of playwrights during that era.
→ Take note of the question set, and structure your answer carefully to ensure that you answer it.
→ Focus your answer on the play that you have seen in the theatre not on the historical information.
→ Reference to the original production conditions should serve to focus your answer on how the modern director has shaped the production.

For example, in 2007, the Octagon Theatre, Bolton and Northern Broadside collaborated on a new interpretation of Aristophanes, *Lysistrata* (a set text for Unit 4 Edexcel). The following extract indicates how knowledge of the original production conditions informs the evaluation of the live performance:

'Lysistrata is an anti-war play. Athens, where the play was originally set, had been at war with Sparta since 431BC. Aristophanes' plays demonstrate his criticisms of the attitudes of leading figures of Athenian society, either for their support of the war or for their philosophies. The production I saw was set in a mill town in northern Britain against a backdrop of racial violence; the women want to stop violence on the streets and occupy the factory: this is Aristophanes' Acropolis and its treasury. The set was a simple rostrum and scaffold with a backing and floor cloth marked out as a street map. In 411BC Aristophanes' play would have been presented in an amphitheatre with the audience a long way from the action whereas we were seated around a thrust stage and felt intimately involved with the action.'

Exam practice   30 minutes   answers: page 161

Write two paragraphs analysing the contribution made to the production by one actor and explain how he/she used performance skills to engage you.

Answers
Responding to live theatre

Preparing for the theatre visit

Checkpoints

1 In **promenade** performances, the audience follows the action to different parts of the performance space. The **auditorium** is the area in a theatre where the audience sit (or stand).

2 There are many examples of **political** play writing, including:

- *The Permanent Way* by David Hare, which exposed the deficiencies of Railtrack in four major train crashes.
- *Stuff Happens*, which was an indictment of the decision to go to war in Iraq.
- David Edgar's *Destiny* (1976) about the National Front during the period that saw the birth of the Anti-Nazi League and Rock Against Racism in Britain.
- David Mamet's *Glengarry Glen Ross*, which is about selling real estate but also about ambition and deception.

Exam practice

Kindertransport by Diane Samuels at Hampstead Theatre
First produced: Soho Theatre Company produced *Kindertransport* at the Cockpit, 1993. The play was co-winner of the 1992 Verity Bargate Award, winner of the 1993 Meyer Whitworth Award.
Diane Samuels went to Cambridge, then worked as a drama teacher in inner London secondary schools and then as an education officer at the Unicorn Theatre for Children before becoming a full-time writer in 1992.
Historical background: When the first 30,000 Jews were detained and placed in concentration camps, the Movement for the Care of Children from Germany was formed in England. The rescue operation, known as 'Kindertransport', would see nearly 10,000 unaccompanied Jewish children travel from Germany to England where they would settle into English families who wanted to help. Of course, most never saw their homeland or their parents again. It is estimated that some 2,500 Kinder eventually emigrated to North America.
Other works: Recently, *Mrs Gorsky* about an American mother, housewife and communist spy, for the Birmingham Rep Theatre. Samuels was awarded a Science on Stage and Screen Award by the Wellcome Trust in 2001 to undertake an experimental collaboration with three medical specialists, playwright Sarah Woods and visual artist Alexa Wright to make an innovative piece of documentary, visual theatre about the nature of pain. She is currently a participant in Exiled Writers Ink's writing and dialogue group 'Across the Divide' for Jewish, Muslim, Israeli and Palestinian writers.
Hampstead Theatre: The auditorium is designed to be as flexible as possible in both staging and seating configurations. The seating capacity can increase from 140 to 325. The space is intimate and the audience are never far from the action.

Reviews:

- The play is an unforgettably moving experience.
- A plot twist in the second act, however, gives the piece real dramatic bite.
- This harrowing tale of loss and survival is sensitively directed by Polly Teale and presented by the excellent Shared Experience Theatre Company.
- Shared Experience puts a living past upon which no dust settles in front of us and leaves us to make our own judgements. This is theatre at its most truthful.

Expectations: I expect the play to be harrowing at times but engaging and with a powerful message. I wonder what the plot twist at the end will be. I also expect there to be significant use of physical images, as I know that this is a feature of Shared Experience's style. I am anticipating that the play will ask questions that I will be thinking about long after I leave the theatre.

Semiotics: signs and systems

Checkpoints

1 **Iconic** signs: the disabled badge; a wheelchair; fish and chips.
   Symbolic signs: no-entry sign; a red cross; a green light.

2 A **coup de théâtre** is a sudden and unexpected event that startles the audience. The single skull signified the Rwandan genocide; this is the iconic image associated with the horrific event. The designer subtly placed the skull on the set but no reference was made to it so the audience made the connections. The cabbages were shaped and stacked like the pictures of skulls with which the audience were familiar. When they were brutally hacked with the machetes, the audience connected the act with the destruction of people so the cabbages were, for that instant, human heads. The shutter dropping made a crashing sound, which drew attention to the revealed skulls. Thus, the connection was reinforced. The play ended but the system of signs communicated to the audience that the massacre in Rwanda had begun.

Taking notes and initial responses

Checkpoint

1 **Set design** includes the colour, shape, texture and structure of the performance space, including entrances and exits, furniture and set dressing.
   The **lighting rig** is the positioning of the lanterns on the lighting bars above the space and in the auditorium.
   A **costume plot** is the overall appearance of the costumes when seen together. It includes each individual costume that one actor wears and the necessary changes. A costume plot will plan and time every costume change.

2 **Impact** refers to a moment or section that had a strong or lasting effect on you as a member of the andience.

Reading the director's concept

Checkpoints

1 **Reception**: the way in which something is received. **Production**: the way in which something has been made.
2 Nicholas Hytner, Artistic Director of the National Theatre; Michael Boyd, Artistic Director, RSC; Phyllida Lloyd; Deborah Warner; Richard Eyre; Trevor Nunn; Jude Kelly.

Exam practice

Comfort me with Apples by Nell Leyshon, directed by Lucy Bailey
The play explored the parallel between the loss of family farming communities in rural England and the sterility of modern society. The production examined family relationships and the relationship with the land. There was an elemental quality to the concept. The stage floor resembled the earth, even when the scene was in a room. Trees soared into the air, but were barren and the stage was covered with real apples, the smell infusing the air in the theatre. There was an atmosphere of decay pervading the production – family relationships had disintegrated and the unpicked apples were decomposing.

The meaning created by the director was that modern society has lost its way and the values of the past have been eroded. The commuter villages that have replaced the apple orchards are sterile, just as the family in the play had become fragmented and emotionally fruitless.

Analysing the production (1)

Checkpoints

1 Lighting terms include: gel, lantern, fresnel, spotlight, birdie, gobo, cross-fade, wash, blackout, state, fade.
2 **Material** and **texture** can signify:
   • wealth or royalty: velvet, satin, and ermine
   • sexuality: fishnet, leather and silk
   • authority: sharply tailored wool suits, crisp cotton shirts.

Exam practice

• The sound created the location: cicadas, birdsong, lapping sea.
• Some sounds were indicated by the text: thunderstorm, gunfire. Others were additional: car brakes screeching, tolling of a church bell.
• The sound of the sea and the birds created an idyllic mood, which was broken by the events in the play, signified by the gunfire and gathering storm.
• The sound of cars, police sirens and the loud music and raised voices from the club created the world beyond the stage. There was also the sound of a baby crying.

• The music enhanced the atmosphere while also suggesting the location. At one point, the actors sang drunkenly. The song was a discordant version of the tune used earlier in the play. This signified the destruction of the natural order by the violent events.
• The most significant impact of the sound design came when the baby suddenly stopped crying after a series of gunshots. No reference was made to this in the text and the audience were left to draw their own conclusions.

Analysing the production (2)

Checkpoints

1 The acting in **melodrama** would be exaggerated with grand gestures, many lines would be addressed to the audience and there would be few subtle moments. **Naturalistic** acting would recreate the character and setting exactly. Voice and movement would be completely believable and gestures would capture the individual characteristics of the role.
2 A **monologue** is a long speech by one actor; if the actor is alone on the stage the speech is known as a **soliloquy**. An **aside** is a line delivered to the audience but not heard by the other characters on stage. Asides are features of comedy, especially in Shakespearean and Restoration plays.

Exam practice

Measure for Measure: Théâtre de Complicité, 2006
I was particularly engaged by Ajay Naidu, who played Lucio. His use of exaggerated gesture and movements captured the audience's attention and enabled them to understand the humour in the text. Lucio was a comedic character. When he spoke to the Duke, who was dressed as a Friar, without realising who he was, he played on the sexual innuendo – '. . . *was to put a ducat in her clack-dish* . . .' – with a vulgar sexual gesture and a mime of drinking. This actor had the ability to command the stage whenever he entered. His movements were swift and agile; he leapt onto a ladder or bounded across the stage. The actor's physical work was in the style of Complicité, whose approach is non-naturalistic.

His voice was also effective. A clipped delivery with a light vocal tone kept the comic mood to all his scenes. He often addressed the audience directly, the informality of his tone engaging us in his comical activities. The actor was most effective in holding a pause, often accompanied by hilarious facial expressions. This added to the absurdity of the scenes; he had exact comic timing. His posture always reflected his personality; he held a particular position for several seconds before moving sharply. Lucio's mischievous nature was captured physically, vocally and expressively in this performance.

Revision checklist
Responding to live theatre

1	Understand how the theatre space will influence the performance style.	Confident	Not confident **Revise** page 146
2	Appreciate the importance of researching the work of the playwright.	Confident	Not confident **Revise** page 146
3	Use critical reviews to sharpen your analytical skills.	Confident	Not confident **Revise** page 147
4	Determine which resources will be of use in preparing for the theatre visit.	Confident	Not confident **Revise** page 147
5	Understand the term 'semiotics' and its system of signs.	Confident	Not confident **Revise** page 148
6	Identify the differences between the terms 'icon' and 'symbol'.	Confident	Not confident **Revise** pages 148–149
7	Define 'coup de théâtre' and 'mise-en-scène'.	Confident	Not confident **Revise** page 149
8	Understand how to read the signs in the different aspects of performance.	Confident	Not confident **Revise** page 150
9	Use de Bono's Six Thinking Hats to analyse a performance.	Confident	Not confident **Revise** page 150
10	Identify visual, emotional and thematic moments from a production.	Confident	Not confident **Revise** pages 150–151
11	Use a mind mapping technique to record responses.	Confident	Not confident **Revise** page 151
12	Define production and reception in relation to theatrical performances.	Confident	Not confident **Revise** page 152
13	Understand the process of establishing the director's concept.	Confident	Not confident **Revise** page 152
14	Appreciate the differences between types of director.	Confident	Not confident **Revise** page 153
15	Analyse the technical elements of the production using the correct terminology.	Confident	Not confident **Revise** pages 154–155
16	Understand how music and sound create meaning.	Confident	Not confident **Revise** page 156
17	Evaluate voice, movement and gesture in specific detail.	Confident	Not confident **Revise** page 158
18	Understand how to evaluate relationships in the performance.	Confident	Not confident **Revise** pages 158–159

By the end of this chapter you should be able to:

Resources

This chapter offers some final information and advice as you prepare for your AS and A2 exams. The first section lists and explains the **assessment objectives** used by examiners to determine your grade. It is very important that you know and understand how your work will be assessed. There is also a section giving final tips for success in all areas of the examination, not simply the written exam. This section covers coursework, performance exams and written exams. Finally, a **glossary** details the important practitioners and terminology.

Exam themes

It is useful to have your own copy of the exam specification. You can obtain one from the board's publication department or by downloading the specification from the board's website. You can also obtain past papers, which are very helpful in preparing for your final exam.

AQA
Publications Department, Stag Hill House, Guildford, Surrey, GU2 5XJ
www.aqa.org.uk

Edexcel
Edexcel Publications, Adamsway, Mansfield, Nottinghamshire, NG18 4FN
www.edexcel.org.uk

WJEC
245 Western Avenue, Cardiff, CF5 2YX
www.wjec.co.uk

Topic checklist

	Edexcel		AQA		WJEC	
	AS	A2	AS	A2	AS	A2
Assessment objectives	○	●	○	●	○	●
Final tips	○	●	○	●	○	●

Assessment objectives

In each of the specifications, there are four assessment objectives, which are common to AS and A2 level examinations. Look carefully at your specification to see the exact percentages that are examined for each unit of the course. The assessment objectives cover all elements of the A level course.

WJEC

AO1 Demonstrate the application of performance and/or production skills through the realisation of drama and theatre

AO2 Demonstrate knowledge and understanding of practical and theoretical aspects of drama and theatre using appropriate terminology

AO3 Interpret plays from different periods and genres

AO4 Make critical and evaluative judgements of live theatre

Edexcel

AO1 Demonstrate the application of performance and/or production skills through the realisation of drama and theatre

AO2 Demonstrate knowledge and understanding of practical and theoretical aspects of drama and theatre using appropriate terminology

AO3 Interpret plays from different periods and genres

AO4 Make critical and evaluative judgements of live theatre

AQA

AO1 Demonstrate the application of performance and/or production skills through the creation and realisation of drama and theatre

AO2 Demonstrate knowledge and understanding of practical and theoretical aspects of drama and theatre using appropriate terminology

AO3 Interpret plays from different periods and genres

AO4 Make critical and evaluative judgements of live theatre

Quality of written communication

The quality of written communication is assessed in all AS and A2 assessment units where candidates are required to produce extended written material. You should:

→ ensure that text is legible and that spelling, punctuation and grammar are accurate so that meaning is clear
→ select and use a form and style of writing appropriate to purpose and to complex subject matter
→ organise relevant information clearly and coherently, using specialist vocabulary when appropriate.

Final tips

This section gives you some final hints to help you to achieve in this examination. The advice is not confined to the written exam because a significant part of all A level Drama and Theatre Studies specifications is the practical performance of scripted or devised theatre. There are some words of advice about portfolios and notes – the coursework elements.

Coursework

→ Keep a journal, diary or log throughout the process – do not leave the writing until the last minute.

→ Try to allow time for your teacher/lecturer to read a draft so that you can act on their advice.

→ Research and read around the text or theme so that you can demonstrate your wider knowledge in the coursework.

→ Consider the most effective way to communicate your ideas. Continuous prose is not the only method that you can use.

→ Remember to evaluate and analyse when you are writing about devised or scripted performance – do not simply *narrate* the process.

→ Make sure that you are clear about the headings and structure given by the examination board.

→ Read through the coursework carefully to check for errors before handing it in!

Practical examinations

The chapters on Devised theatre (pages 108–121) and Performing scripted plays (pages 126–141) have advice about the whole process. You should read these before and during the process. The following points are the key things to remember:

→ Choose the theme or text carefully and not in a hurry.
→ Manage group work with sensitivity and structure to avoid conflict.
→ Define roles and responsibilities early in the process.
→ Research your theme and role in detail.
→ Be clear about your rehearsal aims and set objectives at the end of each session.
→ Make sure that you attend all rehearsals.
→ Learn lines (for the scripted play) well before the examination.
→ Work on specific acting or design skills to improve your performance.
→ Be organised and well prepared on the day of the examination.

Take note

A very good mark in the practical exam and for the coursework elements will put you in a strong position before the final written examinations. You have the chance to gain marks at regular points during the course and you should ensure that you take advantage of this, especially if your strengths lie in performance or design rather than in written examinations.

Exam revision

Some Drama and Theatre Studies examinations allow you to take notes on texts or productions or an annotated text into the exam. You should regard the preparation of your text or notes as having equal importance with revision.

- → Well-prepared, legible and appropriate notes will enable you to locate information quickly in the exam; jumbled notes will slow you down in the exam.

- → Annotate your text in conjunction with revising the work on the play; in the exam you will find that you know exactly where to find the scene or moment that supports your answer.

- → Notes on live theatre productions should be clear, readable and concise. Do not copy out pre-prepared answers: you should be equipped to address the question set in the exam. **Colour code** or divide your notes into **sections** so that you can access them quickly. **Diagrams** and **charts** are often useful ways to summarise information effectively.

- → Create notes on live theatre compared with the original productions by creating a diagram that evaluates key scenes from the live performance with reference to original production conditions. For each scene indicate:

  - → how it was performed live, with your **evaluative comments**

  - → how it might have been performed originally.

> **Example**
>
> *Much Ado About Nothing* (The Church)
> - → RSC 2006 – cross towered from flies, echo effect, dimmed lighting
> - → Globe – daylight, actors bring on torches to indicate darkness, inner stage used as altar, no scenery

Revision techniques

- → Mind maps or charts
- → Revision cards condensing information
- → Read, cover, repeat – useful for facts or dates
- → Revise a topic, then answer a past paper to test your knowledge
- → Colour code information to categorise themes

All revision should be *active*. Re-reading the same page or lying in the sun with a book open will not ensure that your brain has assimilated the information.

Examination technique

- → Make sure that you know exactly what the exam paper will look like, which texts or sections you must answer and how many questions you need to do. The 'rubric' on the paper will give you this information, but in the heat of the moment it is easy to become confused.
- → Read the question carefully. Many questions have a focus and a specific point. For example, if the question asks you to evaluate the use of *stage space* in relation to the *audience*, you must make sure that both aspects of the question are covered.
- → Plan your answer – this may be a quick diagram, chart or list. It is a good way to 'empty' your initial thoughts onto paper and you can go back to this and tick off points as you make them in your answer.
- → Time your answers carefully: do not spend too long on one question and then leave no time for the final answer. You will lose more marks than you gain.
- → Allow time to read through what you have written so that you can correct any simple errors.
- → Try to write clearly: examiners mark hundreds of scripts and there is little time for deciphering handwriting.

> **Take note**
>
> The **rubric** is the instructions printed on the examination paper. It tells you how many questions to answer and other important information about how to answer the questions.

Drama and Theatre Studies is an exciting and rewarding course; you will become very close to your group and feel enormously proud of your performances. Many examiners comment that it is a privilege to watch this high-quality, inventive work. I hope that this guide will help you to achieve your best and that you enjoy your A level course. Good luck!

Index

Glossary

Absurd

Plays written between the two World Wars reflecting the idea that life did not make sense.

Accent

A style of speech from a particular country or area.

Alienation/*Verfremdungseffekt*

Brechtian term meaning 'to make strange'. Brecht sought to remind the audience that the action was not real.

Amphitheatre

A round building containing tiers of seats. Originated from the Greek theatre. The Olivier Theatre at the National Theatre is a good example.

Antagonist

A character who opposes the protagonist. The clash makes the play dramatic.

Apron

The front of a stage that juts out in front of the proscenium arch.

Aside

A comment made by an actor to the audience but not heard by other characters on stage.

Auditorium

The space in a theatre where the audience are seated.

Auteur

A director who is considered a co-author because he/she significantly revises the original play.

Avant-garde

New and experimental work.

Barn door

A metal device with four shutters that slots onto the front of a lamp to prevent spill.

Blank verse

Unrhymed poetry based on iambic pentameter, used in Shakespearean and Jacobean plays.

Box set

Set depicting the inside of a room, in which the audience looks through the invisible 'fourth wall'.

Chorus

Originated in Greek theatre; a character or group of characters provide a summary or narrative link.

Climax/Anti-climax

Climax is a moment of great or culminating intensity in a narrative, a turning point in a plot or dramatic action. An anti-climax is a disappointing decline after a previous rise in dramatic action.

Cross-fade

Lighting changes from one state to another without going to blackout.

Cue

A marker – spoken or technical – for a line, action or sound effect.

Cyclorama

A cloth with a uniform surface extending around and above the stage, used for the projection of light, designs or shadow.

Declarative

A statement, giving information.

Dénouement

Moment of untangling of the plot.

Dialect

A form of a language which is peculiar to a specific region or social group.

Dialectic

The clash of opposites and the resulting conflict. Often applied to Brechtian theatre.

Dialogue

The spoken language of a play.

Direct address

An actor speaks to the audience rather than to another character.

Dramatic irony

The audience know something of which one or more of the characters is unaware.

Duologue

A conversation between two characters.

Epic

Brechtian term for his plays that covered extended periods of time.

Epilogue

A final section of a play acting as a summary, leaving the audience thinking about the key themes or aspects.

Eponymous

Having the same name – Hamlet is the eponymous hero of *Hamlet*.

Exposition

Giving the audience the background information in the opening scenes.

Flood

A lantern that covers the area with a wash of light. Cannot be focused.

Follow spot

Used for highlighting one character – often used in pantomime and musicals.

Forum theatre

Theatre in which the audience participate in the action, developed by Augusto Boal.

Fourth wall

The imaginary wall through which the audience sees a room. Associated with naturalistic drama.

Fresnel

A lantern that gives a soft-edged light.

Gel

Material placed in front of a lantern to provide colour.

Genre

A dramatic form that has identifiable characteristics.

Geste

Brechtian device. An attitude expressed as a symbolic gesture.

Gestures

Physical actions which expose the underlying theme of the play.

Gobo

Metal or similar material, cut out and shaped, then placed in front of a lantern to project an image, e.g. prison bars, dappled sunlight.

Ground plan

A diagram indicating the positioning of furniture, doors, entrances and exits on a stage set.

Imperative

An instruction, command or advice.

Inflection

A variation in intonation or pitch of the voice.

Interrogative

Asks questions.

Intonation

The rise and fall of the voice while speaking.

Juxtaposition

Placing close together in order to make a comparison.

Lighting state

Lights set at particular levels. When there is a change of lighting, a new 'state' is used. The lighting may return to an earlier 'state' at another point in the play.

Limelight

The burning of lime sticks, introduced in 1816, gave a bright white light used to illuminate important actors.

Melodrama

Originated in France and became popular in 19th-century England. Stock characters with good triumphing over evil.

Mise-en-scène

Literally, what is 'put in the scene'. Refers to how the director, designer and performer have interpreted the play.

Monologue

A lengthy speech for one person.

Montage

Used by Brecht and in film. The putting together of short sections or scenes that are dissimilar.

Morality play

Late 15th/early 16th-century drama of moral instruction using personified or abstract characters, e.g. 'Envy'.

Narrative

The story of the play.

Pace

The speed of the play or the delivery of dialogue.

Pause

Moments of stillness or silences; pause can be 'voiced' with a cough or 'er' and 'um' or 'unvoiced' and silent.

Plot

The story of the play.

Preset

Lighting that has been programmed into a board or where the next cue has been set up in advance.

Profile

A lantern that gives a hard-edged spot.

Prologue

An introductory section to a play; an entry into the piece for the audience.

Promenade

The audience moves from one location to another, following the action of the play.

Proscenium arch

An architectural partition that designates the outer limit of the stage, introduced in the 18th century.

Protagonist

The main character of a play.

Proxemics

The physical relationship between the actor and the audience or between the actors on the stage.

Psycho-technique

The use of voice, language, expressive movement and rhythm, associated with Stanislavski.

Pun

A humorous play on words, dependent on the words having a double meaning.

Rake

An auditorium or stage that is sloped, with the rear section above the front. Used to enable the audience to see the action clearly.

Reception

The understanding of the play by the audience, who construct their own meaning from the performance.

Rhythm

The effect produced by the combination or arrangement of formal elements such as length of scenes, dialogue or timing to create movement, tension and emotional value.

Rigging

The erecting of lights on the grid and focusing them onto the stage space.

Semiotics

The signs and symbols in a play that are decoded by the audience.

Soliloquy

A speech by one character who is alone on the stage. Often used to share emotions with the audience.

Sub-plot

A secondary plot running alongside the main story of the play.

Sub-text

The information, not made directly clear by the playwright, learned from reading between the lines.

Thrust stage

The stage juts out into the audience who surround it on three sides. The Elizabethan theatres such as The Globe and The Swan had thrust stages.

Traverse staging

The audience are positioned on either side of a 'corridor' in which the action takes place.

Verfremdungseffekt

Brechtian term, meaning to 'make strange'. A distancing of the spectators from the emotions of the play.